TRS-80 Interfacing

Book 2

by

**Jonathan A. Titus, Christopher A. Titus
and David G. Larsen**

D1421730

Howard W. Sams & Co., Inc.
4300 WEST 62ND ST. INDIANAPOLIS, INDIANA 46268 USA

Preface

In this book, the second of two books on interfacing the popular TRS-80* computer from Radio Shack, we will be introducing you to some of the advanced interfacing techniques that will allow you to do real things with your computer. You will find that these techniques can be applied to computer applications in your home, in a research laboratory, in a school laboratory, or in situations where it is just simply fun to experiment with some of the things that a computer can do. Some of these interfacing techniques can be applied with little difficulty, while others will require a careful analysis of the device or instrument that is to be interfaced to the computer.

In particular, you will learn how the computer can be used to drive high-current and high-voltage loads with open-collector chips, with triacs, with solid-state relays, with transistor drivers, and other interface circuits. You will learn how the computer can be used to generate voltage and current signals that can be used in a variety of control applications, from controlling servo motors in an X-Y plotter, to controlling a programmable power supply. You will also learn how the computer can be used to measure unknown voltages and currents that may arise from solar collector temperature sensors, level detectors, and other voltage-output transducers. Since many computers are being used to control devices that are located at some distance from the central processing unit (CPU), we have spent a great deal of time describing the use of asynchronous-serial communication schemes, and we have provided remote control circuits that allow you to control Universal Asynchronous Receiver/Transmitter (UART) chips, analog-to-digital converters, digital-to-ana-

---

* TRS-80 is a trademark of Radio Shack, a division of Tandy Corp.

log converters, and other devices that can be located from several feet from the computer to several thousand feet from it. We will also introduce you to several new interface/controller chips, such as the Intersil ICL7109 A/D converter, and the Motorola MC14469 remote control chip.

Since the basics of TRS-80 interfacing have been covered in detail in *TRS-80 Interfacing, Book 1*, Howard W. Sams & Co., Inc., Indianapolis, IN 46206, we have not reviewed them here to any extent, and we expect that you have mastered the basics of input port construction, output port construction, device addressing, and simple software development. You will also find that we have skipped over a detailed discussion of the internal operations of many of the interface devices that are described. We don't feel that this is information that is necessary to the design of interface circuits, although you may find that it is "nice to know," once the interface has been tested, and is operational. Likewise, we doubt that there are many readers who can provide a detailed description of how automatic transmissions work, yet we all depend upon them.

The actual uses of the interface circuits that we describe are up to you. While we will describe how to control high-voltage loads, and how to measure small voltages, what you do with these ideas is entirely up to you, whether you decide to build a small rocket engine tester, or an egg sorter. You will find that the circuit descriptions are as complete as possible, and that we have included pin numbers for most of the complex circuits, so that you can use them directly. Likewise, the software examples are complete, and you can use them as they are, or modify and adapt them for your own purposes. We have tried to avoid the use of "general" block diagrams and simple flow charts that do little to increase your understanding of the principles of interfacing computers to external devices.

Since we have provided fairly complete examples, we have decided not to include experiments in this book. Doubtless, some of our readers will miss this, but since the circuits and programs are useful, as is, we expect that many readers will experiment with these as they wish, making up for the lack of experiments.

In this book, some simple assembly-language programs are introduced and explained. These programs deal with simple X-Y displays, controlling a USART chip, and interrupt service subroutine operations. As in the first TRS-80 interfacing book, a knowledge of assembly-language programming is not necessary, but it can be quite helpful, particularly if you are going to try to use interrupts. For additional information on assembly-language programming, we refer you to *8080/8085 Software Design, Books 1 and 2*, and *Z-80 Microprocessor Programming & Interfacing, Book 1*, Howard W. Sams & Co., Inc., Indianapolis, IN 46206. The majority of the programs have been written in BASIC, and we have not used "tricks" to perform special functions in the programs. We are sure that some readers will be able to "shorten" the programs, to make them a bit more efficient, but efficiency was not our goal; simplicity and ease of understanding seemed more important.

Many of the concepts and techniques detailed in this book have been incorporated into a formal course, *TRS-80 Interfacing and Programming*, taught periodically through the Virginia Polytechnic Institute's Extension Division. For additional information about specific course offerings, we suggest that you call the Virginia Tech Center for Continuing Education (703) 961-5182, or Dr. Chris Titus of The Blacksburg Group, at (703) 951-9030. These courses are also offered on an in-house basis.

The Blacksburg Group continues to be interested in adding new titles to the "Blacksburg Continuing Education Series,™" and we are interested in talking with readers who have ideas for new books, or who may have outlines or manuscripts in preparation. A complete packet of information for prospective authors is available upon request from The Blacksburg Group, Inc., P. O. Box 242, Blacksburg, VA 24060.

In conclusion, we hope that you enjoy reading this book on TRS-80 interfacing techniques, and we hope that you will find at least a few ideas and circuits that will inspire you to do some interesting and creative things with your computer.

David G. Larsen, Christopher A. Titus
and Jonathan A. Titus
"The Blacksburg Group"

Contents

Motors, Lamps, Bells, and Whistles

Whenever people are faced with a microcomputer interfacing task in which the computer will be used to control so-called real world devices, they are also faced with the need to control, or drive, devices that may require high voltages, high currents, or both. Whether your computer will be controlling a few light-emitting diodes (LEDs), or a high-power motor, you will need to concern yourself with electronic devices that can easily translate the logic signals of the computer into the proper voltages and currents that will be compatible with the external devices that are to be controlled. The drive circuits that will be described in this chapter will range from low-current and low-voltage, to high-current and high-voltage device controllers. Of course, there will always be alternative methods that may be used, that will accomplish the same interfacing task, so rather than provide an exhaustive coverage of many, many different driver circuits, we have chosen to provide a sampling of typical circuits that you should find to be readily adaptable to your interfacing needs. We will place our emphasis on the *hardware* aspects of these interface circuits, since the software that may be used to control these drivers should be second nature at this point.

OBJECTIVES

At the end of this chapter, you will be able to:

- Design circuits that use open-collector gates and decoders to drive low-voltage and low-current devices.

- Describe the use of open-collector decoders for memory expansion decoding.
- Describe the different types of peripheral drivers and transistor arrays currently available.
- Design high-current lamp-driver circuits.
- Discuss surge currents in lamp-driver circuits.
- Design driver circuits that use transistor arrays.
- Design addressable latch-driver circuits.
- Design solid-state relay circuits for controlling motors, lamps, and other line-voltage operated devices.
- Discuss the use of optical couplers for isolation.

OPEN-COLLECTOR CIRCUITS

The simplest driver circuits already exist within the SN7400-series of integrated circuits. These devices have output transistors in which the collector lead of the transistor is uncommitted, and is provided as the output of the particular gate, decoder, multiplexer, or other *open-collector*-type function. A typical open-collector device is represented by the circuit diagram shown in Fig. 1-1.

In this circuit, which happens to represent an inverter function, the output terminal is the uncommitted collector of the output transistor. Notice, though, that the emitter terminal of the transistor is connected to the ground signal. This means that the output of the transistor will be connected to the ground signal when the transistor is conducting. However, the unconnected transistor collector will have no voltage associated with it when the transistor is no longer conducting. Unlike other SN7400-series devices, the open-collector device does not have a logic one output. The other SN7400-series

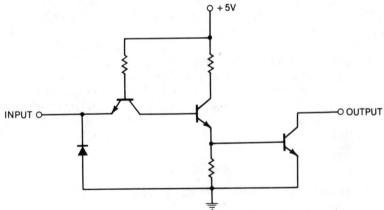

Fig. 1-1. Schematic diagram for an SN7405 open-collector inverter circuit.

devices have a "committed" collector, so that the output is "pulled-up" to a logic one, when the output transistor is not conducting. Additional internal circuitry is used to perform the pull-up function. It is important that you realize that most SN7400-series devices have a logic one, or a logic zero, output state, but that without some sort of pulling-up action, the open-collector devices simply provide a path to ground, or block it. At this point, you may be wondering why anyone would be interested in these devices.

The open-collector devices were quite important in computer circuits prior to the widespread availability of three-state devices, since the open-collector devices could act as if they were "disconnected" from a signal line. In this way, they could either pull-down a signal line, or they could be disconnected from the line, allowing other devices to control it. If the devices on such a bus had distinct logic one outputs, the presence of logic one and logic zero states on the bus at the same time might cause some devices to burn out. Since none of the open-collector devices can generate a distinct logic one output, a simple pull-up resistor was used to cause the bus to be in a logic one state, unless one of the open-collector gates was pulling it down to ground through its output transistor. Many of the early minicomputers, such as Digital Equipment Corporation's PDP-8 family, used the open-collector bus technique. A typical open-collector bus shown in Fig. 1-2. In this circuit, the individual bus drivers are connected to the bus, one at a time, so that data present at their inputs are transferred onto the bus, and to the receiving device, in this case, a simple inverter. To simplify the distinction between open-collector gates, and "normal" gates, we have used the "double-bar" at the input side of open-collector devices.

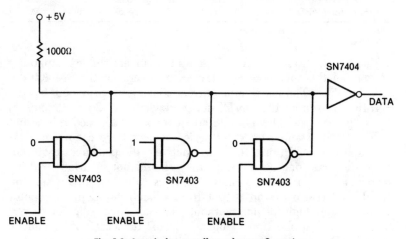

Fig. 1-2. A typical open-collector bus configuration.

In three-state bus systems, it is important that only one output to the bus be activated at one time. In open-collector bus systems, this is not a problem, since the activation of two or more bus drivers will not increase the current flow on the bus, since the current is limited by the 1000-ohm pull-up resistor at the end of the bus. You should note that in the open-collector bus circuit shown in Fig. 1-2, data is passed through the open-collector drivers, but the data is inverted, a logic one becomes a logic zero, while a logic zero becomes a logic one. The receiving inverter circuit reconstructs the data properly. The standby condition of bus is a logic one.

While open-collector devices are still frequently used in computer buses, and in interfaces, they are being replaced by three-state buses, and three-state bus drivers. Three-state buses have their advantages, but open-collector devices are still popular because they have the capability of making, or breaking, a circuit path to ground. In this way, they are readily adapted to driving low-current and low-voltage devices, such as small reed relays and LEDs. Actually, the open-collector devices "sink" current to ground, but the word driver is more frequently used for devices of this type. If you are going to be driving a few low-voltage, low-current devices, you will find that the open-collector devices are ideal.

Table 1-1. Current-Sinking Capabilities of Some SN74-Series Devices

Device	Family				
	74—	74H—	74L—	74LS—	74S—
—00 Quad NAND	16	20	3.6	8	20
—03 Quad NAND	16	20	3.6	8	20
—05 Hex INVERTER	16	20	3.6	8	20
—12 Tri NAND	16	20	3.6	8	20
—22 Dual NAND	16	20	3.6	8	20

Note: All currents in milliamperes, at a maximum of 5.5 volts.

The information in Table 1-1 shows the current sinking capability of some of the open-collector devices in several of the SN7400 device families. The maximum current sinking is provided by the SN74H-series and the SN74S-series devices, at 20 milliamperes (mA) per output. This is quite adequate for small reed relays and LEDs. While standard SN7400-series devices have a current sinking capability of 16 mA, they have active pull-up devices that generate the logic one output, and they should not be used to drive relays, LEDs, or other nonlogic devices, directly. Likewise, you should not try to use an output from a latch, flip-flop, or counter to drive a nonlogic device, without using an open-collector driver. Some typical application of open-collector devices for the control of an LED indicator and a low-current relay are shown in Fig. 1-3.

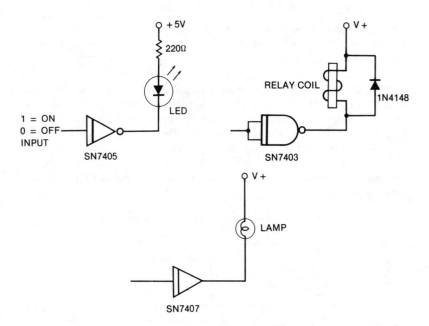

Fig. 1-3. Typical uses of open-collector driver circuits.

You should note that the maximum voltage that can be applied to the open-collector devices listed in Table 1-1 is +5.5 volts.

In some applications, however, it would be useful to have open-collector devices that could handle higher voltages, and higher currents. There are other devices within the SN7400-series that have these capabilities. These open-collector devices are listed in Table 1-2. Note that all of these devices are contained in the SN7400 series, and not in the SN74LS-, SN74S-, or other families. Buffers, inverters, and gates are all available with the high-voltage and high-current capabilities. These types of devices are frequently used in those applications in which some high-voltage load must be driven by the computer, for example, a +12-volt relay. The high-voltage

Table 1-2. Maximum Current and Voltage Levels for Some Open-Collector Devices

Device	I_{MAX} (mA)	V_{MAX} (V)
7406 Hex INVERTER	40	30
7407 Hex BUFFER	40	30
7416 Hex INVERTER	40	15
7417 Hex BUFFER	40	15
7426 Quad 2-input NAND	16	15
7433 Quad 2-input NOR	48	5.5
7438 Quad 2-input NAND	48	5.5

open-collector devices are also used as interface circuits between the transistor-transistor logic (TTL) family, and other logic families in which higher voltages are used to represent the logic one and logic zero logic levels. An example is an interface between a TTL circuit, and a circuit that uses complimentary metal-oxide semiconductor (CMOS) logic chips. A sample circuit is provided in Fig. 1-4. This interfacing technique is important if you will be using the CMOS family of devices for external digital circuits. The CMOS family is frequently used in industrial applications, since it has more noise immunity than the TTL family, and it finds use in remote, or battery-powered applications because of its low power consumption.

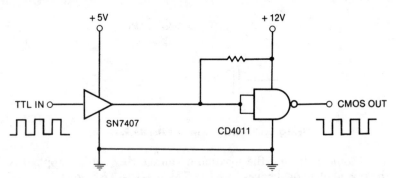

Fig. 1-4. Using an open-collector buffer as a TTL-to-CMOS interface element.

In the interface shown in Fig. 1-3, you will note that a diode has been placed across the coil of the relay. Since the diode serves no purpose when the circuit is powered, you may ask why it has been included. You must remember that when the power is removed from a coil, the "collapsing" flux tends to induce an opposite electromotive force (emf) in the device, generating a voltage. In most relays, this can be significant. Just place your fingers across the terminals of an operating 6-volt buzzer, and you will feel the high voltage that is generated in this way. To prevent such high-voltage spikes from damaging the open-collector driver chip in a relay driving application, a small-signal diode is provided to shunt the back emf so that it will not harm the driver circuit. This is good design practice, and whenever relays are used, such shunts, or protection diodes, should be used in the interface.

Also, as shown in Fig. 1-3, incandescent lamps may be driven by open-collector drivers, although the trend is to use LEDs for front panel indicators, pilot lamps, etc. If you choose to use an incandescent lamp, you should remember that these lamps have a high *inrush* current when the filament is cold. These currents can be present for tens of milliseconds, and they can often exceed the current rating of the driver that is being used to drive the lamp. We will discuss this more when we talk about driving lamps that require 117 volts ac line voltage. In general, incandescent lamps require drivers with high current ratings, so that the inrush currents can be safely handled.

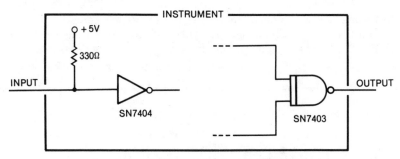

Fig. 1-5. A typical input and output on an instrument.

If you are going to be interfacing commercially available electronic devices and instruments, you will often encounter TTL-compatible inputs that have pull-up resistors associated with them, as shown in Fig. 1-5. You will also encounter outputs from instruments that are driven by open-collector devices, as shown in Fig. 1-5. While standard TTL outputs could probably drive the inputs with pull-up resistors, this is not recommended. In fact, most instruments of this type will be some distance from the computer or interface, so open-collector drivers are the best choice. A typical example of this is shown in Fig. 1-6. One of the reasons for using open-collector drivers is that they can drive long lines with fairly high currents, making the signals less susceptible to having noise induced upon them. The open-collector devices are also used to reduce the effect of the resistance of the wire used as the signal conductor. In the example provided in Fig. 1-6, each of the open-collector drivers will be sinking 11 mA when a logic zero is transmitted on each of the signal lines.

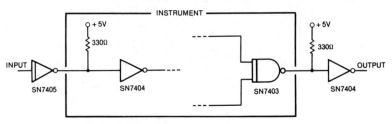

Fig. 1-6. Interfacing open-collector devices with standard instrument I/O lines.

OPEN-COLLECTOR DECODERS

While open-collector gates are quite useful, there are often cases in which other open-collector functions are needed. The most common requirement is for open-collector decoders. In the standard SN7400 family, there are three decoders that are worth describing: the SN74145 high-current decimal decoder, the SN74159 four-line-to-16-line decoder, and the SN74141 high-voltage decimal decoder.

The SN74145 decimal decoder is shown in block diagram form in Fig. 1-7, along with its pin configuration, or *pinout*. This decoder

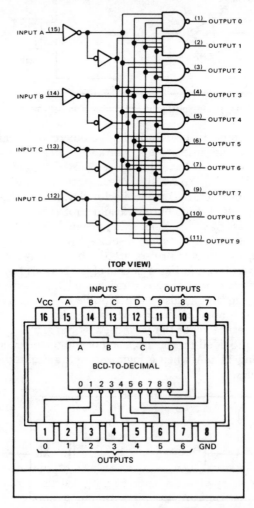

Fig. 1-7. Block diagram and pin configuration for the SN74145 decoder chip.

will accept four bits (four lines) of binary information, decoding the binary value, so that one of the 10 outputs provides a conducting path to ground. Only 10 outputs have been provided, 0 through 10, so not all of the 16 possible binary input states can be decoded. Only the binary values 0000 through 1001 are valid binary inputs, with all other binary input codes causing all of the output transistors to be turned off, or *blanked*. This chip is particularly useful for driving LED or incandescent lamps in displays, since each output transistor can sink up to 80 mA at a maximum of 15 volts. Thus, the decoder can also be used to pulse relays and other devices.

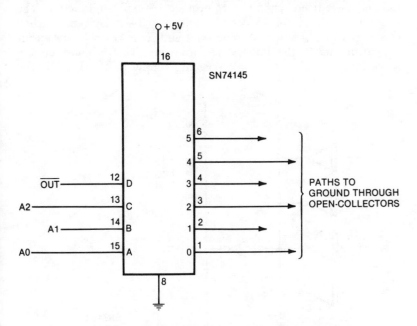

Fig. 1-8. Using an SN74145 decoder to provide short current-sinking pulses for control.

Frequently, there are cases in which high-current pulses must be generated by the computer, for strobing external instruments and circuits. Open-collector gates or inverters could be used along with a standard device address decoder to provide these pulses, or an SN74145 decoder could be used instead, to provide both the decoding and driving functions on one integrated circuit. The schematic diagram shown in Fig. 1-8 shows how this type of open-collector decoder may be used to provide short, high-current paths to ground for use by external devices. Note that this circuit assumes that the required pull-up, or voltage-sourcing device, is provided in the interface to which the decoder is connected. The device address decoding scheme shown in Fig. 1-8 is for nonabsolutely decoded addresses, so the high-current pulses may be generated by several different device address codes.

An additional use for open-collector devices is shown in Fig. 1-9. Note that the outputs of several open-collector devices have been connected together, and to a pull-up resistor, as well. While the outputs of standard SN7400-series devices cannot be connected together if they are to work properly, you have seen that open-collector outputs may be connected in this way. In the decoder circuit shown in Fig. 1-9, the open-collector devices (inverters and buffers) have been configured to provide a NAND gate function. The D input on the SN74145 decoder will only be a logic zero when the proper combination of logic ones and logic zeros is present at the six inputs to the buffers and inverters. This is considered a NAND function, since the logic ones are simply buffered, while the

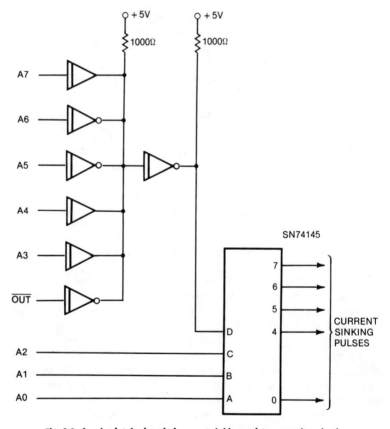

Fig. 1-9. An absolutely decoded current-sinking pulse generating circuit.

logic zeros are inverted to logic ones. The unique state of the NAND gate occurs when all of the inputs are logic ones. The unique output of the NAND gate is a logic zero. When the D input of the SN74145 decoder is a logic zero, the decoder is enabled, and the proper open-collector output from the decoder is turned on, sinking current to ground. In the interface shown, eight pulses can be generated under software control, through the use of statements such as OUT 152,0. You should recall that when a command such as this is executed, the computer outputs the eight-bit binary device address on the address bus, while generating the OUT pulse for synchronization. While the data value, zero in this case, is placed on the data bus, the decoder circuit does not require it, nor is it used elsewhere in the computer system.

In this example, we stated that the SN74145 decoder will be enabled only when its D input is a logic zero. This is not really the case, since the decoder will always accept and decode four binary bits. However, if you ignore the use of the "8" and "9" outputs of the decoder, you can consider the D input to be an enabling input, since the decoder can only enable, or turn on, one of the remaining outputs, "0" through "7," when the D input is a logic zero.

In the SN74145-based decoder schemes that have been illustrated in Figs. 1-8 and 1-9, the decoders have been used to generate short pulses. If you require that the open-collector output be enabled for a period that exceeds the length of the OUT pulse, a latch would be required. In this case, a data value would be transmitted to a latch, which would in turn be wired to an SN74145 decoder. The outputs of the decoder could be turned on, one at a time, for as long as the associated binary value was present at the inputs of the decoder. By using a circuit such as this, it would be possible to have the computer turn various devices on and off for long periods. It is important to remember, though, that when a decoder circuit is used, only one of the devices connected to the outputs of the decoder may be controlled at any time. If some of the interfaced devices are to be controlled by the computer, such that their operation may be independently, and perhaps simultaneously, controlled, then individual outputs must be made available. A simple latch circuit could be used for this function, provided that open-collectors are used for each of the outputs. In a configuration such as this, eight devices may be controlled by an eight-bit latch. Since the individual bit positions are independent of one another, the eight devices may be controlled independently. The two different types of port-controlled open-collector interfaces are shown in Fig. 1-10.

The SN74159 decoder is a 4-line-to-16-line decoder, as shown in Fig. 1-11. The integrated circuit is an open-collector replacement for the SN74154 decoder. All of the 16 possible outputs are provided, and two enabling inputs are also provided, making the SN74159 fairly easy to use. While this decoder does not have the

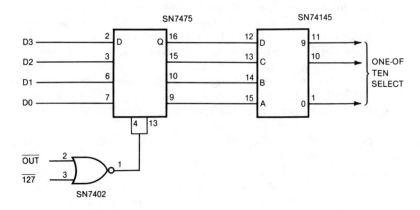

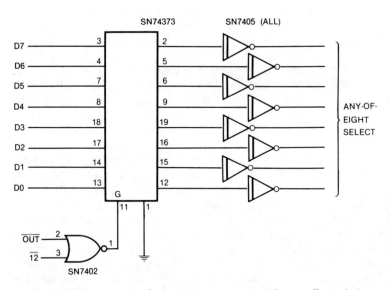

Fig. 1-10. Two ways to use latched output ports to control open-collector devices.

high-current and high-voltage capability of the SN74145, it is still quite useful for controlling interface circuits, such as the one shown in Fig. 1-6. The SN74159 decoder may be used to generate pulses in a manner that is similar to that already described for the SN74145 decoder (Figs. 1-8 and 1-9).

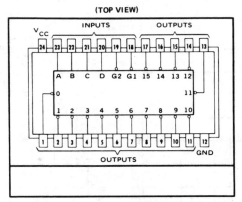

Fig. 1-11. Pin configuration for the SN74159 open-collector 4-to-16-line decoder chip.

The SN74159 may also be used when additional memories are to be added to a small computer system, in which it is desired to mix blocks of memory chips which may contain different numbers of memory bytes. For example, there are memory chips that contain 1K (1024), 2K, and 4K bytes of memory. The SN74159 decoder may be easily used to provide the chip select signals for all of these different "sized" chips, since its decoded outputs may be connected together. The decoder scheme in Fig. 1-12 shows a circuit in which the memory address lines have been used to decode the available memory addresses, dividing them into 1K blocks. Since a 2K block would require two chip select signals, and a 4K block would require four chip select signals, the necessary chip select signals are simply connected together, instead of being gated together with additional gate circuits. Of course, a pull-up resistor must be furnished for each of the three resulting chip-select signals, so that a logic one is actually generated for each line, when the outputs of the decoder are inactive. There are many other circuits in which an open-collector decoder such as the SN74159 may be useful. You should remember that you cannot simply connect the outputs of a standard SN7400-series decoder to perform the same function. Only open-collector gates may be connected to provide these gating functions.

The last open-collector circuit that is generally useful is the SN-74141 decimal decoder. This decoder has been fabricated specifically to drive high-voltage, gas-filled, cold-cathode indicator tubes, in a one-of-ten configuration. The SN74141 decoder is typically used in circuits that drive gas-filled displays, whether they are individual neon indicator lamps, or more complex numeric indicators such as Nixie® tubes. While these types of readout devices are

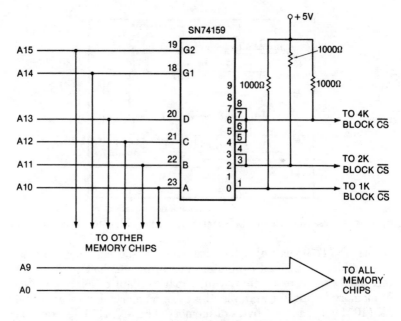

Fig. 1-12. Using an open-collector decoder to generate chip select pulses for blocks of memory.

generally not used in new designs, they are commonly found in older equipment. The SN74141 is used to drive individual gas-filled indicators, such as NE-2 and NE-2H neon lamps, or display panels. Care is required in interfacing high-voltage displays, since it is easy to connect the high voltages to the wrong points in a breadboarded circuit, destroying it. Whenever gas-filled indicators are used, a series, current-limiting resistor must be used, since conducting gas-filled indicators offer almost no resistance in the circuit.

There are quite a few other types of open-collector circuits in the SN7400 family of devices, but most of these are seven-segment decoder driver circuits, used to drive seven-segment LED displays. Some other gating circuits are also available, but in most cases they will not be used in interface circuits, such as the ones described in this chapter.

PERIPHERAL DRIVERS AND TRANSISTOR ARRAYS

In this section, we will describe some of the integrated circuits that have been developed specifically so that TTL-compatible devices can be used to control relays, LEDs, and incandescent displays, to mention only a few possible uses. Peripheral driver circuits are those in which a driver transistor and a gate have been integrated in a single circuit. There are generally two peripheral drivers per integrated circuit package, and the transistor may, or may not, be directly connected to the output of the gate. Various configurations of drivers are possible, using NAND, NOR, AND, or OR gates. Transistor arrays come in many different configurations, using transistors that have been designed for special purposes. We have limited our scope so that only those transistor arrays that are generally used in computer interfacing have been included.

Peripheral Drivers

Peripheral drivers are integrated circuits that include a logic gate, and a driver transistor. Depending upon the driver chosen, or the application in which the driver is to be used, the transistor and the output of the gate may be connected, or they may be unconnected.

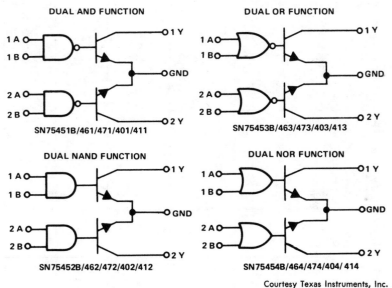

Courtesy Texas Instruments, Inc.

Fig. 1-13. Logic diagrams for some typical dual peripheral driver chips.

These chips are probably best represented by the Texas Instrument's SN75400 family. Table 1-3 summarizes the current drive capabilities, and voltage limits for these devices. In most cases, the subfamilies contain a selection of NAND, NOR, AND, and OR gates that are used to control the driver transistor, or output transistor. Typical examples of dual peripheral driver chips are shown in Fig. 1-13. The functional diagram and pin configuration for the SN75450B, SN75460, and SN75470 chips is shown in Fig. 1-14. While these

Table 1-3. Characteristics of SN75400-Series Peripheral Driver Chips

Maximum Off-State Voltage	Minimum Latch-Up Voltage	Maximum Recommended Output Current	Typical Delay Time	Output Clamp Diodes	Drivers Per Package	Input Compatibility	Device Type and Package −55°C To 125°C	Device Type and Package 0°C To 70°C	Logic Function
15 V	15 V	300 mA	15 ns		2	TTL, DTL		SN75430 J,N SN75431 JG,P SN75432 JG,P SN75433 JG,P SN75434 JG,P	AND* AND NAND OR NOR
30 V	20 V	100 mA	22 ns		2	ECL		SN75441 J,N	OR
30 V	20 V	300 mA	21 ns		2	TTL, DTL	SN55450B J SN55451B JG SN55452B JG SN55453B JG SN55454B JG	SN75450B J,N SN75451B JG,P SN75452B JG,P SN75453B JG,P SN75454B JG,P	AND* AND NAND OR NOR
35 V	30 V	300 mA	33 ns		2	TTL, DTL	SN55460 J SN55461 JG SN55462 JG SN55463 JG SN55464 JG	SN75460 J,N SN75461 JG,P SN75462 JG,P SN75463 JG,P SN75464 JG,P	AND* AND NAND OR NOR
35 V	30 V	500 mA	33 ns		2	TTL, DTL		SN75401 NE SN75402 NE SN75403 NE SN75404 NE	AND NAND OR NOR
50 V	50 V	350 mA	1 µs	YES	7	TTL, DTL, CMOS, P-MOS 14-V to 25-V P-MOS TTL and 5-V CMOS 6-V to 15-V P-MOS, CMOS		ULN2001A† J,N ULN2002A† J,N ULN2003A† J,N ULN2004A† J,N	INVERTING BUFFER

Device	Package	Function	Military Device	Pkg	Input Compatibility	Logic Levels	Strobe	t_{pd}	Output Current	V_2	V_1
SN75470	J,N	AND*	SN55470	J	TTL, DTL	2		33 ns	300 mA	55 V	70 V
SN75471	JG,P	AND	SN55471	JG							
SN75472	JG,P	NAND	SN55472	JG							
SN75473	JG,P	OR	SN55473	JG							
SN75474	JG,P	NOR	SN55474	JG							
SN75475	JG,P	NAND			TTL, DTL, MOS	2	YES	100 ns	300 mA	55 V	70 V
SN75476	JG,P	AND			TTL, DTL, MOS	2	YES	100 ns	300 mA	55 V	70 V
SN75477	JG,P	NAND									
SN75478	JG,P	OR									
SN75479	JG,P	NOR									
SN75411	NE	AND			TTL, DTL	2		33 ns	500 mA	55 V	70 V
SN75412	NE	NAND									
SN75413	NE	OR									
SN75414	NE	NOR									
SN75416	NE	AND			TTL, DTL, MOS	2	YES	100 ns	500 mA	55 V	70 V
SN75417	NE	NAND									
SN75418	NE	OR									
SN75419	NE	NOR									
SN75466†	J,N	INVERTING BUFFER			TTL, DTL, CMOS, P-MOS	7	YES	130 ns	350 mA	60 V	100 V
SN75467†	J,N				14-V to 25-V P-MOS						
SN75468†	J,N				TTL and 5-V CMOS						
SN75469†	J,N				6-V to 15-V P-MOS, CMOS						

*With output transistor base connected externally to output of gate.
†0°C to 85°C

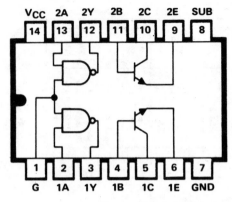

Fig. 1-14. Functional diagram and pinout for SN75450B, SN75460, and SN75470 peripheral driver chips.

chips are pin-for-pin equivalents, the current driving ranges are different, as noted in Table 1-3.

The dual peripheral drivers in which the output transistor has been connected to the gate are very similar to the open-collector devices that have been described previously. The peripheral drivers have the ability to sink higher currents that can be handled by

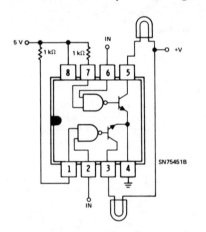

Fig. 1-15. Using the SN75451B driver chip to drive two lamps.

the open-collector devices, and they can handle higher voltages, too. A typical application of an SN75451B driver is shown in Fig. 1-15, in which two incandescent lamps are driven, independently, by the same chip. A second application is shown in Fig. 1-16. In this example, an SN75475 driver is used to control two 48-volt relays. Since this chip contains internal diode clamps, or shunts, external diodes are not required to protect the drive transistor.

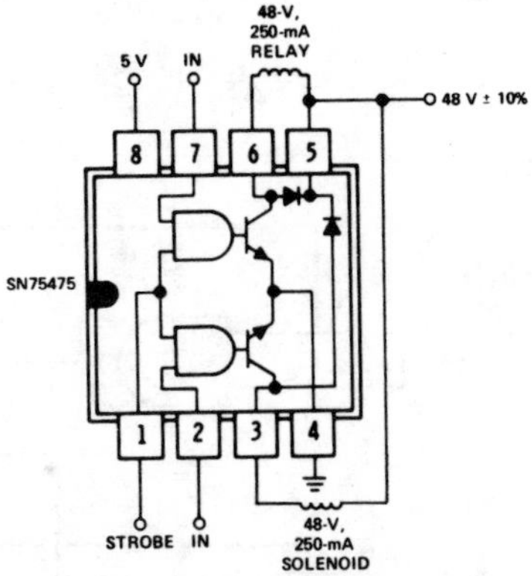

Fig. 1-16. Using the SN75475 peripheral driver to drive two relays.

Courtesy Texas Instruments, Inc.

There are many cases in which LEDs are not particularly useful as indicators, such as those in which an indicator is to be visible from some distance, visible in both high-level and low-level lighting conditions, visible from varying angles, and where a variety of colors is required. Since LEDs cannot answer all of these needs, incandescent indicators are frequently used. These lamps have higher current requirements than do LEDs, and in many cases they require higher drive voltages, too, generally between 12 and 28 volts. Incandescent lamps have high inrush currents when the filaments are cold, and since these currents can frequently reach *ten times* the normal operating current of the lamp, special precautions are required when driving incandescent lamps with peripheral driver chips. There are a number of methods that may be used to reduce the inrush current, and several will be described. The simplest method for reducing the inrush current through a cold filament is to keep the filament warm. This is conveniently done by placing a "keep alive" resistor in parallel with the driver circuit, between the lamp and ground. This is shown in Fig. 1-17. The value of the resistor is chosen so that the current flowing through the lamp is about one-tenth of the fully operational current of the lamp. In the example shown, a 6-volt, 150 mA lamp has been used with a 150-ohm resistor. The value of the resistor was chosen so that the lamp would be unlit, but with about 40 mA flowing through it. In most cases, one-half, or one watt keep-alive resistors are used.

A surge limiting resistor may also be used in series with the lamp, so that the peak current is limited when the lamp is first turned on, as shown in Fig. 1-18. In this circuit, the SN75450B driver has been used, and the output of the gate has been directly connected to the base of the transistor. You must remember that in this type of a circuit, it is the transistor *and* the resistor that will be limiting the

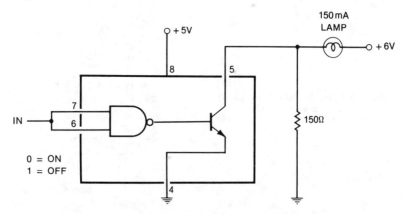

Fig. 1-17. Using an SN75451A as a lamp driver, with a keep-alive resistor.

current, and not the resistor alone. It is not difficult to calculate the limiting current, which is essentially the emitter voltage divided by the emitter resistance. The emitter voltage is the output voltage of the gate, less the emitter-base voltage, or 3.3 volts and 0.95 volts, respectively:

$$I_L = \frac{V_{OH} - V_{BE}}{R_E}$$
$$= \frac{2.35 \text{ volts}}{6.8 \text{ ohms}}$$
$$= 0.345 \text{ A, or } 345 \text{ mA}$$

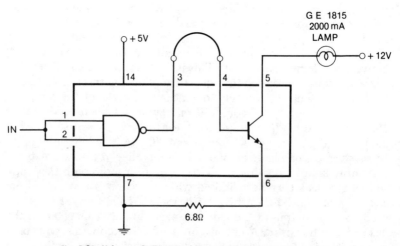

Fig. 1-18. Using an SN75450B driver with current limiting resistor.

The transistor saturates at this point, limiting the flow of current to about 340 mA. Since the filament starts to heat up quickly, the current starts to drop back to its normal level, or about 200 mA for the GE-1851 lamp shown in the circuit. The maximum surge current must not be allowed to exceed the maximum surge level for the SN75450B driver, and also, the current must not be limited by the saturation of the transistor when it is normally in its on state. Thus, the surge current limit defined by the equation should be higher than the normal current flowing through the lamp when it is on.

An alternate method of turning on incandescent lamps involves the use of two driver circuits, one that is used for the normal switching, and another that is used for the current limiting switching. In the example shown in Fig. 1-19, a monostable circuit has been configured with a 390-ohm resistor and a 500 μF capacitor. When the input control line of the lamp goes to a logic one, the current limiting circuit starts to conduct current through the lamp. After the RC network has "timed-out," the current limiting network is bypassed by the connection through the other driver directly to ground. In the circuit shown in Fig. 1-19, the lamp has a "warm-up" period of about 200 ms, before the second driver makes the direct connection to ground.

Driving relays is somewhat simpler than driving lamps. As was noted previously, a diode is generally placed in parallel with the coil of the relay in relay driver circuits, with the polarity of the diode the reverse of the current flow. This shunts the back emf that is generated when the relay is turned off. It is also important to take other protective measures so that the output transistor is protected properly, too. When the transistor is turned off, the voltage on the collector will tend to increase almost instantaneously,

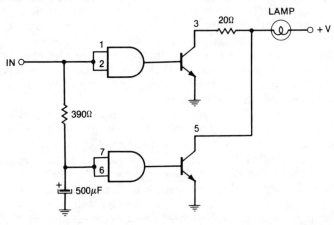

Fig. 1-19. Using two SN75452A drivers for current control in a lamp-driver circuit.

reaching the voltage that is used to drive the coil of the relay. (In this circuit, the collector of the transistor is connected to the coil, the emitter is connected to ground, and the base is connected directly to the output of the gate.) If the collector reaches this voltage very quickly, the drive transistor may be destroyed. To reduce the speed at which the collector voltage increases, after the transistor has been turned off, a small capacitance is added to the circuit, between the collector and ground. A typical circuit in which a capacitor is used is shown in Fig. 1-20. The protective diode can be removed if the peripheral driver chip contains protective diodes.

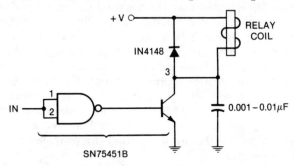

Fig. 1-20. A completely protected relay-driver circuit.

We noted previously that there are some peripheral drivers in which the output transistor is not connected to the gate within the chip. In these drivers, of which the SN75450B is an example (Fig. 1-14), the silicon material upon which the chip has been fabricated—its substrate—is not connected to ground. Thus, the transistor may be used with voltages that are more negative than ground, by connecting the substrate pin on the integrated circuit package to the more negative voltage. The unconnected base is useful, too, since a resistance may be placed between the output of the gate and the input of the base, so that the current flow through the resistor may be limited. We doubt that these applications will prove to be very important in normal interfacing tasks, so we have not provided any specific examples.

There are some other important points that should not be overlooked in the discussion of peripheral driver circuits. Since relays, lamps, LEDs, and other devices will frequently have supply voltages that are higher than the +5-volt used in TTL circuits, it is important that these higher voltages *not* be applied prior to applying the TTL supply voltage. If there is a chance, as there always is, that the higher drive voltages will be present without the +5-volt TTL supply, there should be some provision for backing up the peripheral chips with their own power supply. Probably the simplest type of back up would involve deriving the logic supply voltage for the peripheral driver chips from the voltage used to drive the higher voltage relays, lamps, etc. A simple voltage regulator could be used. In this way, whenever the drive voltage is applied to the system, so is the logic supply for the peripheral drivers. Separate TTL chips could have their own +5-volt power supply.

For additional information about peripheral driver circuits, we refer you to *The Peripheral Driver Data Book* (Texas Instruments, Inc., Dallas, TX 75222), and *Linear and Interface Circuits Applications* (Texas Instruments, Inc., Dallas, TX 75222), from which much of the information in this section was obtained.

Transistor Arrays

There are many different types of transistor arrays that are readily applied to interfacing tasks in which high-current and high-voltage peripheral devices must be controlled. Examples of transistor arrays include the RCA Corporation's CA3096AE, an integrated circuit in which there are three npn and three pnp transistors, and more complex devices such as the Sprague ULN-2800A-series chips that will be described in more detail, later. The main characteristic of these transistor arrays is that they are easily interfaced with TTL-compatible circuits, to provide the capability of driving relays, LEDs, seven-segment displays, incandescent lamps, and other peripheral devices. Some of the transistor arrays require a few additional components to provide the proper input voltages, current levels, etc. We suggest that you carefully review your interfacing requirements when you explore the possibility of using transistor arrays in your designs. There are many applications in which the transistor drivers are better suited than say, peripheral driver chips, or open-collector chips. Most transistor arrays do not come with the NAND, OR, NOR, or AND gates that are found associated with peripheral driver chips. However, if these gating functions are not required on the same chip, then the transistor arrays should be carefully considered. In fact, there are usually more of them in a given integrated circuit package than there are comparable peripheral driver circuits.

The example illustrated in Fig. 1-21 shows the use of a Sprague ULN-2803 or -2805 driver to drive eight incandescent lamps. Since protective diodes have been included on the chip for relay applications, they have been cleverly used in this circuit for a lamp-test feature. Whenever the lamp-test switch is closed, current will flow through all eight diodes, causing each of the lamps to light. Unlit lamps would indicate burned-out filaments. Many of the drivers in the ULN-2800A family are presented in Table 1-4. There are different types of devices for use with the different types of logic

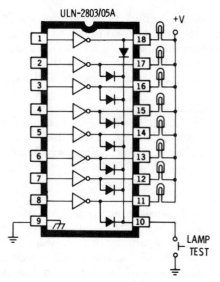

Fig. 1-21. Circuit diagram showing the ULN-2803/05A used as a lamp-driver circuit.

Courtesy Sprague Electric Co.

families; that is, TTL, CMOS, PMOS, and various combinations, at different operating voltages. The use of a ULN-2813A chip as a relay driver is shown in Fig. 1-22. Note that the internal protective diodes have been connected to the +V power supply to shunt the back emf that is generated whenever a relay is turned off.

An application in which one LED is lit within a matrix of LEDs is shown in Fig. 1-23. An SN74145 decoder, with open-collector outputs, has been used to provide current sinks for the individual rows of LEDs, and an RCA CA3082 has been used to source the voltage

Table 1-4. Sprague ULN-2800-Family Characteristics

$V_{CE(MAX)} =$ $I_{C(MAX)} =$	50 V 500 mA	50 V 600 mA	95 V 500 mA
	Type Number		
General Purpose PMOS, CMOS	ULN-2801A	ULN-2811A	ULN-2821A
14-25 V PMOS	ULN-2802A	ULN-2812A	ULN-2822A
5 V TTL, CMOS	ULN-2803A	ULN-2813A	ULN-2823A
6-15 V CMOS, PMOS	ULN-2804A	ULN-2814A	ULN2824A
High Output TTL	ULN-2805A	ULN-2815A	ULN-2825A

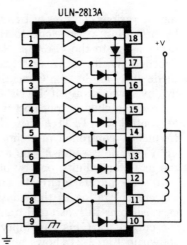

ULN-2813A

Fig. 1-22. Using the ULN-2813A as a relay driver. Note internal protective diodes.

Courtesy Sprague Electric Co.

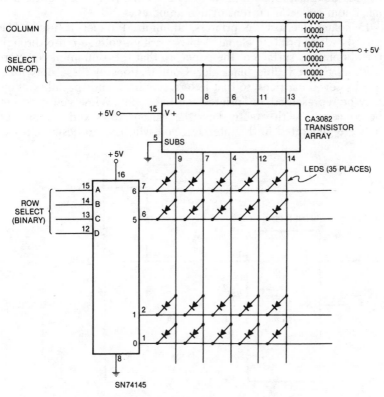

Fig. 1-23. Controlling an LED display matrix with a CA3082 driver, and an SN74145 decoder.

for the various columns of LEDs. In this circuit, one LED is selected by providing a row code to the SN74145 decoder, and a column drive signal to the CA3082. Note that the column selection is not decoded. While this may seem like a simple-minded example, the diode array might be a General Instruments MAN-2A, or equivalent five-by-seven array of LEDs used for alphanumeric displays. Of course, a latched output port would be required if a computer were to control the LED matrix display. Seven-segment displays are frequently controlled in a similar manner, with current sinks turning the various segments on and off, and current sources selecting the individual digits, one by one.

In some interface circuits, currents may be required that exceed the current rating of the transistors on a transistor array chip. In cases such as this, external transistors may be used to further boost the current carrying capability of an interface circuit. The circuit shown in Fig. 1-24 shows how a 2N4901 transistor may be driven by one of the transistors in a ULN-2803 array. The 2N4901 has a maximum collector current of five amperes.

In some electrostatic printers, aluminized paper is used. The print head, or printing element, passes a high-voltage pulse through the aluminized surface of the paper, so that the aluminum is vaporized, leaving a visible black dot. Combinations of these dots form five-by-seven matrices, so that letters, numbers, and special symbols may be represented, or "printed" on the paper. While you need not be concerned with exactly how the various rows and columns of dots are generated in the interface, you will have to design circuits

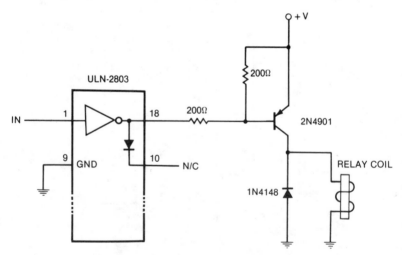

Fig. 1-24. Using an external transistor to boost the current driving ability of a transistor array.

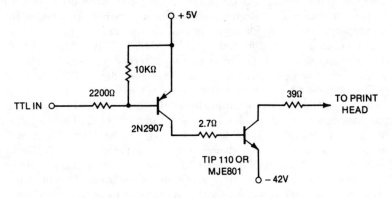

(A) Developing −42V at emitter of TIP110 or MJE801.

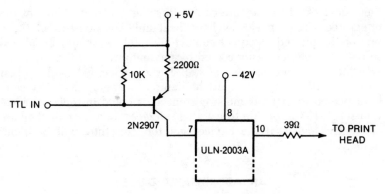

(B) Developing −42V at pin 8 of ULN-2003A.

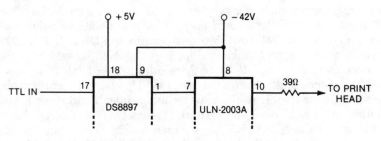

(C) Developing −42V at pin 8 of ULN-2003A.

Fig. 1-25. Three print-head driver circuits for an electrostatic printer, showing various solutions to the high-voltage driving problem.

that can deliver −42-volt pulses to the print head upon command of the interface. This would seem to be a possible application for a transistor array, or for a peripheral driver chip. Actually, there are a number of circuits that may be used to solve this problem. The circuits in Fig. 1-25 illustrate the different ways in which the electrodes may be controlled so that they will deliver the required −42-volt pulses to the aluminized paper. Only one of the circuits is shown, although seven duplicate circuits are required for a seven-row dot-matrix printer. The Texas Instruments TIP110 and Motorola MJE801 transistors are Darlington pairs. The ULN-2003A is a Sprague 50-volt, 500 mA driver, while the DS8897 is a National Semiconductor gas display driver, used in this application to drive the print-head transistor drivers. Future developments will probably yield simpler solutions to this particular interfacing problem.

It is important to remember that there is a voltage drop in *all* of the peripheral drivers and transistor arrays that have been described. Therefore, there will be some heat generated by all of these devices when they are conducting high currents. Some of the integrated circuit packages have heat-sink fins substituted for a few of the unused electrical contact pins. These should be placed so that they can be easily cooled by passing air, or so that they can be attached to an efficient heat sink. If the devices get too hot, their current-carrying capacity must be derated, meaning that they can't be expected to carry as much current as is noted in their specification sheet. If you decide to use these devices, be sure that they are efficiently cooled. If the devices get too hot, they will burn out quickly.

AN ADDRESSABLE DRIVER

There is a particularly useful series of interface circuits that you may want to use. These devices are called addressable latches or addressable drivers, since the chips have internal latches, decoders, and high-power transistor outputs. In the devices manufactured by Signetics, each of the latches' outputs has the ability to either sink or source about 300 mA. Two devices are available, the NE590, which is the current sinking chip, and the NE591, which is the current sourcing chip. Both of these addressable latch chips have eight independently controlled outputs. The latch is addressable, since each of the eight bits may be independently addressed, and either set (logic one), or cleared (logic zero). A general block diagram of the NE590/NE591 is shown in Fig. 1-26, while the pin configurations for both chips are shown in Fig. 1-27. The NE590 is contained in a 16-pin package, and the NE591 is contained in an 18-pin package. The main difference between these chips, aside

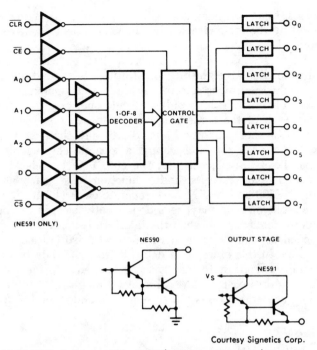

Fig. 1-26. Block diagram of the NE590/591 addressable latch/driver chip.

from the sinking or sourcing of current, is in the use of two additional pins on the NE591 for control of the chip-enabling logic, and for connection to the positive current-sourcing power supply. In

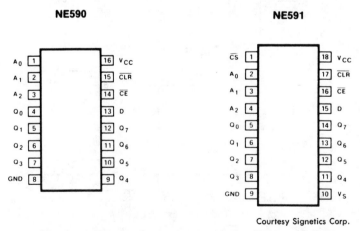

Fig. 1-27. Pin configurations for the Signetics NE590 and NE591 addressable latch/driver chips.

most cases, this supply voltage will be +5 volts, the same voltage as is used by the logic circuits, but in some situations, it can be a maximum of +7 volts.

The NE590/NE591 acts like a normal latch circuit, except that instead of loading an eight-bit word through to the outputs in parallel, an individual bit is selected by three address inputs, and the addressed bit is latched, as either a logic one, or a logic zero. In this way, each of the eight bits may be turned on, or turned off without disturbing the other bits. Since only three address bits are used to address the latch circuit, a separate chip enable ($\overline{CE}$) input has been provided so that the chip may be selected using the remaining address bits, and a function pulse, such as $\overline{OUT}$. Both the NE590 and NE591 have separate clear ($\overline{CLR}$) inputs, so that the eight outputs may be independently cleared at the start of a control sequence, or when the interface is first turned on.

A typical interface circuit in which the NE590 is used is shown in Fig. 1-28. In this example, a data bit from the data bus is used to provide the logic state that is to be latched into the particular bit that is addressed by address bits A2 through A0. Note that the remaining low address bits, A7 through A3, and the $\overline{OUT}$ function

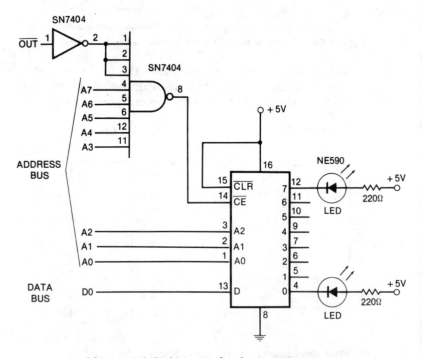

Fig. 1-28. A typical LED-driving interface for the NE590 (current sink).

Table 1-5. Output Commands for Control of the NE590 (See Fig.1-28)

Transistor	ON Command	OFF Command
Q0	OUT 248,1	OUT 248,0
Q1	OUT 249,1	OUT 249,0
Q2	OUT 250,1	OUT 250,0
Q3	OUT 251,1	OUT 251,0
Q4	OUT 252,1	OUT 252,0
Q5	OUT 253,1	OUT 253,0
Q6	OUT 254,1	OUT 254,0
Q7	OUT 255,1	OUT 255,0

pulse, have been gated together to generate the chip enable pulse that controls the actual latching process. In this interface circuit, eight separate device addresses are required, one per bit, while the least-significant bit in the data word transferred by each output command determines whether the addressed transistor switch is on or off. (In the NE590/NE591, logic 1 = transistor on, and logic 0 = transistor off.) In this example, the software instructions shown in Table 1-5 would be used to control the addressable latch. In each case, you must remember to provide the proper data word, so that the corresponding transistor is turned on, or off, as required. Unlike a conventional latch in which all eight data bits are loaded simultaneously, the bits in an addressable latch are loaded one at a time.

Table 1-6. Output Commands for Control of the NE591 (See Fig.1-29)

Transistor	OFF Command	ON Command
Q0	OUT 96,0	OUT 104,0
Q1	OUT 97,0	OUT 105,0
Q2	OUT 98,0	OUT 106,0
Q3	OUT 99,0	OUT 107,0
Q4	OUT 100,0	OUT 108,0
Q5	OUT 101,0	OUT 109,0
Q6	OUT 102,0	OUT 110,0
Q7	OUT 103,0	OUT 111,0

An alternate interfacing circuit is shown in Fig. 1-29, in which the NE591 has been used to source current for the displays. In this example, the data input of the latch is not connected to the data bus, but to one of the address bits, instead. Now, the state of address bit A3 determines whether a logic one, or a logic zero is latched, controlling the respective output transistor. It is not necessary to provide a specific data bit in the output instruction, since the output instructions themselves are used to control the latch. A list of the control software commands for this circuit is shown in Table 1-6. While the data values specified in this table are all zeros, the actual data value is irrelevant (don't care), since the data has no effect upon the latch.

The outputs of the NE590/NE591 chips should be treated as simple current sinks and current sources. The outputs may be used to drive lamps, LEDs, relays, displays, and other devices that require high currents. Since the outputs of the latches may be independently controlled, the latch provides an easy means for generating control pulses that may be used to control external devices, such as the instrument shown in Fig. 1-5. We have used the NE590 in this way to control one part of the interface circuit for a Diablo Hytype I printer. Normal TTL devices did not have the current driving capability, nor did they provide the needed functions in a single chip.

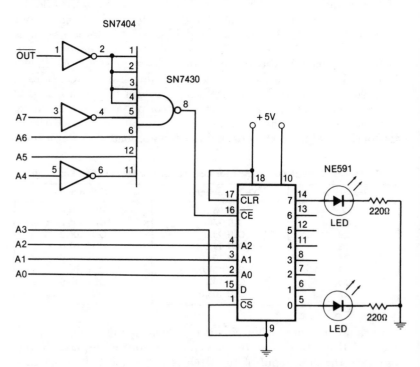

Fig. 1-29. An alternate LED-driving interface for the NE591 (current source).

CONTROLLING AC LINE LOADS

There will probably be applications in your computer system, in which it will be necessary to have the computer control loads that are powered by 117 volts, alternating current, or what is frequently called *line voltage.* The buffers, open-collector chips, and transistor arrays that have already been described cannot control high-voltage, high-current ac loads. One simple solution is to have the computer control buffer chips that in turn control relays, which further control the power to the loads that require line voltage. This is certainly an acceptable way to solve the problem, and it is used in some systems although there are simpler, and more reliable ways in which this task can be accomplished. In this section, we will describe some of the circuits that may be used to allow a small computer to control 117 V ac.

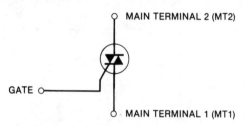

Fig. 1-30. Schematic representation of a triac switch device.

Simple Solid-State Controllers

Probably the simplest electronic switch that can be used to control 117 V ac loads is the *thyristor,* or *triac* semiconductor device, shown in Fig. 1-30. There are other semiconductor switches, but this discussion will be limited to the triac. The triac device has a gate input that is used to control the flow of current through the device. The simplest use of the triac is shown in Fig. 1-31. In this circuit, the triac will not conduct any current when the switch is

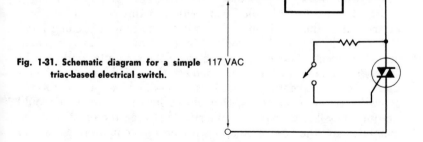

Fig. 1-31. Schematic diagram for a simple triac-based electrical switch.

open, but it will conduct current when the switch is closed. For interfacing purposes, it is preferable to have the computer control the switch so that the current through the load is controlled. An example of such a computer-controlled line switch is shown in Fig. 1-32, in which three triac devices have been used. You should be able to recognize the main triac (T3) that has been used to control the current through the lamp (load). You should also be able to see how a second triac (T2) has been used in place of the mechanical switch that was shown in Fig. 1-31. This switching triac is controlled by a third triac (T1). A logic input turns a transistor on and off, controlling the triac-based switch. The +5-volt supply used in

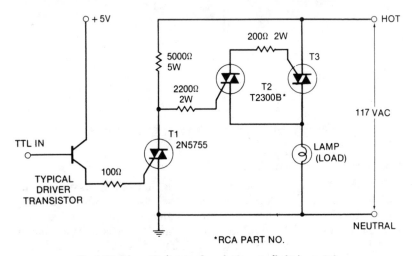

Fig. 1-32. Schematic diagram for a logic-controlled triac switch.

this circuit is the logic supply voltage. Since an incandescent lamp has been used as the load, the additional circuit components have been added to control the inrush current. We have used this as a simple example, merely to show how triac devices may be used to control line loads. A detailed explanation of this circuit is not necessary, since simpler circuits can perform the same switching function. One thing about this circuit (Fig. 1-32) may bother you. There are direct electrical connections between the computer and the 117 V ac line voltage. In the circuit shown, there will be no problems under normal operating conditions, but should a person drop a screwdriver, or other conductive object into the circuit, it would be quite possible to make a connection between the circuits of the computer and the line voltage, destroying the computer. We would like to have some means of protecting the computer from such a disaster.

An *optical coupler* could be used to isolate the computer circuits from the line voltage control circuits. Such a device is shown in cutaway form in Fig. 1-33. An infrared light-emitting diode (IRED) is placed above an infrared-sensitive photodetector. When the IRED is conducting, the infrared light is passed through a "light-pipe," to the detector. The incident infrared light causes current to flow through the detector. Of course, when the IRED is off, current ceases to flow through the detector, or at least it flows at a much reduced rate. In this way, the input signal that turns the IRED on and off is isolated from the photodetector, since there is no electrical connection between the IRED and the detector.

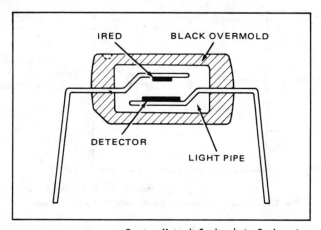

Fig. 1-33. A cut-away view of an optical coupler chip.

The Motorola Semiconductor group has developed an optical coupler that is designed to work directly with triacs and logic levels. This device, the MOC3011, allows the computer to control the IRED, while the infrared light is detected by the photodetector, which is used to control the triac. In this way, the computer may be used to control triac circuits, but without any direct electrical connections with them. The pin configuration for the MOC3011 is provided in Fig. 1-34. Two simple control circuits are shown in Fig. 1-35. These circuits illustrate how the MOC3011 may be used in triac circuits to control resistive (lamp) and reactive (motor) loads.

If you plan to use the MOC3011-type circuit in a number of different interfaces, it would be wise to protect the IRED side of the optical coupler. This can be done with a simple network of parts; a diode to protect against reversed polarity connections, and a transistor to limit the current through the IRED. This protective circuit is shown in Fig. 1-36, which provides a good general-purpose line control circuit, as well. The 2N6071B triac can handle about 4 amperes at 117 V ac. It is important to keep in mind the voltage drop across the triac, since this will generate some heat. If you choose to use this particular circuit, it would be a good idea to use a heat sink for the 2N6071B package. If you plan to control devices that require higher line voltages, say 240 V ac, you cannot use the MOC3011 alone, since it cannot withstand the higher voltage. However, you can double-up the MOC3011 devices so that the voltage

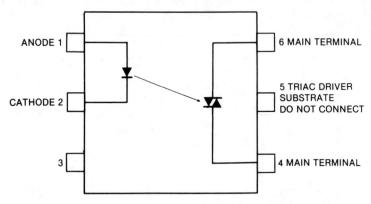

Fig. 1-34. The pin configuration for the MOC3011 optical coupler.

(240 V ac) is equally divided across them. This is shown in Fig. 1-37. Two one-megohm resistors have been used to provide the voltage divider circuit. The protection network on the inputs to the optical coupler has been left out, for clarity.

Solid-State Relays

If you are not particularly excited about the prospect of building a triac-based line switch for each of the line loads that you wish to control, then pre-packaged solid-state relays are an attractive alternative. All of the necessary triac, and other solid-state circuits are molded into a package that simply requires installation in the load circuit, and some simple connections to the computer interface. The schematic diagram of a typical solid-state relay is very similar to that shown in Fig. 1-36. Some typical solid-state relays are shown in Fig. 1-38. These devices are available in a wide variety of sizes and shapes, and with various voltage and current levels. Solid-state relays have their advantages and disadvantages, some of which are listed in Table 1-7. Most solid-state relays can be used in either 117 V ac, or 220 V ac circuits, and relays with current-carrying

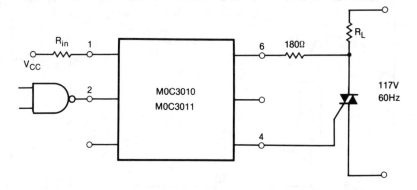

(A) Resistive loads.

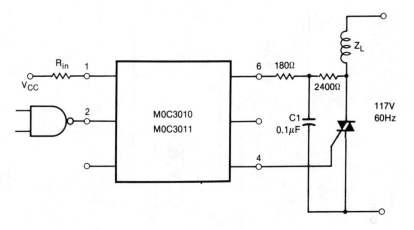

(B) Reactive loads.

Courtesy Motorola Semiconductor Products, Inc.

Fig. 1-35. Two simple triac controllers for resistive loads and reactive loads.

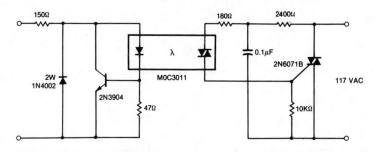

Courtesy Motorola Semiconductor Products, Inc.

Fig. 1-36. A general-purpose triac controller with a protected logic input.

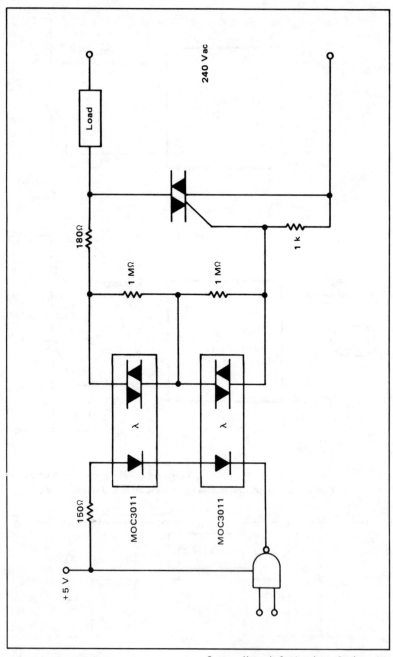

Courtesy Motorola Semiconductor Products, Inc.

Fig. 1-37. Using MOC3011 optical couplers to control 240 V ac triac switches.

Fig. 1-38. Photograph showing the physical characteristics of various solid-state relays.

capabilities of up to 45 amperes are available. Since most solid-state relays are optically coupled to the load-controlling triac, there is substantial voltage isolation between the control and line sides of the relays. This isolation is often several thousand volts, generally running between 1500 and 2500 volts on commercially available models.

Table 1-7. Advantages and Disadvantages of Solid-State Relays

Advantages	Disadvantages
Wear-resistant, no moving parts to wear out.	Require heat sinks, due to the voltage drop in the switching semiconductor.
Quite, contact cleaning is not required.	Generally, just ac loads can be switched.
Directly compatible with TTL and other logic families.	Different contact arrangements are difficult to obtain, most are normally open.
Repeatable performance.	Can be expensive.

Solid-state relays must be used in interfacing applications with some care. When these devices are used to control the high voltages and high currents associated with line loads, it is not always possible to know where in a 117 V ac, 60 Hz (or 50 Hz) cycle, the load will be turned on. If the relay happens to be at the peak voltage when it is turned on, there will be a sudden rush of current through the solid-state relay. This high current can often exceed the maximum current rating of the solid-state relay in use. The instantaneously high current can also cause the solid-state relay circuit to radiate a great deal of electromagnetic noise, over a wide spectrum of frequencies. This noise can be picked up by computer circuits, causing malfunctions, bad data values, and other problems. These problems may be substantially reduced by using a technique called *zero-voltage switching*. When zero-voltage switching is used in a solid-state relay, the relay will only start to conduct voltage, when the alternating voltage applied to it on the load side reaches zero, even if the controlling side of the relay has been activated somewhere in the middle of a voltage cycle. The zero-voltage crossing points

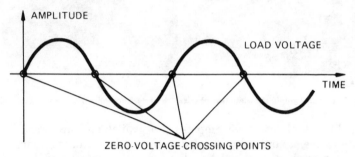

Fig. 1-39. Zero-voltage crossing points in a 117 V ac waveform[4].

are shown in Fig. 1-39, while the timing relationship between the on command and the actual turning on of the load is illustrated in Fig. 1-40. The maximum delay in turning on the solid-state relay is about 8.3 milliseconds, the period of half a cycle at 60 Hz. In most applications in which solid-state relays are used, this will be an insignificant period. Since there is some additional circuitry in zero-voltage switching solid-state relays, to detect the zero-crossing point, some current will be drawn through the load by the relay, even when it is off. This doesn't generally exceed a few milliamperes, however. Actually, most zero-voltage switching solid-state relays don't switch at exactly zero volts, but within about one to five volts of the zero-crossing point.

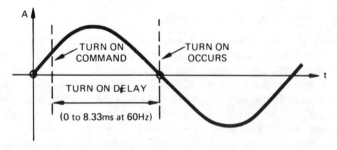

Fig. 1-40. Timing relationship between the turn on command, and the actual zero-voltage switching point[4].

By way of an example, consider a control system in which an incandescent lamp is to be turned on and off by a solid-state relay. The problem of inrush current has already been discussed, but it is an important consideration in the selection of solid-state relays. We will assume that the cold resistance of the filament is 2.4 ohms, and the on resistance is 24 ohms. This ratio is quite reasonable for an incandescent bulb. In calculating the worst case conditions, we will assume that the lamp is turned on when the voltage (117 V ac) is at its peak. Thus, the instantaneous current through the lamp is about *70 amperes:*

$$I_{PEAK} = \frac{V_{PEAK}}{R_{COLD}}$$

$$= \frac{120\sqrt{2}}{2.4}$$

$$= 70 \text{ amperes}$$

If we assume that the switching takes place at 5 volts, which is very close to the zero-voltage point, then the instantaneous current is greatly reduced, being about 2 amperes, instead of 70. Most solid-state relays can operate at high currents for a few cycles, so while start-up and inrush currents may be high, they can frequently be tolerated if they are only present for a few cycles. For example, a solid-state relay that is rated at a maximum current of 10 amperes can handle a peak current of 50 to 60 amperes for one or two cycles, 30 amperes for 10 cycles, or 15 amperes for 100 cycles.

Since the triac devices will continue to conduct current until the gate signal is removed, you may be wondering about the use of zero-voltage switching to turn them off. Actually, the triacs take care of this themselves, since it is the nature of the triac to continue to conduct until the voltage across the triac reaches zero volts, even if the gating signal had been removed elsewhere in the cycle. No special turn-off circuitry is required.

RELAY PROTECTION

Since solid-state relays are frequently used with inductive loads, such as motors, or large relays, it is possible for such loads to generate a back emf when they are turned off. Such emf, or voltage spikes, may be "detected" by the triac in the solid-state relay, causing it to turn back on. It is advisable to use a "snubber" circuit across the load outputs of the solid-state relay, if this appears to be a problem. The snubber circuit helps to reduce the voltage spikes, so that the relay will not be re-energized. Typical snubber circuits are shown in Fig. 1-41. Likewise, glitches or transient high-voltage

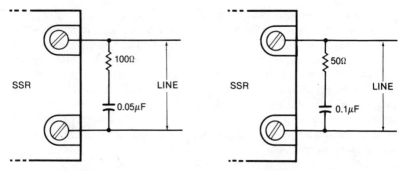

Fig. 1-41. Typical snubber circuits for use with solid-state relays.

spikes on the power lines may also cause solid-state relays to turn on.

Since triacs are used in solid-state relays, they will cause a voltage drop in the load circuit, which will generate heat, in direct relation to the current that is being switched by the relay. Unless you will be using solid-state relays to control fairly low-current devices, the relays should be provided with heat sinks. A typical relationship between the temperature of a relay, and its ability to carry current, is shown in Fig. 1-42. Typically, a 7-ampere solid-state relay can only be used to switch a 1.5 ampere load, unless heatsinking is provided[4]*.

There are other considerations that must be carefully evaluated before solid-state relays can be used in an interface. Most relays

---

* Numbers in parentheses refer to references at the end of the chapter.

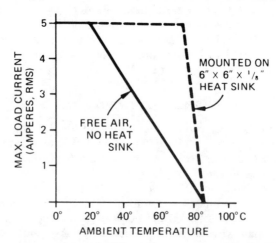

Fig. 1-42. Load current *versus* temperature for a solid-state relay[4].

must have a minimum current passing through them when they are turned on, and there are upper and lower limits on the voltages that may be applied to both the control and load sides of the device. In almost all cases, you will find that solid-state relays are not universal, and that one relay will not suit all of your needs. If you wish to apply solid-state relays to interfacing tasks, we suggest that you take the time to contact some of the manufacturers listed at the end of the chapter, since they will be able to provide you with specific information on the various relays that they manufacture. Many of the manufacturers have written application notes that describe specific applications, general guidelines, and other useful information.

Before we end our discussion of solid-state relays, and other devices that are used to control what can generally be called nonlogic devices, there is one other type of protective device that should be considered. This is the metal-oxide varistor, or MOV. These devices can be used in a variety of different ways to protect computers, control circuits, interfaces, power supplies, and other important parts of a computer system, from high-voltage transients, or spikes. Rather than describe these devices in great detail, we refer you to the well-written applications manual, available from General Electric[6]. In this manual, you will find out more about how you can protect your investment in computer and other electronic equipment.

Oh, yes, we are sure that some of you are wondering about the bells and whistles mentioned in the title of this chapter. Actually, electromechanical bells are simply relay-like circuits, but be sure

SOME SOLID-STATE RELAY MANUFACTURERS

Douglas Randall
6 Pawcatuck Avenue
Pawcatuck, CT 02891

EI&S
42 Pleasant Street
Stomeham, MA 02180

Elec-trol, Inc.
26477 N. Golden Valley Rd.
Saugus, CA 91350

Gordos Arkansas, Inc.
1000 N. Second Street
Rogers, AR 72756

Gould, Inc.
Controls Division
100 Relay Road
Plantsville, CT 06479

Motorola Inc.
Subsystem Products
P. O. Box 29023
Phoenix, AZ 85038

Opto 22
5842 Research Drive
Huntington Beach, CA 92649

Sigma Instruments, Inc.
170 Pearl St.
Braintree, MA 02184

to use good diode protective circuits, since the back emf is generated rather frequently. Solid-state buzzers solve this problem nicely, and they may be driven by open-collector chips, or peripheral drivers, without a great deal of fuss. Whistles, like fire whistles, are generally controlled by a 117 V ac motor, which can be controlled by a solid-state relay, which may be controlled by an open-collector gate, which may be controlled by a computer, etc.

REFERENCES

1. The Peripheral Driver Data Book, Texas Instruments, Inc., Dallas, TX 75222, 1977.

2. Linear and Interface Circuits Applications, Texas Instruments, Inc., Dallas, TX 75222, 1974.

3. Sprague Integrated Circuit Data Book (WR-500), Sprague Electric Co., Worcester, MA 01606, 1978.

4. Designer's Handbook of Solid-State Relays, Gordos Arkansas, Inc., Rogers, AR 72756, 1977.

5. Stepper Motor Handbook, North American Philips Controls Corp., Cheshire, CT 06510.

6. Transient Voltage Suppression Manual, 2nd ed., General Electric Co., Auburn, NY 13201, 1978.

2

Analog and Digital
Conversions and Data
Processing

It is our purpose in this chapter to introduce you to the ways in which your TRS-80 computer can both control and measure external signals that are represented by voltages and currents. You may be asking yourself, "Why would I be interested in doing this?" When you consider the many physical measurements that can be made through the indirect measurement of a voltage or a current, the usefulness of these measurements will be quickly apparent. Consider the measurement of strain, torque, temperature, pressure, incident light, humidity, and other quantities. Each of these can be converted to a voltage that can be readily measured by a computer system. Likewise, there are many cases in which the computer can be used to generate a voltage, or a current, that can be used to control an external device. While some of the on/off interface circuits have already been discussed, there are other situations in which the computer must be able to generate continuously variable voltages, for the control of servo motors, programmable voltage boosters, function generators, electrochemical plating baths, and other voltage-dependent devices. When we talk about using the TRS-80 to actually measure a varying voltage, we will really be talking about the use of devices called *analog-to-digital* converters, and when we describe those situations in which the TRS-80 will be "generating" a varying voltage, *digital-to-analog* converters will be used. There are special types of control interfaces for each of these devices, and they will be described in this chapter, along with the software that will be required to properly control them.

OBJECTIVES

At the end of this chapter, you will be able to:

- Describe the function of a digital-to-analog converter.
- Describe the relationship between the number of input bits to a digital-to-analog converter, and its resolution.
- Describe the operation of a simple eight-bit digital-to-analog converter interface circuit.
- Use the MC1408 and NE5018, eight-bit digital-to-analog converter integrated circuits.
- Write software to control digital-to-analog converters.
- Describe double buffering for digital-to-analog converters.
- Describe the detailed use of digital-to-analog converters in several applications.
- Describe the interfacing requirements of analog-to-digital converters.
- Design analog-to-digital converter interface circuits, using the AD571 and ICL7109 converter chips.
- Describe the application of analog-to-digital converters in several measurement experiments.
- Describe some simple data processing tasks.
- Develop software to control analog-to-digital converters.

In this chapter, the emphasis will be placed upon the use of digital-to-analog (D/A) converters, and analog-to-digital (A/D) converters, so the discussion will center upon several of these converter devices, rather than on an introduction to the many different types of converters that serve the same purpose. You should be aware, though, that there are literally hundreds of different types of converter products, many of which are general-purpose in nature, and some of which have been designed for very specific purposes. As you read through this chapter, you will be provided with some of the details of the various types of converters that are available.

Some of the information in this chapter will discuss the *processing* of information that has been acquired by the computer from an external source. The topics of averaging, filtering, integrating, etc., will be discussed, since it is important to be able to use the information once it has been acquired. The internal operation of D/A and A/D converters has been covered elsewhere, and we refer you to some of the references at the end of this chapter for some of the details of how these devices actually work. For the most part, we will be treating these converters as if they are the proverbial "black boxes" that are well known in engineering circles. Our main concern, and yours, is in the use of these devices, and not what makes them work the way that they do. Now that we have introduced you to this new series of topics, let us start our discussion with the simplest type of converter, the digital-to-analog converter.

DIGITAL-TO-ANALOG CONVERTERS

Digital-to-analog converters, frequently noted as DACs, or D/A converters, are circuits that have digital inputs and a single analog output. The digital inputs are combinations of logic ones and logic zeros that form a binary number. In the applications and circuits described in this book, these inputs will be compatible with the logic levels that are generated by TTL circuits. Thus, they are TTL-compatible inputs. The analog output provided by a D/A converter is a voltage that is continuously variable between an upper and a lower limit. So that some basic principles can be illustrated, we will assume that a D/A converter is available with four binary inputs, and with an analog output that has a range from 0 to +15 volts. The 16 possible binary inputs range from 0 (0000) to 15 (1111).

Each of the four binary inputs to the converter is weighted, in much the same way that the bits themselves are weighted. In the four-bit D/A converter, the four inputs would have weights of one, two, four, and eight, each being an integer power of two. Since each bit is weighted differently, each bit will "contribute" a different amount to the output voltage of the D/A converter. In this case, the most-significant bit (MSB) has a value of either zero, or eight, so it can contribute either 0 or 8 volts to the output of the converter. The least-significant bit (LSB) will also make a contribution to the total output, this being either 0 or 1 volt. We have assumed that the D/A converter contains the necessary circuitry to accurately add these contributed voltages. In this converter, then, the binary bits have the ability to add either zero, or their particular weight, expressed in volts; that is, 8 volts, 4 volts, 2 volts, and 1 volt. Any voltage between 0 and 15 volts (0, 1, 2, 3, . . . 13, 14, or 15 volts), can be generated by the four-bit D/A converter, through the application of the proper four-bit binary code to the four inputs of the converter. The relationship between the binary inputs, and the voltage output, is shown in Table 2-1.

While the output of the D/A converter was noted as being "continuous," you should note that the output of this four-bit D/A converter is a series of discreet voltages that are easily measured. In fact, the output of every D/A converter will be discreet voltage steps, whether the steps are a few millivolts, or 1 volt.

**Table 2-1. Four-Bit D/A Converter With Voltage Range
From 0 to 15 Volts**

Binary Code Input				Output Voltage
D = 8	C = 4	B = 2	A = 1	(Volts)
0	0	0	0	0
0	0	0	1	1
0	0	1	0	2
0	0	1	1	3
0	1	0	0	4
0	1	0	1	5
0	1	1	0	6
0	1	1	1	7
1	0	0	0	8
1	0	0	1	9
1	0	1	0	10
1	0	1	1	11
1	1	0	0	12
1	1	0	1	13
1	1	1	0	14
1	1	1	1	15

The block diagram for a typical D/A converter is shown in Fig. 2-1. In most commercially available D/A converters, the binary inputs control switches that either add, or do not add, to the total output, a current that is proportional to their weight. It is much easier to switch currents in these devices, than it is to switch voltages. A precision resistor ladder is used to control the individual

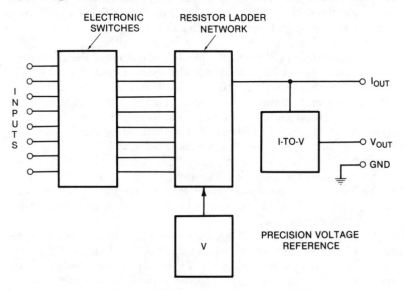

Fig. 2-1. Block diagram of a typical D/A converter.

currents, and you may see the notation "R/2R resistor ladder network," associated with D/A converters.

In computer interfacing, you will probably find little use for D/A converters with fewer than eight bits. In fact, 10- and 12-bit D/A converters are quite common in computer systems. As the number of binary inputs is increased, so is the *resolution* of the converter. This simply means that the voltage steps that are output by the converter, are smaller. Thus, an 8-bit D/A converter would have a resolution of one-part-in-256, and a 12-bit converter would have a one-part-in-4096 resolution. You will probably find that most interfacing tasks that call for an analog control voltage, are easily handled with 8- or 10-bit D/A converters.

Digital-to-analog converters are very fast, converting the applied digital value into the corresponding voltage output within a microsecond. There is no other control required; you simply apply the binary bits, and the voltage output of the converter changes accordingly. Typically, *output ports,* or *latches,* are used in computer interfaces to store binary values for use by D/A converters. You should be familiar with these devices from *TRS-80 Interfacing, Book 1* (Howard W. Sams & Co., Inc., Indianapolis, IN 46206).

Before we get started discussing the interfacing of D/A converters, we need to spend a bit more time discussing the characteristics of the output of the converter. For the purposes of this discussion, we will assume that there is an 8-bit D/A converter available, with its output specified as being within the range of 0 to +10 volts. In this converter, there are 256 different voltages, each of which consists of contributions from the 8 weighted binary inputs. The MSB would contribute 5, or 0 volts, while the next to the MSB would contribute 2.5, or 0 volts, and so on, for each of the 8 bits, as shown in Table 2-2. If you add all of these 8 weighted voltages, as the converter would for a binary input of 11111111_2, or 255, you would find that the total is 9.9609375 volts, and not 10 volts, as was specified. How can this be? Just remember that the MSB contributes one-half of the full-scale voltage, the next to MSB contributes one-quar-

Table 2-2. Voltage Weights for an Eight-bit D/A Converter

Bit Position	Voltage*
Most-significant bit	5.0000000 = ½ of full scale
	2.5000000 = ¼ of full scale
	1.2500000 = $1/_8$ of full scale
	0.6250000 = $1/_{16}$ of full scale
	0.3125000 = $1/_{32}$ of full scale
	0.1562500 = $1/_{64}$ of full scale
	0.0781250 = $1/_{128}$ of full scale
Least-significant bit	0.0390625 = $1/_{256}$ of full scale

*10-volt full-scale converter

ter, and so on. Only an infinite number of bits would be able to have their corresponding voltages added to reach the 10-volt full-scale specification. Actually, the 9.9609375-volt full-scale output is close enough to 10 volts for most interfacing tasks. In fact, the difference between the maximum output from the D/A converter, and the 10-volt maximum that was specified, is 0.0390625 volt, the contribution from the LSB. Ten-bit and 12-bit D/A converters with the same full-scale range have smaller voltage steps, or greater resolution, so that they can more closely approximate the 10-volt full-scale voltage, as noted in Table 2-3. In this discussion, we have provided all of the decimal digits for the calculations of the voltages for each step. In practice, this is not really practical, since most measurements are useful to three significant digits. Thus, the 9.9609375-volt maximum would really be measured at about 9.96 volts.

Table 2-3. Voltage Resolution of Various D/A Converters

Converter	Max Full Scale*	Resolution	% Resolution
8-Bit	9.9609375 volts	0.0390625 volts	0.39
10-Bit	9.9902344 volts	0.0097656 volts	0.1
12-Bit	9.9975588 volts	0.0024412 volts	0.024

*10-volt full-scale converter

Not all converters have the same full-scale voltage output. Some converters are available with a variety of outputs, for example ±2.5 volts, ±5 volts, 0–10 volts and 0–1 volt. Current output D/A converters are also available, having outputs of ±1 mA or 0–10 mA. The converters that have both positive and negative output voltages are called *bipolar* D/A converters, while those that have either positive or negative outputs, are called *unipolar* D/A converters. There are applications for both types. If you need a D/A converter that has a voltage range that is not readily available among the standard converters offered by manufacturers, you can use operational amplifiers (op-amps), to change the range, to add an offset voltage, to invert the voltage, and perform other "conversion" functions on the analog output from the converter. Op-amps are also used to convert the current output by some D/A converters into a voltage.

Just as the converters have different types of outputs, there are devices that have different types of digital inputs, too. Some of the commonly available input codes include binary, binary-coded decimal (BCD), and offset binary. In most cases, the binary input models will be the most useful in computer interfacing applications. Converters are also available with inputs that are compatible with the various types of logic families, for example, CMOS, ECL, and TTL. The wide variety of D/A converters makes them easy to use in computer interface circuits.

D/A Converter Interfacing

As was mentioned previously, most interfaces that use a D/A converter also have latches between the data bus of the microcomputer and the inputs of the converter, since it is necessary to maintain the digital input to the converter for as long as the same voltage output is required. Without the latch function, the D/A converter could not perform any useful function. A typical D/A converter interface circuit is shown in Fig. 2-2. A control pulse is required to activate the latch, and in this circuit, the $\overline{\text{OUT}}$ function pulse has been gated with device address "7," to provide the needed

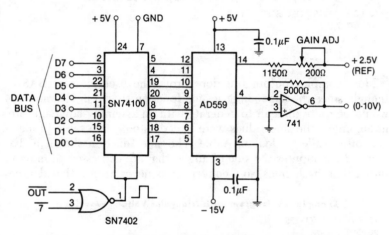

Fig. 2-2. A typical eight-bit D/A converter interface, using an Analog Device AD559 converter.

device select pulse. A typical command that could be used to control this circuit would be OUT 7,100, which would transfer the 8-bit binary value 01100100 to the latch, and thus to the eight inputs of the D/A converter. If a 10-volt full-scale converter is used, an output of about 3.91 volts would result from the execution of this command. Since the D/A converter is under the control of the programmer, various programs can be written to control the voltage output in many ways. The three programs listed in Examples 2-1, 2-2, and 2-3 show how an increasing voltage ramp, a decreasing voltage ramp, and a triangular voltage sweep can be generated. The programs have been written in BASIC, so that they are compatible with the TRS-80 computer. Several other programs that may be used with an 8-bit D/A converter are contained in Experiment No. 11 in *TRS-80 Interfacing, Book 1.* You might be interested to know that the positive ramp program generated a ramp with a

Example 2-1. Program for a Positive Voltage Ramp

```
10 FOR I=0 TO 255
20 OUT 7,I
30 NEXT I
40 GOTO 10
```

period of about 1.5 seconds. An equivalent *assembly-language* program required only six 8-bit bytes of memory, and it was able to generate a similar ramp with a period of *3.6 milliseconds,* or about 400-times faster than was possible with the BASIC program.

Example 2-2. Program for a Negative Voltage Ramp

```
10 FOR I=255 TO 0 STEP −1
20 OUT 7,I
30 NEXT I
40 GOTO 10
```

More complex output functions prove the usefulness of BASIC, though, since the trigonometric sine function shown in Example 2-4 would be quite difficult to generate with an assembly-language program, unless the sine values were already stored in a table in memory, often called a look-up table. The sine function shown in Example 2-4 computes the sine of angles that are expressed in radians, rather than in degrees, so a conversion is necessary, so that degrees

Example 2-3. Program for a Triangular Voltage Waveform

```
10 FOR I=0 TO 255
20 OUT 7,I
30 NEXT I
40 FOR I=255 TO 0 STEP −1
50 OUT 7,I
60 NEXT I
70 GOTO 10
```

are converted to radians. This program also illustrates some other things that must be considered when attempting to use higher-level languages, such as BASIC, and simple hardware interfaces. You should recall that the TRS-80 computer can only transfer eight bits of information to an output device at one time, consisting of values between 0 and 255, inclusive. The values for the sines of different

Example 2-4. Generating a Sine Voltage Function

```
100 FOR I=0 TO 360
110 A=128+INT(127*(SIN(I*0.017453)))
120 OUT 7,A
130 NEXT I
140 GOTO 100
```

angles vary between −1 and +1, so how can an 8-bit D/A converter be used to display a sine function, such as the one generated by the program listed in Example 2-4?

The full-scale range of the sine values must be converted to the full-scale range of the D/A converter, and the *bipolar* sine values must be converted to *unipolar* values for use by the D/A converter. These functions are performed in Example 2-4, at line No. 110. Note that if the sine of an angle is zero, the resulting value for the variable, A, is 128, which when transferred to the D/A converter, will place the output voltage at the middle of the output range. The sine of the unknown angle is multiplied by 127, so that the sines of the angles between 0 and 360 degrees will be converted to values between −127 and +127. When these values are added to +128, the resulting range of values for A is +1 to +255, values that are readily output to the output port of the D/A converter. The INT command is used to generate integer values of the sine, although this command could have been left out of the program, since the OUT command of the TRS-80 ignores fractional portions of values that are to be output.

You will find many applications for D/A converters in which either a particular function (positive ramp) or particular set of data values (sines of angles) may be required. In most cases, BASIC programming steps may be used to convert this information so that it may be output to binary D/A converters for use by a plotter, a display, or to control an instrument.

Practical D/A Converter Circuits

Now that you have seen a few of the things that a D/A converter can do, it is useful to look at a few other D/A circuits. The Motorola MC1480-8 integrated circuit is an 8-bit D/A converter sub-system that contains the current switches used in a complete D/A converter. Since this device costs only a few dollars, it has been quite popular for use in small computer systems. It requires a few external components, as well as an output port latch circuit. A typical circuit in which the MC1408-8 is used is shown in Fig. 2-3. An external operational amplifier has been used in this circuit to provide the necessary current-to-voltage conversion, so that the circuit will provide a 10-volt full-scale output. An external reference voltage is also supplied by the MC1408-8, 2.5 volts in this example, which flows through a 1250-ohm resistor to provide a known current flow of 2 mA. This means that the output of the MC1408-8 converter will be 2 mA at full-scale. A 5000-ohm feedback resistor is used in the op-amp circuit, to provide the 10-volt full-scale output, computed using Ohm's law, I = E/R. An LM318 op-amp, or equivalent, has been selected for its high performance characteristics. The use of voltage references will be discussed in more detail later, since this topic is quite important if the particular D/A converter that you will be using requires a stable, external reference source.

Another typical 8-bit D/A converter interface is shown in Fig. 2-4, in which a Signetics NE5018 D/A converter chip has been used. In this circuit, additional circuit components have been added, so that the output of the converter may be adjusted for the maximum voltage output desired, and so that the offset may be adjusted, too. The full-scale adjustment allows you to adjust the output of the circuit, so that its maximum is very close to 10 volts, or 9.96 volts

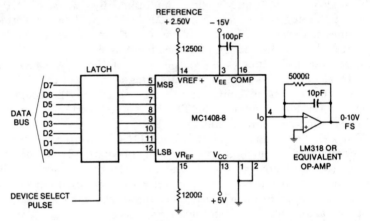

Fig. 2-3. A typical eight-bit D/A converter interface, using a Motorola MC1408-8 converter.

for true 8-bit conversions. The offset adjustment allows the output of the converter to be set at exactly zero for an input of 00000000_2. Most converter circuits can be adapted so that they include controls for full-scale and offset adjustments. Some converters may be configured so that either a bipolar, or a unipolar output is available. This can be done fairly easily with the NE5018, so that the output of the converter may be either ±5 volts, or 0 to 10 volts.

Two important features have been incorporated into the NE5018. One of these is the availability of an on-chip voltage reference circuit. The other is the presence of on-chip latches for the eight data bits. A simple latch enable ($\overline{LE}$) signal is supplied by the computer to transfer eight bits of information from the data bus to the internal latches. This does away with the need for an output port circuit, when the NE5018 is used. It has been our experience that the NE5018 is a very useful and convenient D/A converter circuit for general-purpose use. It is available for about $10.00. The NE5018 may be used without the full-scale and offset controls, simply by removing the four control resistors from the circuit.

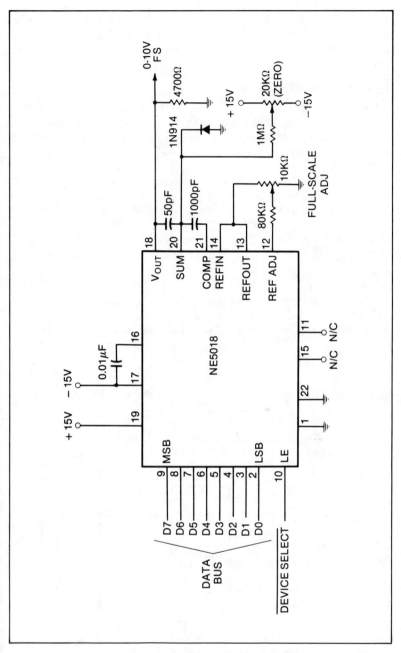

Fig. 2-4. An eight-bit D/A converter interface using the Signetics NE5018, with an internal latch.

Of course, there are many other 8-bit converters available from a number of different manufacturers. A representative list of some of these has been included at the end of this chapter, for your reference.

Higher Resolution Converters

There are situations in which analog control voltages are required, but with resolutions that are greater than that available from 8-bit converters. A four-fold increase in resolution is available when 10-bit D/A converters are used in place of 8-bit converters, but interfacing these devices to an 8-bit computer such as the TRS-80, presents some interesting problems. You will recall that the TRS-80 computer can only transfer 8 bits at a time, and that it is impossible for it to transfer a 10-bit value to an external device, all 10 bits at the same time. On the surface, the solution would seem to be trivial, since an 8-bit latch could be used for eight of the bits, and a 2-bit latch could be used for the remaining bits. Data transfers could take place through the use of one OUT command to transfer part of the data word (eight bits), and another OUT command to transfer the remaining part of the data word (two bits). Of course, two separate device addresses would be required for the proper control of the interface. Such an interface is shown in Fig. 2-5. If you attempted to use this circuit, along with the program listed in Ex-

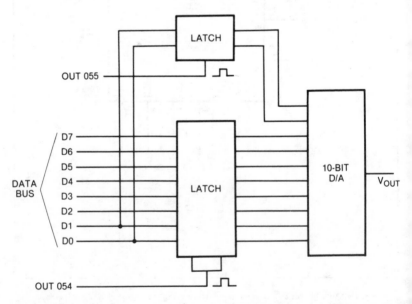

Fig. 2-5. Block diagram for a 10-bit D/A converter interfaced to an eight-bit computer.

**Example 2-5. A Positive Ramp Generator Program for a 10-bit
D/A Converter**

```
10 FOR I = 0 TO 1023
20 M = INT(I/256)
30 L = I − (256*M)
40 OUT 54,L
50 OUT 55,M
60 NEXT I
70 GOTO 10
```

ample 2-5, to generate a positive voltage ramp, you would observe
a number of glitches, or errors, in the output voltage. These errors
occur since the complete 10-bit binary value is not applied to the
inputs of the converter at exactly the same time. The BASIC program takes several milliseconds to execute each of the program
steps.

To eliminate such errors in the loading of 10-bit values to D/A
converters, a technique called *double-buffering* is used. A simple
double-buffered D/A converter circuit is shown in Fig. 2-6. The
MC3410 D/A converter chip has been chosen for this example, since
it is very similar to the MC1408-8 device that has been described
already. Note that the least-significant bits have two sets of data
latches between the data bus, and the inputs of the converter, while
the two most-significant bits have only one latch. As was the case
in the 10-bit D/A converter interface circuit shown in Fig. 2-5, two
separate latch control signals have been used, but there is a significant difference in the operation of these two interfaces. In the
double-buffered interface, the eight least-significant bits are loaded
into Latch No. 1 when the low-byte strobe (LBS) signal is generated by the computer. This latch retains the information that has
been transferred to it and presents it to the inputs to Latch No. 2.
Since Latch No. 2 has not been actuated, there is no effect upon
its outputs to the D/A converter. When the two most-significant
bits are transferred to the interface by the activation of the high-
byte strobe (HBS) signal, these bits are loaded into Latch No. 3.
The HBS signal also transfers the information from Latch No. 1
to Latch No. 2, so that the 10-bit data word is presented to the inputs of the D/A converter as a complete set of 10 bits. All that was
required in this new interface was an additional 8-bit latch circuit,
controlled by the HBS signal.

With the double-buffered 10-bit D/A converter, an error-free
ramp may be generated, since no glitches will be observed. In the
circuit shown in Fig. 2-5, the glitches are observed during the tran-
sitions from binary inputs of 0011111111 to 0100000000, from
0111111111 to 1000000000, and so on. The reason for the glitches
has been explained; the 10-bits of information are not transferred

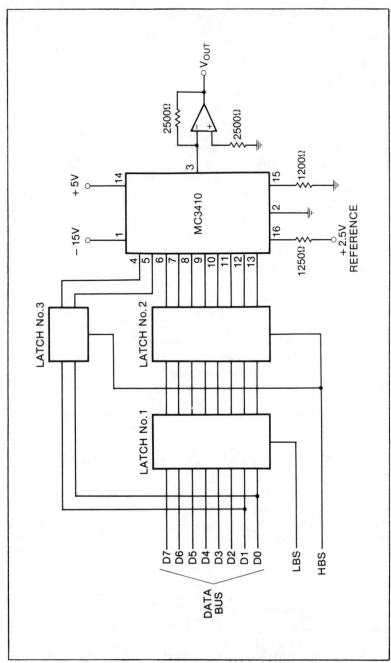

Fig. 2-6. A simple double-buffered 10-bit D/A converter interface.

to the inputs of the converter simultaneously. However, the actual errors, themselves, may not be quite so obvious. Assuming that the eight least-significant bits are transferred to the converter first, the transition from 0011111111 to 0100000000 would actually be from 0011111111 to 0000000000, and then to 0100000000.

A second approach to double-buffering is shown in Fig. 2-7. In this interface circuit, an Analog Devices AD561, 10-bit converter has been used. This converter contains an internal voltage reference, so it is fairly easy to use. In the interface circuit, a second latch has been used for both the least-significant bits, and for the most-significant bits, requiring three control lines. Here, the LBS

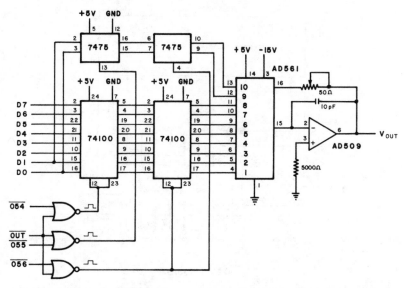

Fig. 2-7. A double-buffered 10-bit D/A converter interface, using Analog Device AD561.

signal loads the LSBs into an 8-bit latch, while the HBS signal loads the MSBs into a separate latch. The HBS signal *does not* transfer the new data word to the inputs of the D/A converter. A separate control signal, load D/A converter (LDAC), is used to transfer the separately formed portions of the complete 10-bit word to the converter. In this way, either the MSBs, or the LSBs, may be loaded into the interface circuit first, without disturbing the other bits. Only when the LDAC signal has been actuated, will the actual transfer to the converter take place. This double-buffering scheme provides a bit more flexibility than the one shown in Fig. 2-6, but it does require the use of an additional 2-bit latch, and a third control line. The program listed in Example 2-5 may be used with this interface, but an additional command would have to be included, so that the LDAC line would be pulsed by the computer:

55 OUT 56,0

Just as 8-bit D/A converters are being constructed with on-chip latch circuits, 10-bit D/A converters are being constructed with all of the necessary circuitry for the double-buffering functions. An example of this type of converter is the Analog Devices AD7522LN, as shown in Fig. 2-8. You should be able to distinguish the LBS, HBS, and LDAC signals. This chip costs about $20.00, which is

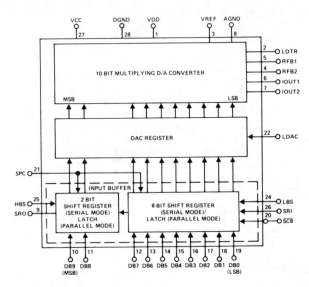

(A) Block diagram.

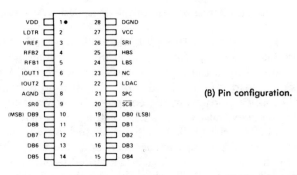

(B) Pin configuration.

Courtesy Analog Devices, Inc.

Fig. 2-8. The schematic diagram and pin configuration for the AD7522LN 10-bit double-buffered D/A converter chip.

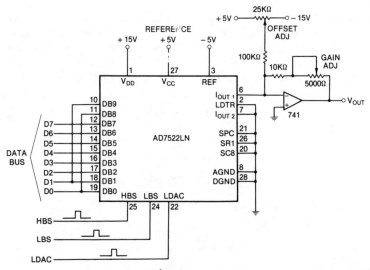

Fig. 2-9. Schematic diagram for a D/A converter interface, using the AD7522 double-buffered converter chip.

quite reasonable, when you consider that much of the interface circuitry has been provided on the converter chip. This converter does require an external reference, and a complete interface circuit is shown in Fig. 2-9. Both full-scale (gain) and offset control potentiometers have been included in this circuit, as has an op-amp for voltage output.

Reference Voltages

In many digital-to-analog converter circuits, an external voltage, or current, reference is required, to provide a reference upon which the final output of the converter is based. It should go without saying that a converter is only as good as its reference, although this relationship is frequently overlooked. If you use a voltage reference that is unstable, or that varies with temperature, supply voltage, or current, then the output of the D/A converter will vary, too. The best way to avoid these problems is by using a stable voltage reference source. There are many reference devices available, with one of the easiest to use being the Analog Devices AD580. This three-terminal reference can be operated with supply voltages that are between 4.5 volts, and 30 volts, to provide a steady 2.5-volt output (±1%). Since the AD580 is quite inexpensive, it can be used easily in those D/A converter circuits that require a 2.5-volt reference. The AD580 is shown in Fig. 2-10. You can also make a "poor man's reference," using a standard voltage regulator chip, such as the 78L05 five-volt regulator. This is shown in Fig. 2-11, in a configuration that uses a resistor divider network to obtain the 2.5-volt reference voltage. Voltage regulators have a possible error of about ±10%, so you may find that it is advantageous to use a standard reference voltage supplying chip, rather than a regulator, or you may wish to try to use a variable voltage regulator device, such as an LM117-series, or a 78MG00-series device. If a voltage regulator is used,

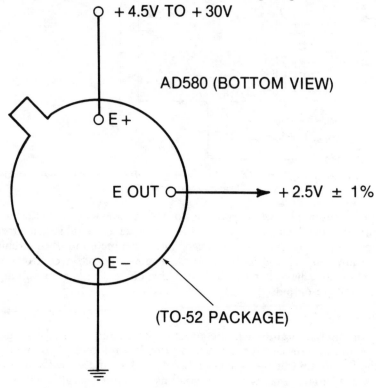

Fig. 2-10. Bottom view of the AD580 +2.5-volt voltage reference chip.

the voltage output by the D/A converter will only be as accurate as the voltage reference supplied by the regulator chip. It has been our experience that voltage regulator reference supplies work well for general experimental, and student laboratory use, while most practical applications demand the use of a commercially available reference chip.

You should also pay careful attention to the power supplies that are used to power the D/A converters in a computer interface circuit. These supplies should provide *clean,* ripple-free voltages that are well regulated. In fact, it is best if separate power supplies are used to power the converters and any associated analog circuitry,

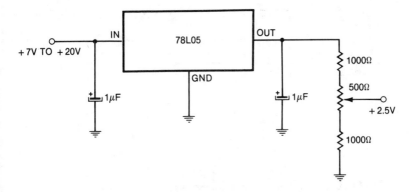

Fig. 2-11. A "poor man's reference," using a 5-volt voltage regulator chip.

since noise that is induced on the supply voltages from relay driving, lamp driving, etc., will invariably show up superimposed upon the analog signals that are generated by the D/A converters. It is also very easy to be careless in the design of interface circuits, since we tend to forget that ground lines carry substantial amounts of current. Current differences, and voltage differences on these ground connections can result in additional noise being added to the signal of the converter. The best solution to the problem of grounding is to use separate ground lines for the analog signal processing portions of your interface circuit, returning this ground directly to the power supplies of the analog circuit. Of course, a common ground is required between the power supplies of the digital circuit and the power supplies of the analog circuit. Such a connection should be made with heavy gauge wire. When breadboarding and testing interface circuits, the analog and digital ground paths are frequently treated as if they were the same. For most purposes, this will work without too much difficulty, but this should not be done when the actual interface is finally built for its end use.

D/A CONVERTER APPLICATIONS

There are many situations in which a D/A converter may be used to control a voltage-dependent device, of which servo motors, frequency synthesizers, voltage amplifiers, variable-gain amplifiers, programmable filters, and crt displays are typical examples. There are many others that will be obvious as you tackle new interfacing tasks. Rather than try to cover many different applications, we will provide a rather simple example that illustrates the power of D/A converters.

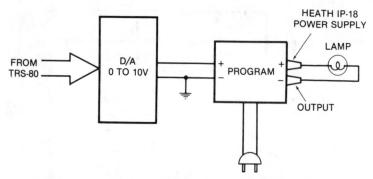

Fig. 2-12. Using a D/A converter to control a programmable power supply.

In this example, a simple incandescent lamp is to be cycled through a number of voltage changes for quality control purposes. A D/A converter is the obvious choice for generating the different voltages, but the converter by itself, even with an op-amp, cannot drive the lamp with enough current to light it. What is really needed is a high-powered D/A converter. The problem is readily solved by using a voltage-programmable power supply that will accept an external voltage, generating the same voltage at its output, but at higher currents. In this example, a Heath IP-18 power supply was used, since it has the remote-program feature, along with a 0- to 15-volt output, at a maximum of 500 mA. The output of the D/A converter was simply connected to the remote programming input on the rear of the power supply, as shown in Fig. 2-12. The gain and offset controls of the converter were adjusted so that the voltage output by the power supply was equal to the voltage generated by the various commands in the control program.

A program was written so that the lamp could be cycled between zero and an upper voltage limit that was entered into the computer by the test operator. A listing of the control program is shown in Example 2-6. You might ask, "Why would anyone want to cycle

Example 2-6. Lamp Test Program

```
 10 INPUT "LAMP VOLTAGE";V
 20 M=V*25.5
 30 FOR I=0 TO M
 40 OUT 6,I
 50 FOR T=0 TO 30: NEXT T
 60 NEXT I
 70 FOR I=M TO 0 STEP −1
 80 OUT 6,I
 90 FOR T=0 TO 30: NEXT T
100 NEXT I
110 GOTO 20
```

incandescent lamps?" There could be manufacturing situations in which it is necessary to cycle a new lamp design through 10,000 such cycles before the design could be given its final approval. The computer can do an excellent job of performing these tests. Instead of a lamp, other devices could be cycled in a similar manner: electrochemical electrodes, circuits for use in spacecraft, etc. In fact, you might want to run a device through a number of tests, not to see whether or not it would fail, but rather to see how it performed after the tests had been performed. If there was some way in which the intensity of the lamp could be monitored (by the computer, of course), then a complete lamp testing system could be built. The computer could also perform the functions of quality control reporting, generating a report sheet at the end of a day or shift, showing how the lamps, or other devices, performed during a given run through the production equipment. If the computer had the ability to "draw" graphic pictures, as the TRS-80 does, bar graphs, or histograms, could be generated, showing the number of failures in each lot that was processed by the computer. We will talk more about measurements in this chapter, so this should give you an idea of where you are headed.

Actually, the lamp testing program can be expanded, so that other tests can be run, too. In the program listings for Example 2-6, you will note that two statements have been used in the program, at lines 50 and 90. These commands provide time delays between each voltage step. These time delays could be lengthened, or removed, to create other test conditions. With the time delay commands taken out of the program, the test program took about two seconds to make the triangular voltage swing from 0 to 6 volts, and then back to 0. Additional program steps might be added so that an upper and lower voltage limit could be entered by the operator, along with the period of the voltage ramp. There are other refinements that could be added, too.

While a D/A converter may be used to control a device, such as the programmable power supply, two or more D/A converters are frequently required for control purposes. One of the most frequent uses of a dual D/A converter system is for the display of data on an oscilloscope, or on an X versus Y plotter, sometimes just called an X-Y plotter. Through the use of such instruments, the computer can be programmed to position an electron beam, or a pen, at a particular point on the display, and to either cause a point of light to be seen, or a dot on a piece of paper to be printed. When a number of such points have been generated by the computer, a complete picture may be observed, whether it is a graph of the units sold versus selling price, or a plot of map contours. Since it is very easy to examine a graphical representation of information, these types of displays are frequently incorporated into small computer systems. We will spend some time describing the use of D/A converters to control both X-Y plotters and oscilloscopes.

USING D/A CONVERTERS FOR GRAPHICS

In general, much of the information that is output to an oscilloscope or an X-Y plotter has been acquired from some process that varied with respect to time. For instance, the temperature of a greenhouse might be monitored every 15 minutes for 24 hours. The resulting temperatures could then be displayed, with respect to the time at which they were measured. In another application, the price of a stock might be entered into the computer at 3:00 pm each day, for 30 consecutive days. At the end of the 30-day period, the price of the stock could be plotted with respect to the dates on which the prices were observed.

You will note that one quantity is generally plotted *against* another quantity; in our examples, temperature *against* time, and price *against* time. Most plots involve one quantity that changes at a known rate, since it is easy to make measurements in this way, and since the resulting plots and graphs are easy to interpret. In our examples, we chose *time* for the continuously changing axis, with the stock prices and temperatures forming the unknown values that were plotted. There are probably dozens of other similar examples that come to mind, in which one quantity is continuously changing, while the other is being measured.

Digital-to-analog converters are frequently used to control both X-Y plotters, and oscilloscopes, since both are voltage-dependent devices. In each case, the voltage applied causes a proportional movement in either a pen carrier, or an illuminated spot on the face of the scope. Since the plotter and oscilloscope are both capable of presenting two-dimensional information, two D/A converters are used, one for the horizontal, or back-and-forth motion, and one for the vertical, or up-and-down movement. These movements are made on the X and Y axes, respectively. Since each of the D/A converters can be treated independently, as can any other I/O device, it is possible to control one axis, without affecting the other. Thus, the position of the pen, or electron beam, can be positioned anywhere in the display area. (We have assumed that the D/A converters and the display instrument have been adjusted properly.)

If two 8-bit D/A converters are used to control a plotter, there are 256 different positions for the pen along each of the two axes, providing the capability to "address" any one of 65,536 different points on the display area at which the pen can leave a mark. This provides a great deal of flexibility in terms of what you can display with the plotter. We will spend some time discussing the use of X-Y displays that are controlled by two D/A converters, since this type of device provides an ideal way of plotting information for later use. A block diagram of a typical dual D/A converter interface is shown in Fig. 2-13. Each D/A converter is controlled independently of the other. In this example, one of the D/A converters generates the continuously changing linear voltage ramp that moves the plotting device from left to right, while the other D/A converter supplies the actual information that is to be plotted. An X-Y

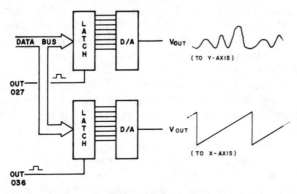

Fig. 2-13. Using two eight-bit D/A converters for X-Y display control.

plotter would only require a single scan in which to plot the values, while an oscilloscope would require multiple scans, one right after the other, in order to "refresh" the display on the phosphorescent screen. It is probably obvious, then, that the interface shown in Fig. 2-13 is being used to control an oscilloscope display, since the linear ramp is followed by another linear ramp, and so on, while the data output is also being repeated.

The transfer of information to the two D/A converters must take place in a synchronized manner, so that the proper X- and Y-axis voltages are applied to the device in the proper sequence. The program in Example 2-7 provides the steps that transfer the X- and Y-axis information to the two D/A converters, point by point. Note that the array of information that would be plotted by this program must have been generated previously, and the array is limited to 256 eight-bit values. As you look through this program, you may wonder where the X-axis values are being generated, to form the increasing values for the display. Since the array subscript is incremented by one each time that a new data value is obtained from the memory of the computer, this subscript value is also used as the X-axis value. In this way, the subscript value performs two

Example 2-7. A Simple Display Program

```
200 FOR T=0 TO 255
210 OUT 6,T:OUT 7,A(T)
220 NEXT T
230 GOTO 200
```

functions: it locates a specific data value in the array, and it locates the position at which the plotter is supposed to plot the information.

In this example, the program has been written so that when a display of the data has been completed, another complete display will start again, so that an oscilloscope may be used to observe the plotted information. When the program was run, however, it took the TRS-80 almost three seconds to display the 256 data points. This means that this type of a BASIC program is fairly limited in its ability to display information on an oscilloscope.

If a plotter were to be controlled by this program, there would have to be some means of controlling the up and down motion of the pen, otherwise the plotter would constantly be drawing lines, even when the computer repositions the pen to being a plot. Some time-delay steps would also have to be added to the program so that the plotter would have enough time to move from point to point before the pen was dropped onto the paper to leave a mark. While the beam of an oscilloscope may be able to reposition itself very quickly, up to one second may be required to allow the plotter to move to the next data point to be plotted. The pen control interface is rather simple, since most plotters have an external pen-control signal that may be used to control the position of the pen carrier. A typical interface is shown in Fig. 2-14. This circuit uses two output commands for pen control, so that only simple statements in the plotting program are required to control the pen. The

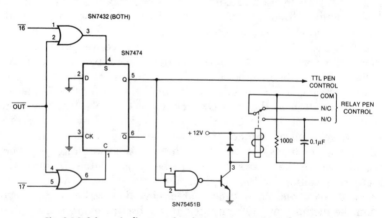

Fig. 2-14. Schematic diagram of a plotter pen-control interface circuit.

circuit uses a standard flip-flop circuit, in which the OUT 16,0 command moves the pen up, and the OUT 17,0 command moves the pen down. The pen takes a few milliseconds to change its position, so time delays for this must be included in the plotting program, too. Since some plotters have a TTL-compatible pen-control input, this has been shown in the pen control interface circuit, along with the relay contact connections which may be used with those plotters that have pen-control signals that are not compatible with TTL levels. A standard peripheral driver circuit has been used to drive the relay, and a snubber circuit has been included to help protect the computer interface from responding to any noise induced on the control lines by the operation of the pen-control circuitry of the plotter. Since it is impossible to know the characteristics of the control circuitry for each plotter, it is possible that one plotter will have its pen in the up position, when another plotter will have its pen in the down position, after execution of a pen-up command, OUT 16,0. This polarity is easily changed, either by switching the OUT 16,0 and OUT 17,0 commands in the program, or by switching the connection from the Q to the $\overline{Q}$ output on the flip-flop.

A plotter control program is shown in Example 2-8. Additional software delay statements have been used in this program so that the plotter will have enough time to move to the next point to be

Example 2-8. A Complete Plot Program

```
200 OUT 17,0
210 FOR T=0 TO 100:NEXT T
220 OUT 7,0:OUT 6,0:FOR T=0 TO 500:NEXT T
230 FOR J=0 TO 255
240 OUT 6,J:OUT 7,A(J)
250 FOR T=0 TO 100:NEXT T
260 OUT 16,0
270 FOR T=0 TO 50:NEXT T
280 OUT 17,0
290 FOR T=0 TO 50:NEXT T
300 NEXT J
310 END
```

plotted before the pen is dropped onto the paper. Likewise, the pen is left on the paper for a definite period, and then lifted for a definite period, before the plotter moves on to the next point. This provides enough time so that the pen is not raised or dropped in the middle of one of the movements of the plotter, which would result in a smudge or a streak on the paper. Since this is a plotter control program, only one pass through the program is required. When this program was tested, it took about 2½ minutes to plot all of the information in a 256-element array.

We will provide you with a number of different graphic programs that may be used with either an X-Y plotter, or with an oscilloscope. The plotter control functions have been left out, so if you wish to use these programs, these steps must be added for proper plotter control. Before we explore the use of some of these other display-generating programs, we want to provide you with some software that can be run on the TRS-80, so that an oscilloscope may be used to display data files. Since the display program that was provided in Example 2-7 is quite slow for an oscilloscope display, it cannot be used very well for X-Y displays of information. To speed up the display process, we must turn to *assembly language*, the language that is used to control the internal workings of the Z-80 micro-processor chip within the TRS-80 computer. A simple program that will allow you to continuously display a block or array of 256 data values in X-Y format is required. An assembly-language program can do this quite well, and fast enough so that an X-Y display on the oscilloscope appears to be present continuously. We do not intend to go into great detail about the program and how it works, but a listing is provided, along with the necessary details of using it.

An Assembly-Language Display Program

The assembly-language program that is discussed here is for use with an oscilloscope that has X-Y display capability. It will not work with a plotter, since the TRS-80 is transferring the data to the D/A converters faster than the servo motors and mechanical linkages can possibly react to it. There are no pen control commands, and no time delay statements in this program. In fact, the program requires only 16 bytes of read/write memory, along with the 256 bytes that are used to store the information that is to be displayed. A complete assembly-language program is listed in Example 2-9, for those readers who are interested in how it works. The actual operation of the program is very similar to that for the program provided in Example 2-7.

In order to use the assembly-language program, you must first reserve a portion of the read/write memory of the TRS-80 for the program, and also for the 256-byte data storage area. When you turn on the TRS-80, it asks you, MEMORY SIZE? At this time, type in 20079, and ENTER. This reserves the upper, or last, 400 read-write memory locations for your use. (Remember, we have assumed that your computer has 4K of memory.) A BASIC program that will load the assembly-language program steps into their corresponding memory locations is given in Example 2-10. Each code for an assembly-language step has been placed in the proper sequence in the DATA statement, and READ and POKE commands have been used to place these program steps in their proper read/

Example 2-9. An Assembly-Language Display Program for the TRS-80

Decimal Address		Op-Code	Hex Op-Code	Decimal Op-Code
20079	START,	LXIH	21	33
20080		00	00	0
20081		4F	4F	79
20082	LOOP,	MOVAM	7E	126
20083		OUT	D3	211
20084		07	07	7
20085		MOVAL	7D	125
20086		OUT	D3	211
20087		06	06	6
20088		INRL	2C	44
20089		JNZ	C2	194
20090		LOOP	72	114
20091		0	4E	78
20092		JMP	C3	195
20093		START	6F	111
20094		0	4E	78

write memory locations. Once you have entered the BASIC program, you may run it to transfer the information for the assembly-language program into read/write memory. How can you examine the read/write memory locations to be sure that these values have actually been transferred? A simple PEEK command can be used, for example, PRINT PEEK (20084), should print "7" when it is executed. You may wish to save the short BASIC-language program on a cassette tape for later use, since we will be describing the display of data arrays later in this chapter.

It is easy to run the assembly-language program, once the BASIC "loader" program has been run. When the computer displays READY, type in SYSTEM, and the computer should respond with "*?" Now, type in /20097, the starting address of the program, and hit ENTER. This will start the execution of the short assembly-language oscilloscope display program. Since the BREAK key will be inactive, you can only exit from the display program by actuating the RESET push button that is located near the expansion connector, inside the case of the TRS-80. If you have properly loaded the BASIC loader program, executed it, and started the display program, you should be able to observe that the two D/A converters are causing a somewhat random pattern of points to be dis-

Example 2-10. A BASIC Loader Program for the Display Routine

```
10 DATA 33,0,79,126,211,7,125,211,6,44,194,114,78,195,111,78
20 FOR I=0 TO 15
30 READ A
40 POKE (20079+I),A
50 NEXT I
60 END
```

Example 2-11. A Random Data Generator Program

```
200 N=20224
205 FOR I=0 TO 255
210 A=RND(255)
220 POKE N,A
230 N=N+1
240 NEXT I
250 END
```

played on the oscilloscope screen. There may be some distinct patterns, depending upon what happened to be stored in the read/write memory locations, when the power was applied to the TRS-80 computer. Remember, though, that to use this assembly-language program, a portion of the read/write memory of the TRS-80 must be protected when the computer is first turned on.

Once you understand the operation of the BASIC loader, and the use of the assembly-language program, you may wonder how an array of data may be transferred to read/write memory for later display. Just as the assembly-language program steps were transferred through the use of a POKE statement, so too may the data values. Of course, the data values must be between 0 and 255.

Two BASIC programs have been listed in Examples 2-11 and 2-12. Each will transfer a series of data values to the section of read/write memory that has been set aside for this purpose. This is called the display buffer area. The first program, Example 2-11, generates 256 random data values that will appear to be spread randomly across the screen of the oscilloscope. The second program, Example 2-12, is the sine-generating program that was described previously in Example 2-4. However, the necessary data transfer steps have been included in the new program. The sine program will generate 180 sine values, so not all of the points in the display will be used. They will be displayed, however, since the display program isn't very sophisticated, and it can't tell where the sine values end, and where the random information starts. The typical displays generated by these programs are shown in Figs. 2-15 and 2-16. Remember that these BASIC programs simply *generate* the data that are displayed by the assembly-language program located in the protected read/write memory. You must use the SYSTEM

Example 2-12. A Sine Function Generator Program

```
200 N=20224
205 FOR I=0 TO 360 STEP 2
210 A=128+INT(127*(SIN(I*0.017453)))
220 POKE N,A
230 N=N+1
240 NEXT I
250 END
```

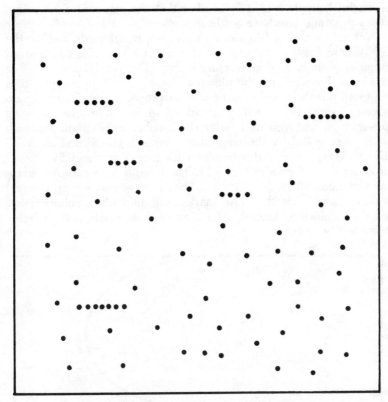

Fig. 2-15. Random data displayed during a test of the display program.

command to start the display sequence if you wish to try either of these program examples.

If you are interested in the use of Z-80 assembly language, we refer you to *Z-80 Microprocessor Programming and Interfacing, Book 1*, Howard W. Sams & Co., Inc., Indianapolis, IN 46206.

Plotter Applications

In many instances, a plot of data points on a blank sheet of paper is not all that is required of a data processing program. It would be convenient if the computer could "draw" a set of co-ordinate scales on the same sheet of paper, so that a reference could be readily established, and labels and scales easily added. Since the plotter may be controlled by the two D/A converters, it is fairly simple to develop a short BASIC program that will draw a box around the data, using the minimum and maximum values that may be accepted by the two D/A converters. Such a program is listed in Example 2-13. (Remember that the pen control and time delay program steps have not been included, for the sake of clarity.)

Not only is a boxed-in plot easy to read, but it lends itself to the addition of small marks along each axis, dividing each into a given number of units, so that labeling is easy. The BASIC program that drew the lines around the plot may be expanded to include steps that will put these scale marks in their proper places. The program given in Example 2-14 may be added to the co-ordinate-drawing program so that you may enter the number of divisions for each axis, when asked by the computer, "X AXIS DIV?" and "Y AXIS DIV?" A typical co-ordinate plot with four Y-axis and five X-axis scale marks is shown in Fig. 2-17. These scale marks are really approximations, since the output of the D/A converter is in discreet voltage steps, and the scale marks, and individual voltage steps may not coincide. Actually, the error is quite small, and probably wouldn't be noticed.

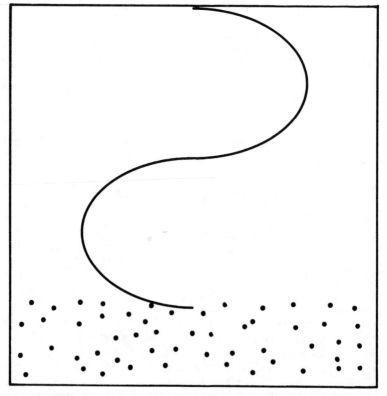

Fig. 2-16. A sine-wave function display. Note that some random data remain since the sine function does not fill the display buffer.

Example 2-13. A Co-ordinate Generator Program

```
 10 OUT 7,0:OUT 6,0
 20 FOR I=0 TO 255
 30 OUT 6,I
 40 NEXT I
 50 FOR J=0 TO 255
 60 OUT 7,J
 70 NEXT J
 80 FOR I=255 TO 0 STEP -1
 90 OUT 6,I
100 NEXT I
110 FOR J=255 TO 0 STEP -1
120 OUT 7,J
130 NEXT J
140 END
```

Since the scale marks are useful, actually completing these lines so that they extend completely across the plot might be even more useful in some cases. The program listed in Example 2-15 links the co-ordinate and scale-drawing programs, and it adds some steps that allow you to decide whether scale marks or complete grid lines are to be drawn. We are sure that a more sophisticated question could be asked by the computer, allowing the answer to be YES, or NO, but this is not the object of these programs. We leave it to you to modify the example programs that we have provided to meet your needs.

Example 2-14. A Scale Mark Generator Program

```
140 INPUT "X AXIS DIV";X
150 INPUT "Y AXIS DIV";Y
160 XA=256/X:XD=XA:YA=256/Y:YD=YA
170 FOR Q=1 TO X-1
180 OUT 6,XA
190 FOR I=0 TO 15
200 OUT 7,I
205 FOR T=0 TO 30:NEXT T
210 NEXT I
220 OUT 7,0
230 XA=XA+XD
240 NEXT Q
250 OUT 6,0
260 FOR Q=1 TO Y-1
270 OUT 7,YA
280 FOR I=0 TO 15
290 OUT 6,I
300 FOR T=0 TO 30:NEXT T
310 NEXT I
320 OUT 6,0
330 YA=YA+YD
340 NEXT Q
350 OUT 7,0
```

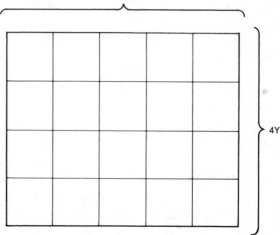

Fig. 2-17. Typical co-ordinates plotted by the TRS-80, by a BASIC control program.

What the question is asking is, "How long should the scale marks be; should they be short, or should they be as long as the respective axis?" The answer determines the length of these marks. The rest of the program remains the same. Modifications could be made to this program, so that the scale marks could be calculated in logarithmic ratios. In this way, semilog and log-log plots could be generated, along with the appropriate scale marks or grids.

X-Y Displays and Line Plots

The plotting systems that we have described so far are really Y versus time, or Y-T displays of information, regardless of the actual labels that are assigned to each of the axes. In each case, there was only one point for each value on the X axis. The sine function is a good example. The computer is generating the sine of an angle, but since an angle can only have one sine value, the result is a continuous function, or one that only has a single value for each value on one of the axes. The time axis has been represented by a steadily increasing value, or voltage, in the case of the D/A converters, which changed with respect to time. There are occasions, though, when the data that are to be displayed are not continuous. Just think back to the program that drew the lines, or box, around the plotted information. The lines are not a continuous plot, since the two D/A converters were controlled independently of each other and each point of the X axis had two or more points associated with it on the Y axis. In fact, the point at which X equalled zero

Example 2-15. A Complete Co-ordinate Plotting Program

```
10 OUT 7,0:OUT 6,0
20 FOR I=0 TO 255
30 OUT 6,I
40 NEXT I
50 FOR J=0 TO 255
60 OUT 7,J
70 NEXT J
80 FOR I=255 TO 0 STEP −1
90 OUT 6,I
100 NEXT I
110 FOR J=255 TO 0 STEP −1
120 OUT 7,J
130 NEXT J
140 INPUT "X AXIS DIV";X
150 INPUT "Y AXIS DIV";Y
152 INPUT "LINES − 0=NO 1=YES";K
154 IF K=0 THEN H=15 ELSE H=255
160 XA=256/X:XD=XA:YA=256/Y:YD=YA
170 FOR Q=1 TO X−1
180 OUT 6,XA
190 FOR I=0 TO H
200 OUT 7,I
210 NEXT I
220 OUT 7,0
230 XA=XA+XD
240 NEXT Q
250 OUT 6,0
260 FOR Q=1 TO Y−1
270 OUT 7,YA
280 FOR I=0 TO H
290 OUT 6,I
310 NEXT I
320 OUT 6,0
330 YA=YA+YD
340 NEXT Q
350 OUT 7,0
```

has 256 different Y-axis values. So, the box is not a continuous function. There are many other functions that are not continuous. Suppose that you wanted to have the TRS-80 draw a circle, or other object on the plotter. There would be great difficulty in drawing it using the Y-T type of display, since the plotter would have to plot two points for each value along the time, or X, axis. How then, do you use the computer to generate odd shapes and other discontinuous functions? The answer should be readily apparent. Each of the D/A converters is used independently, and neither is used to generate a continuously increasing (or decreasing) voltage. In this way, a true X-Y plotter is configured, so that odd shapes, schematic drawings, contour maps, and other such drawings are readily created. Since each point to be plotted has both an X-axis and a Y-axis coordinate, generating the information to be plotted requires twice as much storage space as the information to be plotted with a Y-T program. It is now fairly easy to plot a circle, using the well-known formula,

$$X^2 + Y^2 = R^2$$

When some arrays of information are plotted, some data points are invariably scattered about the plot, so that it is difficult to see a definite relationship in the information. All of the plotting that we have illustrated so far has been point plotting. That is, plotting by individual points, one after the other. The only exceptions have been the plots of the lines, or co-ordinates, that surround the plots, and the scale-mark plots. It would be valuable if the computer could plot straight lines between the various points, so that their relationship would be clear. This means that the computer would be used to "fill-in" the spaces between the two data values that are next to each other on the plot. You can do this with a straight-edge and a pencil. For the computer the problem is not difficult, but it takes a good understanding of the problem before you can begin to think about the programming that is necessary.

When using the computer to complete a straight line between two points, the points must be carefully defined. Since the co-ordinate system has been used so far, we will continue to use it to define the points that are to be connected. When two points are defined, say 64,65 and 196,197, the co-ordinates tell the computer

Example 2-16. A Best Straight Line Generator Program

```
10 INPUT "XI";XI
20 INPUT "YI";YI
30 INPUT "XF";XF
40 INPUT "YF";YF
50 IF (XI>XF) AND (YI>YF) THEN 60 ELSE 70
60 A=XI:XI=XF:XF=A:A=YI:YI=YF:YF=A
70 OUT 6,XI:OUT 7,YI
80 DX=XF-XI:DY=YF-YI
90 IF DX<DY GOTO 250
100 S=DY/DX
110 FOR I=1 TO INT(DX)
120 XI=XI+1:YI=YI+S
130 OUT 6,XI:OUT 7,YI
140 NEXT I
150 END
250 S=DX/DY
260 FOR I=1 TO INT(DY)
270 XI=XI+S:YI=YI+1
280 OUT 6,XI:OUT 7,YI
290 NEXT I
300 END
```

where the points are, so that it will know where to start the straight line, and where to end it. Since the slope of the line between the two points is easily calculated, the "rate of climb" (or rate of descent) for the line drawing is known. The computer program listed in Example 2-16 will plot the best straight line between two points. The basic idea is to calculate the slope, and to use this to determine the increase, or decrease, in one of the outputs of the D/A converter. Since the straight lines can go in any direction, the program must be able to handle both positive and negative slopes, as well as starting co-ordinates that are larger than the ending co-ordinates. The program also determined which of the axes should be used for the linearly increasing axis, so that the maximum number of points is used to fill in the gap between the two points of interest. This program is useful, since it can be used to superimpose trends, slopes and other information on top of plots, as well as to connect points on a plot. You will see another possible use for this type of program, when data processing is described in more detail.

USING ANALOG-TO-DIGITAL CONVERTERS

In this section, we will be describing the use of analog-to-digital converters, also called A/D converters, and ADCs. These devices give the computer the ability to measure an analog voltage, so that physical measurements of pressure, temperature, light intensity, and others may be made available to the computer for processing with BASIC-language programs. In some cases, it will be easy for you to sit down in front of your computer and enter various measurements by using the keyboard, while in other cases, it will be easier to use a sensor, and an analog-to-digital converter that is controlled by the computer. If you are simply converting a single temperature measurement from degrees-Fahrenheit to degrees-Celsius (centigrade), then it is easy to enter the value into a short BASIC program that will perform the conversion. However, if you are trying to measure the indoor and outdoor temperatures of a building every 10 minutes, over a 24-hour period, it would certainly be nice if a small computer could do this, without any actions from the operator. At other times, the measurements that are required will be acquired at such short time intervals, that it will be impossible to record the information fast enough by hand. Again, a small computer is ideally suited to quickly acquire such measurements.

Analog-to-digital converters are not difficult to use with small computer systems. In fact, two specific examples of A/D converter interfacing to the TRS-80 will be described in this chapter. The BASIC-language programs that are used to control the converters will also be discussed in detail.

Converter Interfaces

Most analog-to-digital converters operate by comparing an unknown applied voltage that is to be "converted," to a known voltage, or a series of known voltages. Since A/D converters are specified as having a particular range of input voltages, and a certain number of output bits, their resolution, or resolving power, is readily determined. For example, an A/D converter with a 0 to 10-volt input, and a 10-bit output can resolve any unknown voltage that is within its input range, into a 10-bit binary word, between 0 and 1023. Therefore, the resolution of the converter is one-part-in-1024, or 9.76 millivolts. In most cases, you will use A/D converters that have binary outputs, although other output coding formats are readily available. When A/D converters are used with binary computers, the models with binary outputs are the best bet, since no code conversions—in either software or hardware—are required.

A typical A/D converter is shown in block diagram form in Fig. 2-18. Notice that there is an unknown voltage input connection on the left side of the converter, and there are eight binary outputs on the right side. Unlike D/A converters, A/D converters require some additional control lines, one noted as READY/$\overline{\text{BUSY}}$, and the other noted as CONVERT. The CONVERT pulse must be sent to

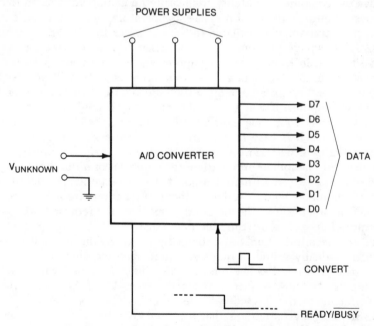

Fig. 2-18. Block diagram of a typical eight-bit A/D converter.

the converter whenever a conversion is required, since the A/D converter is not constantly converting unknown voltages into their binary equivalents. Compared to D/A converters, most A/D converters are rather slow. It can take from 20 microseconds to several milliseconds for A/D converters to perform a conversion, depending upon the technique used for the internal conversion process. Since the computer cannot simply supply a convert pulse and then read the binary data from the outputs of the converter, some type of a synchronizing signal must be provided by the converter to indicate that it has completed the conversion process, and that the binary values present at its outputs are valid. The READY/$\overline{BUSY}$ signal provides the synchronizing function. This output is a logic one when the converter has completed its conversion; that is, when the outputs are valid, and when a new conversion may be started. When this signal is a logic zero, the converter is performing the conversion. These two control signals may have other names, but their function is the same in all converters.

The interface for a simple A/D converter, such as the one shown in Fig. 2-18, should be easy to visualize. An input port is required for the eight bits of data from the converter, a source of the CONVERT pulse is required, and some means for monitoring the READY/BUSY signal must be provided. You have already seen that OUT commands may be used for control purposes, even when data is not transferred, and an input port may be used so that the computer can periodically test the state of the READY/$\overline{BUSY}$ *status flag* of the A/D converter. A simple A/D converter interface circuit is provided in Fig. 2-19. A typical program that could be used to control this interface is shown in Example 2-17. Appropriate steps have been included in the program, so that the voltage measured will be displayed as both the decimal value of the 8-bit binary data word, and also as the actual voltage that has been measured, or converted. These steps are performed by the BASIC-language program, and not by the interface circuitry.

In the control program, the OUT 5,0 command causes the CONVERT input of the converter to be pulsed, initiating the conversion process. Then the computer constantly tests the state of the READY/$\overline{BUSY}$ status flag of the A/D converter. Only when the flag becomes a logic one will the computer proceed to line 170,

Example 2-17. A Control Program for an 8-Bit A/D Converter (see Fig. 2-19)

```
150 OUT 5,0
160 IF INP(12) AND 2=0 THEN 160
170 A=INP(10)
180 PRINT A,A*0.03906
190 GOTO 150
```

where the data input step is executed. The logical AND operation is necessary (line 160), since the state of the other bits from input port 12 must not affect the test process. The logical ANDing with the value 00000010 means that only bit D1 will be tested.

There are applications in which resolution of greater than eight bits is required for the measurement of unknown voltages. Converters with greater resolutions have more than eight output bits, so the interfaces for these converters require additional interface components, since more than eight bits must be transferred to the computer. In the case of a 10-bit A/D converter, eight of the bits would

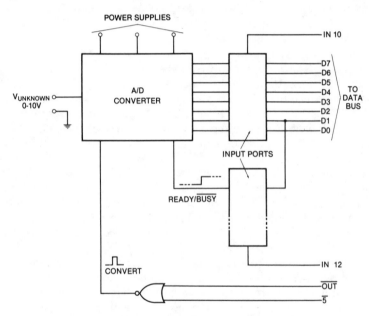

Fig. 2-19. A simple eight-bit A/D converter interface circuit.

use an 8-bit input port, while the remaining two bits would be assigned another 8-bit input port. Some of the remaining bits on this port could be used to monitor the status flag of the converter. Such an interface is shown in Fig. 2-20. The CONVERT input and the status flag output perform the same functions as they did in the 8-bit converter interface circuit. Since some of the 10 bits will be input from one port, while the remaining bits are input from another port, the resulting values must be combined so that the data values are between 0 and 1023, the range possible with a 10-bit converter. The software steps shown in Example 2-18 show how this is done with a scaling factor for the two most-significant bits.

```
200 OUT 5,0
210 M=INP(4):IF M AND 64=0 THEN 210
220 M=256*(M AND 3)
230 L=INP(3)
240 PRINT M+L, (M+L)*0.00977
250 GOTO 200
```

The TRS-80 does not know that the two MSBs that are input at bit positions D1 and D0 should have *decimal* values of 512 and 256, respectively. The computer treats these bits as if they were input at the bit positions with values of 2 and 1, respectively, which is what is expected if you consider these two bits at input port 4, without considering the rest of the circuitry. To scale these bits to their actual "positional" values within the 10-bit data word, multiply them by 256, and then add them to the remaining eight LSBs. Since the eight LSBs did not undergo any "positional" change when they were transferred to the TRS-80, their values do not require any modification. Whenever you are transferring information that contains more than eight bits, such a conversion process will probably be required to recombine the information into a meaningful decimal value that may be processed by the computer.

You will now take a look at two different A/D converters that operate in different ways. The purpose of these discussions is to describe the converters in general terms, to provide some applications, and to allow you to see how the converters are interfaced to the computer. The operation of each converter will not be described

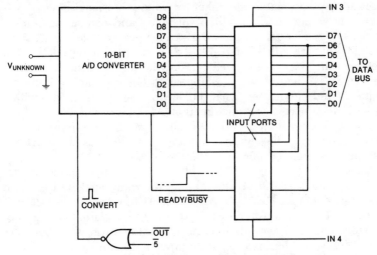

Fig. 2-20. A 10-bit A/D converter interface circuit.

in much detail. There are many different types of conversion techniques, but the two that are represented by these converters are the most popular, and the most widely used.

The AD571 10-Bit A/D Converter

The Analog Devices AD571 A/D converter was briefly discussed in *TRS-80 Interfacing, Book 1,* since the chip was used in one of the experiments. This chip uses the *successive-approximation* conversion technique which compares the unknown voltage to a preset series of voltages that are binary fractions of the maximum voltage that may be measured. Thus, for a converter with an input of 0 to 10 volts, the comparisons would be made with 5 volts, 2.5 volts, 1.25 volts, and so on, for as many bits as there are on the digital output side of the converter. When an unknown voltage is to be converted, it is first compared to 5 volts. If the voltage is greater than 5 volts, the 2.5-volt step is added, and the unknown voltage is compared to 7.5 volts. If the unknown voltage is still greater than 7.5 volts, the 1.25-volt step is added to the test voltage, and the unknown voltage is compared to 8.75 volts. We will assume that the unknown voltage is less than 8.75 volts, but greater than 7.5 volts. In the last test, then, the test voltage was greater than the unknown voltage, so the 1.25-volt step must be removed, or subtracted from the test voltage. Now, the next smallest fractional test voltage, 0.625 volts, is added to the 7.5-volt test voltage, and the test is performed again. In this way, for an 8-bit, successive-approximation D/A converter, there is one test voltage for each of the eight bits, and each one is either added, or not added, to the test voltage, as it attempts to match the unknown voltage. Internal circuits perform the voltage addition, bit sequencing and comparing. An internal D/A converter supplies the various test voltages in the same weights that were listed in Table 2-2. A typical timing relationship between the start of a conversion and the test sequences is shown in Fig. 2-21. The test voltages appear to home in on the unknown voltage, and no matter what unknown voltage is used (within range), the successive-approximation A/D converter will perform one test for each bit position. In most successive-approximation A/D converters, the conversion process is very fast. The AD571 can perform a conversion in 25 *microseconds.*

Since the AD571 is a 10-bit converter, two input ports are required to service all of its digital outputs, which include the status flag, called DATA READY. While the AD571 has three-state output lines, there is no way in which these can be controlled in groups of eight bits, and two bits for direct transfer to the data bus lines of the TRS-80. Thus, two separate input ports are required. A control line for the CONVERT control input must also be supplied to the chip. Since the AD571 uses a 10-bit internal D/A converter to generate the test voltages, a good, stable reference voltage is required. Luckily, the reference source has been integrated onto the same chip. The interface circuit for the AD571 is shown in Fig. 2-22, and the pin configuration for the chip is shown in Fig. 2-23. The power supply lines of the AD571 converter may be set at different voltages, depending upon the circuit in which the chip is to

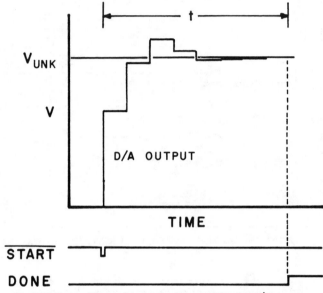

Fig. 2-21. Timing diagram for a successive-approximation A/D converter.

be used. For example, the V+ power supply input (pin 10) may be varied between +5 volts and +15 volts, so that the outputs of the chip may be used with either TTL-compatible chips, or CMOS-compatible chips. Likewise, the V− power supply input (pin 12) may be connected to either −12 volts, or −15 volts, depending upon which of the voltages is found in your computer, or in the interface circuits.

The AD571 may be operated in either the unipolar (0 to 10 volts) or bipolar (±5 volts) mode through the use of a bipolar offset control input, pin 15. If this pin is left "open," or disconnected, then the bipolar mode is selected. If it is grounded, the chip will operate in the unipolar mode. This provides a great deal of flexibility in handling computer interfacing tasks.

Since the AD571 requires a $\overline{\text{CONVERT}}$ pulse that is 2 microseconds long, a device select pulse—a device address gated with $\overline{\text{OUT}}$—cannot be used directly to strobe the $\overline{\text{CONVERT}}$ input, since

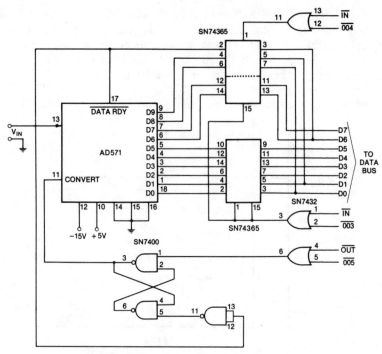

Fig. 2-22. Complete interface for the AD571 10-bit A/D converter.

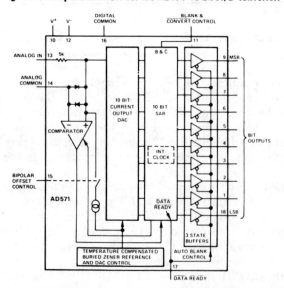

Courtesy Analog Devices, Inc.

Fig. 2-23. Pin configuration and block diagram for the AD571 10-bit converter chip.

the $\overline{\text{OUT}}$ pulse of the TRS-80 is only present for 1.3 microseconds. A cross-coupled NAND gate has been used in this circuit to provide the proper $\overline{\text{CONVERT}}$ pulse timing. An OUT 5 pulse will cause a logic one to be placed on the $\overline{\text{CONVERT}}$ input, and it will remain there until the NAND gate flip-flop circuit is cleared by the $\overline{\text{DATA READY}}$ signal. In this circuit the start-of-conversion signal will be present until it is removed once the conversion is underway.

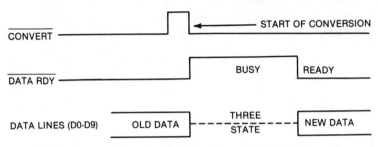

Fig. 2-24. Convert pulse and mode timing diagram for the AD571 converter.

The timing diagram for the conversion sequence of the AD571 is shown in Fig. 2-24. A short $\overline{\text{CONVERT}}$ pulse is applied to the $\overline{\text{CONVERT}}$ input of the AD571 to initiate the conversion sequence. Even though the "start" pulse of the converter is noted as a logic zero signal, a positive, or logic one, pulse is required to start the conversion. The difference comes about because the $\overline{\text{CONVERT}}$ signal performs two functions. Not only does it start a conversion, but it also controls the three-state output lines of the converter. When in the logic one state, the $\overline{\text{CONVERT}}$ input places the three-state outputs in their high-impedance, or disconnected, state, so that they are not connected to the input ports. Since the three-state capability is not being used in the configuration used in this example, we are not concerned with this feature. Nevertheless, the nomenclature of the $\overline{\text{CONVERT}}$ input can be confusing. It is the negative-going edge of the $\overline{\text{CONVERT}}$ pulse that triggers the start of the conversion process, and the $\overline{\text{CONVERT}}$ input must remain in the logic zero state for the conversion to be performed and for the 10 binary outputs to be active. The $\overline{\text{DATA READY}}$ status flag output is a logic one during the conversion process (BUSY) and it is a logic zero when the conversion has been completed, indicating that the 10 output bits may be read by the computer.

One deficiency of the AD571 is that it has a relatively low input impedance, generally between 3000 and 7000 ohms. Since this can load a test circuit that is not capable of providing a great deal of current, about 3.5 mA, to the converter, we suggest the use of a voltage-follower circuit between the output of the sensor and the input of the converter. A typical voltage follower circuit is shown in Fig. 2-25. The various pin configurations will depend upon the op-amp chosen for use in the circuit. A 741-type op-amp, having an input impedance of about 2 megohms, will serve well in most applications.

Before a typical application of the AD571 is illustrated, you need to consider the software used to control this device in a bit more detail. The program shown in Example 2-18 can be used with the AD571, if the converter is used in the unipolar mode. The results of the program will be displayed as the decimal value of the 10-bit data word, and also as the voltage measured. What type of

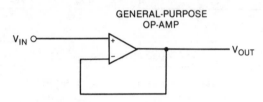

Fig. 2-25. A simple voltage-follower buffer circuit.

program will be used if the converter is to be used in the bipolar mode? The program would have to decide whether the voltage was positive or negative, and perhaps perform some complex calculations. Actually, there isn't much about the bipolar voltage program that is very complex, at all. Instead of starting at zero, the converter starts at −5 volts, so all you have to do is to *offset* the voltage computation by −5, as shown in Example 2-19.

There is one other software consideration. Since the converter only requires 25 microseconds to perform the conversion, you can probably be sure that the conversion has been completed by the time that the TRS-80 starts to test the $\overline{\text{DATA READY}}$ flag. It would be surprising if the data were not ready, since it takes the computer tens, if not hundreds, of microseconds to interpret each of the BASIC commands in the program. There probably isn't any reason why the flag-checking is required for the proper operation of the program. In fact, the program listed in Example 2-19 will run quite well with line 210 written as,

$$210 \quad M = INP(4)$$

Would you want to include the additional flag hardware in your interface? We would suggest that you do, since sooner or later you will probably want to tackle some application that requires high-speed data acquisition and the use of assembly language for programming. When you use assembly language, the flag testing steps

Example 2-19. A Control Program for the AD571 (Bipolar Mode)

```
200  OUT 5,0
210  M=INP(4):IF M AND 64=0 THEN 210
220  M=256*(M AND 3)
230  L=INP(3)
240  PRINT M+L, ((M+L)*0.00977)−5
250  GOTO 200
```

in the program are quite important. You may also find that the flag testing steps in the BASIC program provide an additional way of testing your interface. If the flag is not in the correct state at a particular time, there may be a problem in the interface that can be readily identified. Without the availability of the flag, and the capability to test it under software control, the interface check-out may take longer, and it may be difficult to locate faults.

An A/D Converter Interface Application

In this application, the 10-bit A/D converter will be used to measure the voltage across a light-dependent resistor, or photocell. The photocell is configured as shown in Fig. 2-26, in which the photocell has been placed in a voltage divider network with a 560K-ohm resistor. The value of the fixed resistor was chosen so that the maximum voltage from the output of the photocell would be about 10 volts, the maximum that may be used with the AD571 when it is in the unipolar mode. This means that when no light is illuminating the photocell, its resistance is about 1.02 megohms.

As the light intensity upon the surface of the photocell increases, a corresponding decrease in the voltage from the photocell is observed. As with most cadmium sulfide (CdS) photodetectors, the resistance decreases as the light intensity increases. While the voltage may be measured for various light intensities with a meter, a digital panel meter, or other instrument, we wish to use the computer to assist in these measurements. In this example, we are inter-

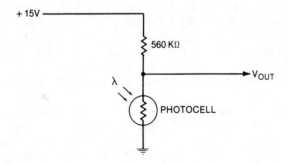

Fig. 2-26. The photocell voltage-divider circuit used in the lamp measurement experiment.

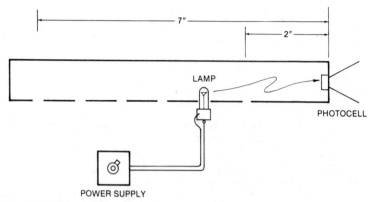

Fig. 2-27. Light-tube experimental set-up. Lamp positions are at 1-inch intervals.

ested in measuring the resistance of the photocell as a function of its distance from a constantly illuminated source. To test this relationship, the photocell is mounted in one end of a cardboard tube that has holes punched in it at 1-inch intervals, starting 2 inches from the photocell. A small 6-volt lamp may be placed in the holes, one at a time, and the voltage across the photocell measured. A diagram of the experimental equipment is shown in Fig. 2-27. Of course, the unused holes are covered during the experiment to prevent stray light from entering and throwing off the results.

Now, the lamp may be moved from hole to hole while the computer is used to control the A/D converter, and to temporarily store the value that has been acquired. In this experiment, the power supply was adjusted so that the voltage across the photocell was just about 10 volts when the lamp was placed in the hole farthest from the photocell. Since the resistance of the photocell decreases with the addition of more light, the voltage across the photocell should decrease as the lamp is brought closer to it. A very simple program was developed so that the voltage at each lamp position could be measured by the A/D converter. This program is listed in Example 2-20. The INPUT Q statement is a "dummy" command that simply allows the computer to stop so that the lamp may be moved before the next conversion sequence is started. The flag of the A/D converter is not tested in this program, and the data for the converter is acquired and processed in a single statement in the program.

When the program was started, the lamp was placed 7 inches from the photocell, so that it could be moved closer each time that the program was rerun through the data acquisition steps, following the actuation of the ENTER key. No data is entered for the dummy variable, Q, but the ENTER key must be depressed, to al-

Example 2-20. Lamp Data Acquisition Program

```
 10 DIM A(6)
 20 FOR I=1 TO 6
 30 INPUT Q
 40 OUT 5,0
 50 P=(256*(INP(4) AND 3))+INP(3)
 60 A(I)=P
 70 NEXT I
 80 FOR I=1 TO 6
 90 PRINT I, A(I),A(I)*0.00977
100 NEXT I
110 END
```

low the computer to go past this variable input command. The results of a typical experiment are listed in Table 2-4. The test was run several times, but the runs were not reproducible, giving values between 807 (7.88 volts) and 853 (8.33 volts) for the 7-inch position of the lamp. Clearly, something was wrong in the experiment when these values were acquired.

We found that the TRS-80 is a very "noisy" computer, generating a great deal of high-frequency electrical noise that is radiated in all directions, and is easily picked up by power supply leads, bus cables, and other interconnections in the interfaces. We found no

Table 2-4. Results of a Single Detector-Lamp Test Sequence

Test No.	Decimal Value	Voltage*
1 (7 in.)	807	7.88
2	773	7.55
3	615	6.00
4	550	5.37
5	412	4.02
6 (2 in.)	263	2.57

*Calculated

suitable way to reduce the noise that was superimposed upon the voltage from the photocell. The noise was substantial, since it caused wide variations in the values obtained from the A/D converter. To remove some of the noise from the signals, a number of tests could be run, and then average values could be calculated for each of the lamp positions. Why not let the computer perform all of the data acquisition and data averaging steps?

The program in Example 2-21 incorporates the averaging steps so that the final voltage values are actually the average of four values acquired one after the other for each position of the lamp along the tube. We have introduced a short time delay into the program at line 60 that will have the effect of spacing each of the data points about one quarter of a second apart while they are be-

Example 2-21. Lamp Data Acquisition Program, with Averaging

```
 10 DIM A(6)
 20 FOR I=1 TO 6
 30 S=0:INPUT Q
 35 FOR R=1 TO 4
 40 OUT 5,0
 50 P=(256*(INP(4) AND 3))+INP(3)
 55 S=S+P
 60 FOR T=0 TO 100:NEXT T:NEXT R
 65 A(I)=S/4
 70 NEXT I
 80 FOR I=1 TO 6
 90 PRINT I, A(I),A(I)*0.00977
100 NEXT I
110 END
```

ing acquired. The averaging technique worked well in the experiment, providing results that were reproducible to within a few percent of each other. Thus, the averaging technique worked well to reduce the noise that was superimposed upon the signal that was to be measured. The averaging technique is a valuable one, and we will discuss it in more detail later. The averaging technique can be implemented in either hardware, or software. One final note on the averaging technique. In this case, four samples were averaged, so the noise was reduced by $\sqrt{4}$, or 2, so that it was twice as low as it would have been in individual measurements.

The experiment still hasn't been completed, though, since the actual results of the experiment are to be represented by the *resistance* of the photocell versus light intensity, or distance from the photocell in this case. Now, you need to add some steps to the program so that the voltage values are converted to resistances. Using Ohm's law ($I = E/R$), you can compare the resistance of the photocell for each of the voltages across it. If "V" is the voltage across the photocell, then the equation:

$$\frac{560000}{(15 - V)} \times V = \text{Detector Resistance}$$

may be used to determine the resistances of the photocell. The complete program is shown in Example 2-22. Column headings could be printed by the program, if they are required. Typical test results obtained by this program are provided in Table 2-5, and the results have been plotted in Fig. 2-28, showing a nice relationship between the distance of the lamp, and the resistance of the photocell. Some of you will probably realize that the plot is not what you would expect for a standard physics experiment in which it is observed that when a light source's distance from a "detector" is doubled, the light reaching the detector is quartered. There are several

Example 2-22. Lamp Data Acquisition and Averaging Program, with Resistance Calculations

```
10 DIM A(6)
20 FOR I = 1 TO 6
30 S=0:INPUT Q
35 FOR R=1 TO 4
40 OUT 5,0
50 P=(256*(INP(4) AND 3))+INP(3)
55 S=S+P
60 FOR T=0 TO 100:NEXT T:NEXT R
65 A(I)=S/4
70 NEXT I
80 FOR I=1 TO 6
85 V=A(I)*0.00977
90 PRINT I,V,((560000/(15−V))*V)
100 NEXT I
110 END
```

reasons why this standard behavior is not observed in this experiment: (1) we do not know that the detector behaves in this way (perhaps it has a nonlinear response to light intensities), (2) the detector may be operating in a region of the visible light spectrum in which it isn't very sensitive, and (3) don't forget that none of the light leaves the tube, much of it being reflected back on the

Table 2-5. Results of a Detector-Lamp Test Sequence Using the Averaging Program

Test	Voltage	Resistance
1	8.7295	779605
2	7.67678	587036
3	6.23082	397900
4	5.26603	302957
5	3.89823	196636
6	2.60615	117755

photocell. The experiment could have been done in a darkened room, with a photodetector that was well matched to the light source, but since this would give the usual physics-lab results, it would take all the fun out of the exercise.

The ICL7109 12-Bit A/D Converter

The second A/D converter that we will discuss is the 12-bit Intersil ICL7109 device. This converter uses the *dual-slope* conversion process, so we will spend a short bit of time discussing how it works, in general terms. The dual-slope conversion technique uses a voltage integration process that sums an unknown voltage over a fixed period of time, called T1. At the end of this period, higher unknown voltages will have higher sums, while lower unknown voltages will

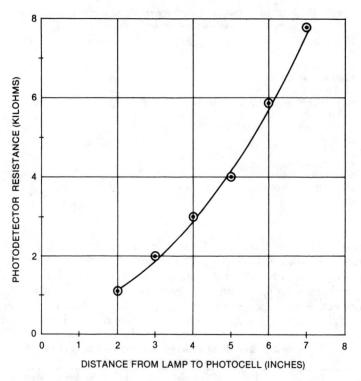

Fig. 2-28. Plot of resistance *versus* distance for the averaged photodetector data values.

have lower sums. The actual conversion process takes place when the integrated value of the applied voltage is reduced at a known rate. Since it will take longer to decrease a high value of integrated voltage than it will to decrease a low value, the period required to cause the integrated voltage to be decreased to zero is a representation of its value, and thus, the unknown analog voltage. The timing diagram for the dual-slope conversion process is shown in Fig. 2-29. The T1 period for two unknown voltages is equal, so that at the end of this integration period, the higher voltage, A, will have summed to a higher total voltage than will have voltage B. This is analogous to water flowing out of two pipes at different rates. After a fixed period, the water flowing out of the pipe with the higher flow rate will have filled more of a container than the flow from the other pipe will have. Once the integration period has ended, the integrated voltage is discharged at a known rate. Since the rate is fixed, the slopes of all of the discharge plots will be equal, as shown in Fig. 2-29. Only the discharge period will change, being longer for the higher initial unknown voltage input. Thus, the dis-

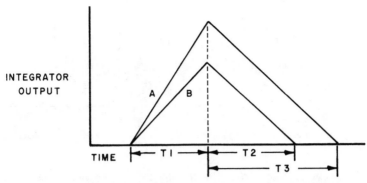

Fig. 2-29. Timing diagram for two different voltages converted by the dual-slope conversion process.

charge period is proportional to the unknown input voltage that is to be digitized.

All of the functions of integrating, discharging, and measuring the discharge period are performed by the integrating, or dual-slope A/D converter. The discharge periods, T2 and T3 (Fig. 2-29) are generally used internally by the converter, to gate a counter that accumulates a binary count that is proportional to the voltage. You do not have to be concerned with this, though, since the converter manufacturers take care of this. You are probably wondering why anyone would choose to use a converter that uses such a slow process. The answer is that the dual-slope A/D converter integrates, or *averages*, the unknown voltage for later measurement, rather than measuring it quickly, and directly, as is the case with a successive-approximation converter. Why is the averaging so important?

You just read about an application in which voltage averaging was quite important, since external noise that was added to the unknown signal contributed significant errors to the measurements. The averaging was done with four values of the unknown signal, so that the noise could be averaged out. The voltage integration technique also averages some noise, since we assume that the noise will add to the signal as many times as it subtracts from it, as shown in Fig. 2-30. The noise has been greatly exaggerated in this figure, so that the actual voltage may be easily seen. The signal is also shown with some periodic noise, such as 60 Hz noise, since it may be easier to see how this adds and subtracts from the signal on a regular basis.

The timing diagram in Fig. 2-31 shows how a dual-slope A/D converter would integrate this noisy signal. The resulting integrated value of the noisy signal would be very close to the voltage that

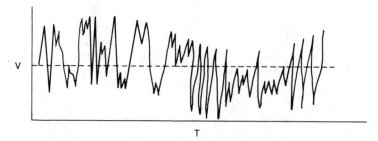

Fig. 2-30. Timing diagram showing periodic (60 Hz) and random noise superimposed upon an analog signal.

would have resulted from the integration of the noise-free signal. Actually, we are most interested in the area under the time-voltage line, as shown in the shaded portion of Fig. 2-31. Once the integration period has ended, the discharging is started, and the period that is required for the integrated voltage to reach zero volts is measured. This represents the actual, average value of the unknown, noisy signal. In this example, the averaging took place during the integration period. In most dual-slope A/D converters, the integration period is set at an integer multiple of a 60-Hz sine wave period, so that line-frequency noise is averaged out. Of course, converters are not perfect, so this is a noise reduction technique, and not all of the noise is eliminated.

Now, the ICL7109 A/D converter will be considered in detail. A pin configuration and test circuit diagram is provided in Fig. 2-32. Only a few inexpensive components are required by the ICL7109 for proper operation. The use of a readily available 3.5795 MHz

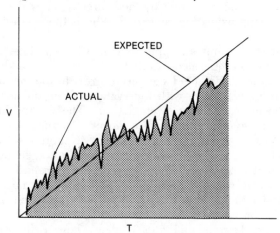

Fig. 2-31. Timing diagram showing the integration of a noisy analog signal, *versus* what is expected for a noise-free signal.

crystal to generate the timing of the control signals allows the converter to operate at 7.5 conversions per second, so that 60 Hz noise is rejected during the integration period. If an external clock signal is supplied, the converter may be set so that it will perform conversions at the rate of 30 per second. The ICL7109 contains an on-chip voltage reference circuit.

On the digital data side of the converter, you will find that there is a high-order byte, and a low-order byte. The low-order byte contains data bits B1 (D0) through B8 (D7), while the high-order byte contains the remaining four data bits, B9 (D8) through B12 (D11), as well as two additional bits; a polarity bit (POL) and an over-range bit (OR). These two bits are useful in detecting the sign, or polarity, of the applied voltage, and also in detecting an error resulting from the use of too high an unknown voltage at the input of the converter. These data bits have three-state outputs, and they are controlled through the use of the low-byte enable (LBEN) and high-byte enable (HBEN) signals. These two inputs allow the data of the converter to be transferred to another device without any additional control or buffering circuitry. Caution must be observed in the use of these three-state outputs, since they can only power one TTL load, and they are not capable of driving long buses. We suggest that this three-state capability *not be used* unless the computer system in which the ICL7109 is to be used is small, having only a few devices on the data bus, so that the ICL7109 will operate properly. The information in Table 2-6 provides brief descriptions for each of the signals of the ICL7109.

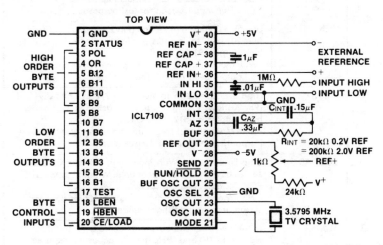

Courtesy Intersil, Inc.

Fig. 2-32. Pin configuration and test circuit for the ICL7109 12-bit dual-slope A/D converter chip.

Table 2-6. ICL7109 Signal Description

Pin	Symbol	Description
1	GND	Digital Ground, 0V, Ground return for all digital logic
2	STATUS	Output–High during integrate and deintegrate until data is latched. –Low when analog section is in Auto-Zero configuration.
3	POL	Polarity, Three-State Output
4	OR	Over-range, Three-State Output
5	B12	Bit 12 (Most Significant Bit)
6	B11	Bit 11
7	B10	Bit 10
8	B9	Bit 9
9	B8	Bit 8
10	B7	Bit 7
11	B6	Bit 6 Data Bits, Three-State Output
12	B5	Bit 5
13	B4	Bit 4
14	B3	Bit 3
15	B2	Bit 2
16	B1	Bit 1 (Least Significant Bit)
17	TEST	Input High–Normal Operation. Input Low–Forces all bit outputs high. Note: This input is used for test purposes only.
18	LBEN	Low Byte Enable–With Mode (Pin 21) low, and CE/LOAD (Pin 20) low, taking this pin low activates low order byte outputs B1-B8. –With Mode (Pin 21) high, this pin serves as a low byte flag output used in handshake mode.
19	HBEN	High Byte Enable–With Mode (Pin 21) low, and CE/LOAD (Pin 20) low, taking this pin low activates high order byte outputs B9-B12, POL, OR. –With Mode (Pin 21) high, this pin serves as a high byte flag output used in handshake mode.
20	CE/LOAD	Chip Enable Load–With Mode (Pin 21) low, CE/LOAD serves as a master output enable. When high, B1-B12, POL, OR outputs are disabled. –With Mode (Pin 21) high, this pin serves as a load strobe used in handshake mode.
21	MODE	Input Low–Direct output mode where CE/LOAD (Pin 20), HBEN (Pin 19) and LBEN (Pin 18) act as inputs directly controlling byte outputs. Input Pulsed High–Causes immediate entry into handshake mode and output of data

Table 2-6. continued

21 cont	MODE cont	Input High–Enables CE/LOAD (Pin 20), HBEN (Pin 19), and LBEN (Pin 18) as outputs, handshake mode will be entered and data output
22	OSC IN	Oscillator Input
23	OSC OUT	Oscillator Output
24	OSC SEL	Oscillator Select–Input high configures OSC IN, OSC OUT, BUF OSC OUT as RC oscillator–clock will be same phase and duty cycle as BUF OSC OUT. –Input low configures OSC IN, OSC OUT for crystal oscillator–clock frequency will be 1/58 of frequency at BUF OSC OUT.
25	BUF OSC OUT	Buffered Oscillator Output
26	RUN/HOLD	Input High–Conversions continuously performed every 8192 clock pulses. Input Low–Conversion in progress completed, converter will stop in Auto-Zero 7 counts before integrate.
27	SEND	Input–Used in handshake mode to indicate ability of an external device to accept data.
28	V	Analog Negative Supply–Nominally $-5V$ with respect to GND (Pin 1).
29	REF OUT	Reference Voltage Output–Nominally 2.8V down from V^+ (Pin 40).
30	BUFFER	Buffer Amplifier Output
31	AUTO-ZERO	Auto-Zero Node–Inside foil of C_{AZ}
32	INTEGRATOR	Integrator Output–Outside foil of C_{INT}
33	COMMON	Analog Common–System is Auto-Zeroed to COMMON
34	INPUT LO	Differential Input Low Side
35	INPUT HI	Differential Input High Side
36	REF IN +	Differential Reference Input Positive
37	REF CAP +	Reference Capacitor Positive
38	REF CAP −	Reference Capacitor Negative
39	REF IN −	Differential Reference Input Negative
40	V^+	Positive Supply Voltage–Nominally $+5V$ with respect to GND (Pin 1).

The ICL7109 converter can be operated in one of two modes, a *direct* mode, or a *handshake* mode. Only the direct mode will be important here, since this configures the chip so that it appears to operate in the same general manner as other A/D converters. A typical interface for the ICL7109 is shown in Fig. 2-33. The three-state output capability of the chip has not been used since a long, heavily loaded bus was involved, as is probably the case in most TRS-80 systems. Four SN74365 (DM8095) three-state buffers were used between the outputs of the A/D converter and the data bus lines of the computer. Two input control signals were used as the device select pulses to the buffers. Note that the $\overline{\text{MODE}}$, CE/LOAD, $\overline{\text{HBEN}}$ and $\overline{\text{LBEN}}$ control signals have all been grounded. A few changes have been made in the basic circuit shown in Fig. 2-32, so that the range of the converter will be ±5 volts. The integration

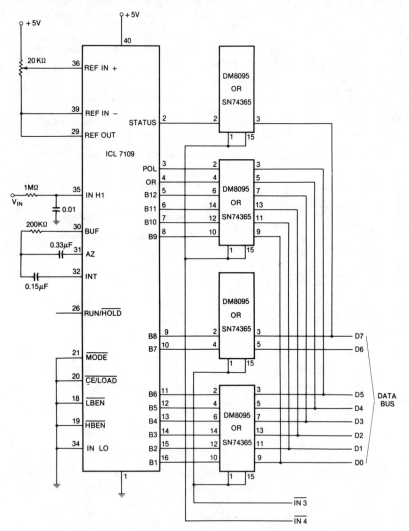

Fig. 2-33. Schematic diagram of an interface for the ICL7109 A/D converter.

resistor, R_{INT}, has been changed to 200 K ohms, and the reference voltage divider has been changed from two resistors, to a single potentiometer. These changes are incorporated into the circuit shown in Fig. 2-33. While this is a typical interface, you will note that there is no connection to the chip to start the conversion sequence. While the ICL7109 is in the DIRECT mode, there are two types of conversion sequences that may be used: the *continuous conversion,* and the *conversion on command* modes. Both of these will be described, since they will be important for various interfacing tasks.

ICL7109 Continuous Conversion Mode

When the RUN/$\overline{\text{HOLD}}$ line of the ICL7109 is held at a logic one, or when it is open (unconnected), the converter will use its internal logic circuits to sequence through one conversion right after another. In this way, the 12-bit binary output is always changing, to reflect the newly digitized voltage. In this mode, the STATUS output of the chip may be monitored to determine whether the chip is converting a voltage, or whether it is performing internal housekeeping tasks, getting it ready for the next conversion sequence.

To help you better understand the timing relationships, a timing diagram has been provided in Fig. 2-34. You should be able to recognize the integration period, and the discharge, or de-integration period. The INTERNAL LATCH pulse is generated by the internal logic circuits of the chip to update the 12-bit data word, to present the value from the latest conversion. The STATUS output is a logic one during the conversion period, and a logic zero after the conversion has been completed. The digital data outputs only change on the negative-going edge of the STATUS signal. The data can be read at any time, or you can wait until the current conversion has been completed before reading the data.

If you choose to read the data only after the latest conversion has been completed; that is, you wish to wait until the STATUS

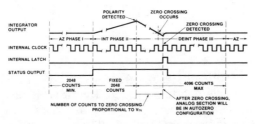

Courtesy Intersil, Inc.

Fig. 2-34. Timing relationships for the ICL7109 A/D converter.

Example 2-23. A Simple Display Update Program for the ICL7109 Converter

```
10 IF(128 AND INP(4))=1 THEN 10
20 PRINT ((15 AND INP(4))*256)+INP(3)
30 IF(128 AND INP(4))=0 THEN 30
40 GOTO 10
```

flag output becomes a logic zero again, you could use the program listed in Example 2-23. In this program, the computer will wait until the STATUS flag goes from a logic one to a logic zero, before it inputs and displays the decimal equivalent of the 12-bit binary value. The program will continue to display the latest conversion value, going through the program again and again. If you wish to obtain a single conversion value at some time in a BASIC program, you could use the program steps listed in Example 2-24. In this se-

Example 2-24. A Single Point Data Acquisition Routine

```
200 A=(INP(4) AND 128)
210 IF A>(INP(4) AND 128) THEN 220 ELSE 200
220 Q=((INP(4) AND 15)*256)+INP(3)
```

quence of program steps, the computer waits for the logic one to logic zero transition on the STATUS output before it acquires a single value from the converter. In both of these program examples, you should note the use of the logical AND operation to mask-out unused, and unwanted, bits, both in the STATUS flag testing, and in the computing of the final data value.

You could input a 12-bit data value at any time, regardless of the state of the STATUS signal, to reflect the current value present at the outputs of the converter, but you would have to be careful in evaluating the value obtained, since it is possible to transfer the 12-bit value to the computer just as it is being updated by the converter, on the negative-going edge of the STATUS output. To prevent this from happening, the program shown in Example 2-25

Example 2-25. A Continuous Data Acquisition Program, with Flag Transition Checks

```
100 A=(INP(4) AND 128)
110 PRINT ((15 AND INP(4))*256)+INP(3)
120 IF A>(INP(4) AND 128) THEN 100
```

tests the STATUS flag signal before and after the data has been acquired. If a logic one to logic zero transition is detected during the course of the acquisition, indicating that the data has been updated, the new data value is acquired. This program could be rewritten, so that only a single data value is obtained, rather than having each new data value acquired and displayed. All of these programs, Examples 2-23, 2-24, and 2-25 have provided examples of sequences of instructions that may be used to acquire data from the ICL7109 when it is in the free-running, or continuous conversion mode. For most applications, this mode is easy to use, but there is another mode that allows the ICL7109 to only perform a single conversion, upon command of the computer.

ICL7109 One-Shot Conversion Mode

Although the ICL7109 does not have a CONVERT pulse input, as such, it does have the capability to perform one conversion at a time, under the direct control of external interface circuits. In this *conversion on command* mode, each of the conversions is "requested," causing the A/D converter to digitize the unknown voltage only once, rather than again and again. The RUN/$\overline{\text{HOLD}}$ input (pin 26) provides the necessary control function to allow the ICL7109 to operate in the one-shot mode. When the RUN/$\overline{\text{HOLD}}$ input is a logic one, the converter is placed in the continuous conversion mode, while a logic zero input will cause the converter to complete its current conversion, update the data outputs, and then stop. This allows the converter to be placed in a standby mode, so that it can be restarted for conversions, as required.

When the conversion on command, or one-shot mode is used, the RUN/$\overline{\text{HOLD}}$ input is kept in the logic zero state, being pulsed to the logic one state when a conversion is requested. There is a definite timing relationship between the RUN/$\overline{\text{HOLD}}$ signal, and the STATUS output signal, and the availability of the digital data. We will assume that when the system has been reset, the RUN/$\overline{\text{HOLD}}$ signal is in the logic zero state. To start a conversion sequence, the RUN/$\overline{\text{HOLD}}$ input is changed to a logic one, indicating to the converter that it is to start a conversion sequence. There are some internal logic functions that must take place, so there is a definite period before the STATUS output goes to a logic one, indicating that a conversion is in progress. When the STATUS output goes to a logic zero, this indicates a conversion has been completed, and that the RUN/$\overline{\text{HOLD}}$ signal should be placed back in the logic zero state. Likewise, the resulting 12-bit data value should be acquired by the computer. There are two ways in which the control of the RUN/$\overline{\text{HOLD}}$ input can be achieved, and we are sure that there are other variations, too. In both cases, the ICL7109 interface circuitry shown in Fig. 2-33 is expanded to include the new control circuits for the one-shot control.

In the first example of one-shot conversion control, a flip-flop is controlled by a program, to provide the proper logic levels for the RUN/$\overline{\text{HOLD}}$ input. The interface circuit is shown in Fig. 2-35. An

Example 2-26. A Single Conversion Control Program (see Fig. 2-35)

```
10 OUT 6,0
20 IF(INP(4) AND 128)=0 THEN 20
40 IF(INP(4) AND 128)=1 THEN 40
50 PRINT ((INP(4) AND 15)*256)+INP(3)
55 OUT 7,0
60 FOR T=0 TO 1000:NEXT T
70 GOTO 10
```

OUT 6,0 command is used to clear the flip-flop, starting the conversion, while an OUT 7,0 command is used to set the flop-flop,
changing the logic level applied to the RUN/HOLD input back to
a logic zero. This interface circuitry must be added to that shown
in Fig. 2-33. A control program that may be used to control this
new interface is listed in Example 2-26. Actually, this interface is
quite general, since both the conversion on command and continuous conversion modes may be used. For the continuous conversion
mode, the flip-flop is simply reset with an OUT 6,0 command, placing the RUN/HOLD input in the logic one state.

A different type of one-shot control interface is shown in Fig. 2-
36. In this circuit, the STATUS signal has been used to clock a flip-
flop, causing it to change the states of its outputs. An OUT 6 pulse
is used to clear the flop-flop, placing the RUN/HOLD signal in the
logic one state, to start a conversion. Once the conversion has been
completed, the logic one to logic zero transition of the STATUS
output clocks the flip-flop, so that the RUN/HOLD signal becomes
a logic zero again, stopping the conversion sequence, so that an-

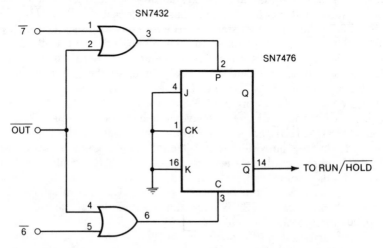

Fig. 2-35. Schematic diagram of a control circuit for the ICL7109, for both single and
multiple conversions.

Example 2-27. A Single Conversion Control Program (see Fig. 2-36)

```
200 OUT 6,0
210 IF(128 AND INP(4))=0 THEN 210
220 PRINT ((INP(4) AND 15)*256)+INP(3)
230 FOR T=0 TO 200:NEXT T
240 GOTO 200
```

other conversion will not take place. Another signal from the flip-flop is used as a status signal to one of the input ports of the computer, to indicate that a conversion has been completed. In this configuration, the ICL7109 appears to be used in the more "traditional" way; that is, a convert pulse is used to start a conversion, and a flag output indicates when the conversion has been completed. A typical control program is shown in Example 2-27. This configuration can be used only if you wish to use the one-shot mode, since it is not very easy to switch back and forth between the continuous conversion and the conversion on command modes. (Note that in the circuit shown in Fig. 2-36, when used with the ICL7109 converter circuit shown in Fig. 2-33, the connection from the STATUS output to the three-state input port is removed, since the STATUS output of the flip-flop provides this function.)

The sample programs that have been provided for the one-shot conversion mode are fairly simple, and are easily rewritten, for use as subroutines, for the acquisition of one or more data values. The single-conversion method is frequently used when a single value is to be obtained, and when it is necessary to obtain the most recently digitized value. The one-shot mode is also useful when assembly-language programs are going to be used to control the converter.

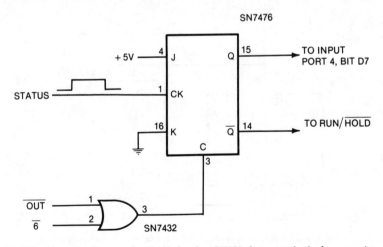

Fig. 2-36. Schematic diagram of a circuit for the ICL7109 that controls single conversions.

Another A/D Converter Interface Application

Now that the 12-bit ICL7109 A/D converter has been interfaced to the TRS-80 computer, it will be applied to a voltage-measuring problem. In this case, it is necessary to measure a temperature, a problem found in many experiments, control systems, solar heater systems, cooling towers, and so on. There are numerous ways in which temperatures can be measured; with thermocouples, thermistors, temperature-dependent semiconductors, and others, being frequently used. In recent years, a number of new temperature sensors have become available. The Analog Devices AD590, and the National Semiconductor LM3911, are representative examples. The AD590 is a two-terminal temperature transducer, while the LM3911 is a four-terminal device. The AD590 lends itself to use in those applications that require highly accurate measurements, while the LM3911 is excellent for general-purpose uses. The LM3911 will be used in this particular application.

The LM3911 is a temperature sensing device that provides a voltage output that is directly proportional to the temperature of the chip. In fact, the output is generally in millivolts-per-degree, so that the conversion from a voltage to a temperature is fairly simple. While the LM3911 may be used in many different types of applications, from use as a thermostat, to use as a simple thermometer, it will be used as a temperature transducer in this application, so that the ICL7109 A/D converter can measure the voltage that it generates. The simplest configuration for the LM3911 is shown in Fig. 2-37, in which the LM3911 has been used to provide a volt-

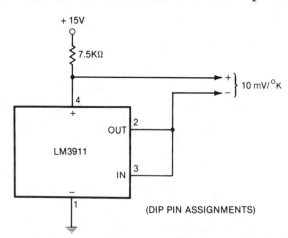

Fig. 2-37. Schematic diagram showing the LM3911 sensor used for
temperature measurement.

age output of 10 millivolts for each Kelvin. The Kelvin temperature scale uses the same units as the Celsius scale, except that the Kelvin scale starts at absolute zero and reaches 273 K at the freezing point of water, which is 0°C, or 32°F. [Note the ° symbol is not used with Kelvins. The SI unit of temperature is the Kelvin, not degree (°) Kelvin.] Room temperature is about 20°C, or 293 K. The conversion from the Fahrenheit to the Celsius and Kelvin scales are as follows:

$$°C = (°F - 32) \times (5/9)$$
$$K = 5/9 (°F - 32) + 273.15$$

The circuit provided in Fig. 2-37 shows the voltage signal that corresponds to the temperature, as being the difference between the voltage at two points in the circuit, neither of which is ground. This is a situation that has not been encountered before, since all of the previous measurements have been made with respect to ground potential. Since the ICL7109 has a *differential* input capability; that is, it can measure the *difference* between two voltages, it might be possible to use this to our advantage. Unfortunately, the more positive of the two voltages produced by the LM3911 is about +7 volts, which is outside the range of the differential input for the ICL7109. Some other means of measuring the signal must be found, or some other "translation" process must be found so that the temperature voltage can be referenced to ground.

A simple differential input op-amp circuit with a gain of one (unity gain) can be used to reference the voltage signal to ground. A typical circuit is shown in Fig. 2-38. A 741 op-amp was used in this circuit, with ±15-volt power supplies. The voltage that represents the temperature of the LM3911 is now referenced to ground, and the output is measured at about 3.03 volts, to 303 K, very close to the actual room temperature. This is the signal that the ICL7109 is to digitize. A simple test program was developed to control the converter in the continuous conversion mode. Example

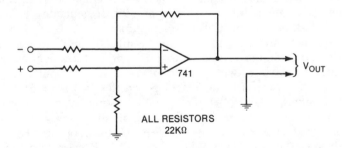

Fig. 2-38. A simple op-amp circuit used to reference a differential signal to ground.

**Example 2-28. A Simple Voltage Display Program for a 12-Bit
A/D Converter**

```
10 IF (128 AND INP(4))=1 THEN 20
20 A=((INP(4) AND 15)*256)+INP(3)
30 PRINT (A*5)/4096;
40 IF (128 AND INP(4))=0 THEN 40
50 GOTO 10
```

2-28 shows the program that acquired the data, and displayed the decimal equivalent of the voltage obtained from the op-amp circuit. The PRINT command converts the decimal equivalent of the 12-bit binary output of the converter into a value that ranges between 0 and +5 volts. When the program was first tested, the voltage displayed by the TRS-80 did not match the voltage that was being generated by the op-amp circuit. This didn't mean that the system wasn't operating properly, but it was an indication that the scale-factor, or gain of the A/D converter was not properly adjusted. To correct the problem, the GAIN potentiometer of ICL7109 was simply adjusted until the voltage output by the op-amp, and the voltage displayed, were equal. Don't forget, that in any system, a certain number of adjustments and test runs will have to be made before the system can provide meaningful results.

Once the gain adjustment of the A/D converter had been made, a simple command was added to the test program to cause it to display the Celsius temperature, along with the measured voltage. The following line was added to the program in Example 2-28:

```
35 PRINT USING "###.#-";((A*500)/4096)-273
```

This converted the voltage to the correct Celsius temperature value. A semicolon is placed at the end of line 30, in the program, to *suppress* the carriage-return function in the display.

Since the LM3911 is a semiconductor device, it requires some power to operate, so its temperature was found to be a degree or two higher than the actual room temperature. In liquids, or moving air, this probably wouldn't be noticed. A complete temperature display program is listed in Example 2-29. It generates a display of both Fahrenheit and Celsius temperatures.

Now, the temperature measurement application will be expanded, so that the computer is used to acquire temperatures over a known period. The software will be written so that the computer will acquire one temperature value each second, for two minutes, a total of 120 values. The LM3911 chip will be quickly cooled with a freezing spray of Freon, typically available as "Freeze Mist," or a similar product, used for cooling electronic components. The temperature of the LM3911 will be measured, as it warms up to room temperature, both in still air, and in moving air, supplied by a small

Example 2-29. A Complete Temperature Display Program for °C and °F

```
 10 CLS:PRINT@ 215,"CELSIUS":PRINT@ 279,"FAHRENHEIT"
 20 IF (128 AND INP(4))=1 THEN 20
 30 Q=((15 AND INP(4))*256)+INP(3)
 40 Q=INT((Q*500)/4096)-273
 50 F=INT((Q*9/5)+32)
 60 PRINT@ 200,"        ";:PRINT@ 200,Q;
 70 PRINT@ 264,"        ";:PRINT@ 264,F
 80 IF(128 AND INP(4))=0 THEN 80
 90 FOR T=0 TO 200:NEXT T
100 GOTO 20
```

fan. A typical data acquisition program is listed in Example 2-30. It has some interesting features that we will briefly describe. A time-delay routine has been placed in the program, so that the temperature information will be acquired at one-second intervals. Actually, the delay period was adjusted during several test runs, so that the values were acquired over the two-minute period. The line printer feature has been used in this program, so that a copy of the results can be obtained for future reference. The LPRINT USING command was used, so that the results of the experiment would be tabulated in neat columns, so that the results would be easy to read. A display-plot routine has also been added, so that the results can be readily seen on the video monitor.

As you look through the program listing, you may wonder why a few additional spaces are printed after each tenth value. Actually, the printer can't "print" spaces, it just marks them off, moving the print head mechanism in the process. Since the carriage-return (re-

Example 2-30. A Temperature Data Acquisition Program

```
 10 DIM A(120)
 20 FOR I=0 TO 119
 30 IF (128 AND INP(4))=1 THEN 30
 40 Q=((15 AND INP(4))*256)+INP(3)
 50 A(I)=INT((Q*500)/4096)-273
 60 FOR T=0 TO 335:NEXT T
 70 NEXT I
 75 Z=0
 80 FOR I=0 TO 119
 90 LPRINT USING "+######"; A(I);
 95 Z=Z+1:IF Z=10 THEN 400
100 NEXT I
110 INPUT Q
120 CLS
130 FOR I=0 TO 119
140 SET (I,((46-A(I))/2))
150 NEXT I
160 GOTO 160
400 LPRINT "  "
410 Z=0:GOTO 100
```

Table 2-7. Temperature Data for Cooled Sensor at One-Second Intervals
(Read Across Each Row)

−34	−34	−34	−33	−33	−33	−32	−32	−31	−31
−30	−30	−29	−29	−28	−28	−27	−27	−26	−26
−25	−25	−24	−24	−23	−23	−22	−22	−21	−21
−20	−19	−19	−18	−18	−17	−16	−15	−15	−14
−13	−13	−12	−11	−11	−10	−9	−9	−8	−8
−7	−7	−6	−5	−5	−5	−4	−4	−3	−3
−2	−2	−1	−1	−1	+0	+0	+0	+0	+1
+1	+1	+1	+1	+1	+2	+2	+2	+2	+2
+3	+3	+3	+3	+3	+3	+4	+4	+4	+4
+5	+5	+5	+6	+6	+6	+6	+7	+7	+7
+7	+8	+8	+8	+8	+8	+9	+9	+9	+9
+9	+9	+10	+10	+10	+10	+10	+10	+11	+11

turning the print head to the left margin) has been suppressed in the LPRINT USING "+######";A(I); command, with the two semicolons, the command at line 400 causes the printer to mark off a few spaces, and then to perform a carriage return. There is no semicolon in this "dummy" command, so its only effect is to cause a carriage return to be generated, so that the next row of figures can be typed directly under the one previously printed. The line-feed function that moves the paper up for the next row is generated by the line printer, or its interface circuitry, whenever a carriage return command is detected.

In this experiment, the LM3911 sensor was cooled to about 240 K, or −33°C with the Freon spray. The chip was allowed to warm up, and the various temperature values were acquired. Two different sets of values were obtained, one set when the LM3911 was simply allowed to warm up on the breadboard, and one when air was blown over the chip with a small fan, similar to the ones used in electronic equipment. The data is presented in Tables 2-7 and 2-8, respectively. Graphs of the temperature changes *vs* time are provided in Fig. 2-39. There is a notable increase in the warming rate of the system in which the fan was used, a good indication that the

Table 2-8. Temperature Data for Cooled Sensor in Fan Air Path
at One-Second Intervals (Read Across Each Row)

−34	−33	−31	−29	−27	−25	−22	−19	−17	−14
−11	−9	−6	−4	−2	−1	+0	+1	+3	+4
+5	+6	+7	+8	+9	+9	+10	+11	+11	+12
+13	+13	+14	+14	+15	+15	+15	+16	+16	+16
+17	+17	+17	+17	+17	+18	+18	+18	+18	+18
+18	+18	+19	+19	+19	+19	+19	+19	+19	+19
+19	+19	+20	+20	+20	+20	+20	+20	+20	+20
+20	+20	+20	+20	+20	+20	+21	+21	+21	+21
+21	+21	+21	+21	+21	+21	+21	+21	+21	+21
+21	+21	+21	+21	+22	+22	+22	+22	+22	+22
+22	+22	+22	+22	+22	+22	+22	+22	+22	+22
+22	+22	+23	+23	+23	+23	+23	+23	+23	+23

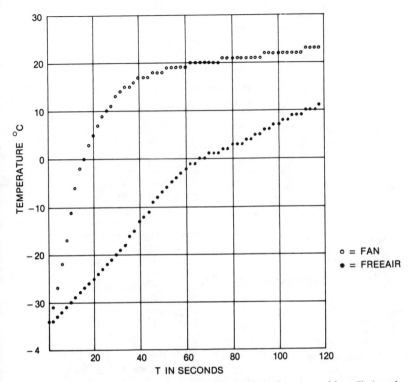

Fig. 2-39. Plots of temperature *versus* time for the LM3911 when warmed by still air and moving air.

fan was doing its job in transporting energy from one place to another, whether it be for cooling, or heating.

This example was not developed as a controlled experiment, but rather as an example of the type of thing that a small computer can do quite nicely. The computer could have taken over some of the other tasks in this experiment, too. For example, the final plot of temperatures and times might have been generated by the computer on an X-Y plotter, controlled by two D/A converters. The computer could have been programmed to start the data acquisition sequence only when the temperature reached a certain level, and so on.

There are some final notes on the LM3911 chip. We found that the pin configurations in the data sheets were sometimes wrong. The errors seem to have crept into the data sheets, since the metal can, transistor-like package for this chip has a different pin configuration than does the eight-pin mini-DIP. Be careful to check on this if you have a data sheet for the LM3911. The LM3911 is specified as being able to operate down to −25°C, yet we were able to operate it down to below −35°C. We don't suggest that you do this on a regular basis, though, if you expect the device to operate in a reproducible manner.

A LIST OF REPRESENTATIVE ANALOG-DIGITAL CONVERTER MANUFACTURERS

Advanced Micro Devices
901 Thompson Pl.
Sunnyvale, CA 94086

Analog Devices, Inc.
P. O. Box 280
Norwood, MA 02062

Analogic Corporation
Audubon Rd.
Wakefield, MA 01880

Beckman Instruments
Adv. Electro-Products Div.
2500 Harbor Blvd.
Fullerton, CA 92634

Burr-Brown
P. O. Box 11400
Tucson, AZ 85734

Data Translation
4 Strathmore Rd.
Natick, MA 01760

Datel-Intersil
11 Cabot Blvd.
Mansfield, MA 02048

Hybrid Systems Corp.
Crosby Drive
Bedford, MA 01730

Intech/Function Modules
282 Brokaw
Santa Clara, CA 95050

National Semiconductor Corp.
2900 Semiconductor Drive
Santa Clara, CA 95051

Signetics Corporation
811 E. Arques Avenue
Sunnyvale, CA 94086

REFERENCES

1. *Microcomputer-Analog Converter Software & Hardware Interfacing,* Howard W. Sams & Co., Inc., Indianapolis, IN 46206, 1978.

2. *Analog-Digital Conversion Notes,* Analog Devices, Inc., Norwood, MA 02062, 1977.

3. *IC Converter Cookbook,* Howard W. Sams & Co., Inc., Indianapolis, IN 46206, 1978.

4. *Datel-Intersil Engineering Product Handbook,* Datel-Intersil, Mansfield, MA 02048, 1979.

5. *Data Acquisition Products Catalog,* Analog Devices, Inc., Norwood, MA 02062, 1978.

6. *Data Acquisition Products Catalog Supplement,* Analog Devices, Inc., Norwood, MA 02062, 1979.

3

Some Practical Data Processing

In the previous chapter, we discussed the use of analog-to-digital converters in computer interface circuits, for the measurement of unknown voltages. While some examples of how the data could be acquired and processed were provided, important topics such as sampling rates, noise, filtering, and others, were not discussed in much detail. These topics are some of the ones that will be described in this chapter, so that you will be able to use and analyze the information that you have acquired from external sources. The information in this chapter is provided as an introduction, since it is impossible to cover all of the different types of data processing tasks that you might find useful. There are a number of excellent references that devote more detail to the treatment of the subjects covered here, and we will note them for you. The use of detailed mathematical formulae has been avoided, as much as possible, since it seems more important to provide usefeul examples and programs that can be used right away. Our main emphasis is upon the development of techniques that you can apply to some specific data processing tasks.

OBJECTIVES

At the end of this chapter, you will be able to:

- Describe the considerations involved in determining data sampling rates.
- Calculate data sampling rates for periodic signals.

- Define "aliasing effect."
- Define inflection points.
- Use a BASIC program to find the inflection points in an array.
- Write a program to scale data values between two defined limits.
- Use ensemble averaging to reduce noise in arrays of information.
- Describe digital filtering.
- Use a BASIC program to filter an array of continuous information.
- Describe the method of least-squares fit.
- Use a BASIC program to find the least-squares fit for an array of information.
- Define linear correlation coefficient.

DATA SAMPLING

Whenever an A/D converter is used to measure an unknown analog voltage, it is important to have an understanding of the phenomenon that is being measured; that is, how fast is the signal changing, is it periodic, what are the maximum and minimum voltages that are to be measured? If you are not careful in interpreting your data, false results can be obtained. The voltage versus time information provided in Fig. 3-1 shows a slowly varying voltage that is defined by the three points that were measured by an A/D converter, connected to an experiment. Before this information is used in any way, it might prove useful to carefully examine the unknown voltage signal that is generated by the experiment. An oscilloscope will work nicely here. A typical oscilloscope plot of the voltage signal is shown in Fig. 3-2 for the same experiment. The

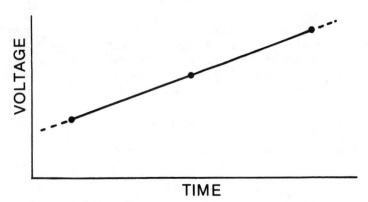

Fig. 3-1. Typical voltage *versus* time measurements made in an experiment.

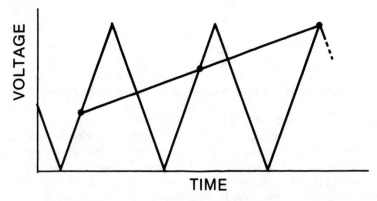

Fig. 3-2. Periodic waveform, with superimposed measurements, showing the effect of aliasing.

points shown in Fig. 3-1 are superimposed upon those in Fig. 3-2 to show how they were obtained when the varying voltage signal was sampled at too-slow a rate. This is called an *aliasing effect,* since the measured voltages are really an "alias" of the periodic triangular wave. Now, the question is, "How fast must the samples be acquired from the A/D converter, so that a true representation of the signal is obtained?"

Of course, the information could be obtained very quickly, but the faster that the computer acquires data, the faster it fills up the available read/write memory. There must be some means of determining the slowest sampling rate for a given signal. The Nyquist relationship states that the minimum sampling rate must be *twice the frequency of maximum frequency component* in a signal that is continuous. Thus, if the maximum *frequency component* is F_{MAX}, then the minimum sampling frequency, F_S, is given by the simple relationship:

$$F_S = 2F_{MAX}$$

It is important to remember that the maximum frequency component of the signal determines the sampling rate minimum, and that in many cases, the maximum frequency of a signal, and its maximum frequency component will be different. This means that a 20-Hz signal may be measured by sampling it at a minimum of 40 points per second, as long as the 20-Hz signal does not contain any frequency components that are above 20 Hz. Of course, you can always sample the 20-Hz signal at *faster* rates.

Since few small computer users have spectrum analyzers available, so that frequency components of a signal can be determined, other techniques must be used to establish the proper sampling

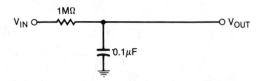

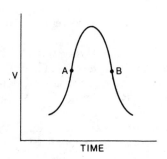

Fig. 3-3. Circuit for a simple low-pass filter with a cutoff of about 1.5 Hz.

rate for unknown signals. Three general techniques are used: (1) trial and error is used to obtain the best reconstruction of the unknown signal; (2) a low-pass filter is used to remove high-frequency components from the signal; and (3) some attempt is made to relate the signal and the measurement rate. In the first case, the technique is fairly simple, but it may take some time to adjust your program so that it acquires information at the proper rate. Simple passive components may be used to construct a filter, as shown in Fig. 3-3, or operational-amplifier-based filters can be used (see *Design of Active Filters, with Experiments*, Howard W. Sams & Co., Inc., Indianapolis, IN 46206). The sampling rate may also be roughly related to the function that is to be measured.

Fig. 3-4. A typical peak, showing the two inflection points, A and B.

If a peak (or valley) voltage is being measured by the computer, as shown in Fig. 3-4, you want to be sure that the computer acquires enough points to accurately characterize the peak. But, where does the peak start, and where does it stop? In a regular peak, there are two points that can be useful in helping you to characterize it. These are the *inflection points* and they occur on the positive-going side, and on the negative-going side of the peak. These points indicate where the slope has gone from an increasing slope to a decreasing slope. For example, when a car starts down a highway, it accelerates to reach a maximum speed, but it must stop accelerating, otherwise it would continue to go faster and faster. The point at which the acceleration stops, and at which the deceleration starts, is the inflection point. This is shown in Fig. 3-4, at points A and B. If you acquire between 10 and 20 points between the inflection points, you will be able to accurately characterize the peak, so that its position (or time) and height are known with little error. The computer could be programmed to determine when the inflection points have been reached, since it can acquire data continuously, evaluating the slopes of the lines between the consecutive points. Thus, the computer would acquire a data value and calculate the slope of the line that would connect this point, and the one that was acquired previously. The slope is temporarily stored. When the next data value is obtained, the slope between it and the previously obtained value is computed, and compared with the slope that was temporarily stored. If the slope is increasing, the computer continues with this sequence until a decrease in the slope is detected. The points acquired during the slope determining steps are simply "discarded," and not used by the computer. Once the inflection point has been reached, the data is acquired.

A simple inflection point-detecting program is listed in Example 3-1. A subroutine starting at line 2000 must be supplied to acquire single values from an A/D converter. A time delay routine could be built into the subroutine, so that data points are only acquired

Example 3-1. Program for Determining Inflection Points on a Continuous Function

```
1500 GOSUB 2000
1510 B1=A
1520 GOSUB 2000
1530 B2=A
1540 S1=ABS(B2−B1)
1550 GOSUB 2000
1560 B3=A
1570 S2=ABS(B3-B2)
1580 IF S2−S1>0 THEN B1=B2:B2=B3:GOTO 1540
1590 PRINT"INFLECTION"
```

at regular intervals. The A/D converter control subroutine has not been shown, for clarity, but many of the programs described in the previous chapter could be readily adapted for use in the inflection point program. In this example, we have assumed that the signal is noise-free, since a noisy signal will cause errors in the determinations of the slope, resulting in the selection of false inflection points. Just as several points were averaged together in the photocell/lamp experiment, the same type of averaging may be used here, too.

Instead of simply having the subroutine at line 200 acquire a single data point for use in the evaluation of the slope of the signal, the computer could be programmed so that the subroutine at line 200 actually acquired a number of data points, averaging them before presenting the averaged value for use in the determination of the slope. In this way, much of the noise could be averaged out.

This is called "boxcar" averaging, or window averaging, since a boxcar-like, or window-like section of the data has been averaged to provide a single data point. This averaging technique would be used only during the determination of the inflection point, as a noise-reducing technique. When the actual data values are to be obtained across the peak, no averaging is used. For those readers who are interested in calculus, the inflection point is also the point at which the second derivative of the function is zero.

A second method involving peak measurement uses the height and width of a typical peak to determine the sampling rate, rather than the inflection points. Once a typical, or representative, peak has been measured, the height of the peak is divided in half, and perpendicular to and through this point, a horizontal line is drawn. This line intersects the peak on the positive-going side, and on the negative-going side. The length of this line between these two intersection points is called the peak-width-at-half-height. If 10 to 20 points are acquired across the peak, from one intersection point to the other, the peak should be fairly well defined. This technique is fairly subjective, since the height of the peak must be determined, and it isn't always possible to accurately determine where the peak starts, and where it ends.

SCALING

Once an array, or a file of data has been acquired, what can be done with it? Probably before any complex data processing or data reducing steps are started, it might be good to examine the information obtained, to be sure that it has been acquired properly. A simple examination of the "raw" data, prior to processing may disclose the fact that the experiment was not connected to the computer properly, or that some malfunction took place. As was noted in Chapter 2, an X-Y, or Y-T display of the information is easy to come by, using either a plotter or an oscilloscope for the display. However, when eight-bit D/A converters are used to control plotters or oscilloscopes, it is impossible to have them accept values that are greater than 255, or less than zero. If a quantity was measured as changing between 2000 pounds per square inch to 4000 pounds per square inch, eight-bit D/A converters could not be used to display these values directly. Likewise, values between −30° C and −50° C couldn't be displayed either, since they are negative numbers, and the D/A converters have no provisions to accept negative binary values.

To display either the pressure, or the temperature information on the plotter or oscilloscope, the raw data must be scaled, so that it has a range that is between zero and 255. The first thing that is done with the data is to adjust its "offset" so that the minimum value corresponds to zero. Then, the remaining values are either multiplied by a scaling factor that either expands or contracts the data values, so that they all fit into the display area, with a resolution of eight bits. Of course, D/A converters with more resolution could be used in the computer system, but they will not add much resolution to a simple oscilloscope, or plotter display. Since the original information has been manipulated to make it "fit" into the display area, it would be useful to know what the lowest value is, what the highest value is, and what the scaling factor is, too.

Example 3-2. A Data Scaling Program

```
 900 INPUT "# DATA POINTS";N
 910 DIM A(N)
 920 FOR I=0 TO N−1
 930 INPUT A(I)
 940 NEXT I
1000 B=100000
1010 FOR I=0 TO N−1
1020 IF A(I)<B THEN B=A(I)
1030 NEXT I
1070 C=−100000
1080 FOR I=0 TO N−1
1090 IF A(I)>C THEN C=A(I)
1100 NEXT I
1110 S=255/(C−B)
1120 FOR I=0 TO N−1
1130 A(I)=(A(I)−B)*S
1140 NEXT I
1150 PRINT "MIN";B,"MAX";C,"SCALE FACTOR";S
1155 FOR I=0 TO N−1
1160 PRINT I, A(I)
1170 NEXT I
1180 END
```

A typical scaling program is provided in Example 3-2. This would probably be found in part of a general-purpose plotter control program, but it is presented here, without these steps. The number of data values to be scaled can be preset, although when eight-bit D/A converters are used, the maximum number of points that can be represented is 256, so the scaling would probably be limited to a 256-element array. The data input steps in this program (lines 910-940) may be left out if the data has been acquired and stored with another program. The minimum, maximum, and scale values are all printed, so that it is easy to label the axes on the plot. The program can scale sets of data that have values that are between 100,000 and −100,000, but these limits are easily changed, as required.

AVERAGING

The use of averaging is quite common in processing data for later evaluation. In the photocell/lamp experiment, several data values were averaged to obtain a single value that represented the voltage across the photocell. The averaging technique helped to eliminate random noise that was superimposed upon the signal that was being measured. As was noted, this is called boxcar averaging, since a number of successive points were averaged to provide a single point. The measurements across a peak may also be averaged using the boxcar method, but this means that the data sampling rate must be increased, since additional points are required for the averaging. If you find that a signal can be defined by acquiring 15 points, and you wish to average 4 points to provide each of the 15, then 60 points must be acquired, so that they can be averaged to provide the 15 points of interest. Thus, the data acquisition rate must be four times what it would have been if only the 15 points were required in the first place.

When the data points are to be averaged, there is a choice that must be made. Are the data points to be averaged after each set has been acquired, or are the points to be stored for later evaluation and averaging? The answer depends upon the speed at which the points are to be acquired, and the amount of memory that is available for the temporary storage of the information. If the points are going to be acquired every second or so, then there is probably time to average them during the acquisition, with time to spare. If the points are to be acquired every 100 milliseconds, or so, the data points should probably be stored for later evaluation. You must carefully evaluate the amount of storage that is required, so that your computer does not run out of memory during the acquisition of information.

While the boxcar averaging technique is useful, it can present some difficulties, since it requires that the computer acquire more points than are actually necessary, and it may take excessive amounts of memory to store the data, or comparatively long periods to average each set of points, as new points are acquired. To eliminate some of these problems, there are two other techniques that should be considered: ensemble averaging, and digital filtering.

When the *ensemble averaging* technique is used, successive sets of information are averaged together to eliminate noise. This means that the experiment, or test, that is generating the information, must be repeated, and except for the noise superimposed on the signal, it must be reproducible. For example, the discharging of a capacitor through a load, or the current passing through a coil, should both be reproducible, while the stress forces in a chimney that is being

demolished, or the temperatures during a given day, are not reproducible, since they cannot be repeated in exactly the same way.
It is important that you not try to apply ensemble averaging to
the evaluation of information from nonreproducible experiments,
since if you do, erroneous results will be obtained.

To illustrate the ensemble averaging technique, an example will
be useful. Let's assume that 10 people are taking part in a physical
exercise program to increase their endurance. The experiment takes
place over 30 days, and each day, the people are to do as many
push-ups as they can, noting the results in a table. At the end of
the 30-day period, someone sits down and averages the number of
push-ups done for each day. The end result is an *ensemble average*
that tabulates the average number of push-ups done for each of
the 30 days. While the results from the different people are certainly not reproducible, this example illustrates the technique.
Many tests are run, and the values that occur at the same times
in each are averaged, to give an average value for that particular
time. Of course, the variable used as the "base" does not have to be
time, it could just as easily be voltage, current, or some other
quantity.

To illustrate the use of ensemble averaging, a noisy sine-wave
signal will be averaged with a number of similar sine waves, in
which only the noise portion of the signal has varied. Instead of
developing a complex circuit to generate the sine wave, add the
noise to it, and then digitize it, the TRS-80 can be used by itself
to generate the noisy signals through the use of the SIN function
to generate the sine wave, and the use of the random number
(RND) generator to generate the noise. The program used is illustrated in Example 3-3. The program initializes an array of 180
points, and then generates a sequence of sine values, such that the
values range between 64 and 192. A random number generation
step is included in the program to generate some random noise.
Another random number generation sequence is used to determine
whether the noise should be added to, or subtracted from, the sine
signal. The signals are all added together in a single array, and then
averaged at the end, by dividing the accumulated value for each
"point" in the sin function by the number of sine waves generated.
In the program listed in Example 3-3, eight sine waves are generated, with noise, and then averaged, to help remove the noise. The
resulting values are stored in read/write memory for later examination with an oscilloscope display program (see Example 2-9).

A single sine wave with superimposed noise is shown in Fig. 3-5,
with the ensemble-averaged waveforms for 4, 8, and 16 different
waveforms shown in Figs. 3-6, 3-7, and 3-8, respectively. You should
be able to see that as the number of sine waves that are averaged

Example 3-3. Sine Wave and Noise Generator Program

```
500 DIM A(180)
510 FOR J=0 TO 180
520 A(J)=0
530 NEXT J
540 FOR E=0 TO 7
550 J=0
560 FOR I=0 TO 360 STEP 2
570 A=128+INT(64*(SIN(I*0.017453)))
580 B=RND(8)
590 IF RND(100)>50 THEN A(J)=A(J)+A+B ELSE A(J)=A(J)+A-B
600 J=J+1
610 NEXT I
620 NEXT E
630 N=20224
640 FOR J=0 TO 180
650 POKE N,A(J)/8
670 N=N+1
680 NEXT J
690 END
```

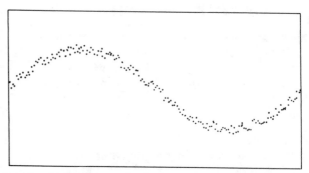

Fig. 3-5. A plot of a TRS-80-generated sine wave, with random noise super-imposed upon it.

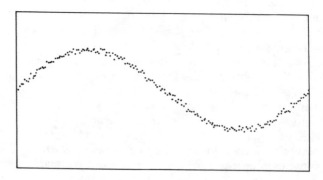

Fig. 3-6. Ensemble average of four noisy sine waves.

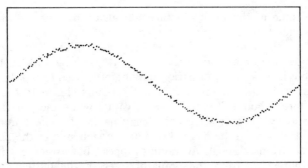

Fig. 3-7. Ensemble average of eight noisy sine waves.

is increased, the noise is decreased. Remember, though, that the reduction in noise also means that more experiments or tests must be performed to provide the raw data that is used in the averaging process. As noted previously, this technique is only useful if multiple sets of data are available. One final note on the ensemble averaging program shown in Example 3-3. This program takes about three minutes to process eight noisy sine waves, so if you wish to run it, remember to be patient. If you are processing arrays of information that have been acquired at some other time, the averaging should not require as much time, since software steps were used in our program to actually create the sine values, and to add the noise to the signal.

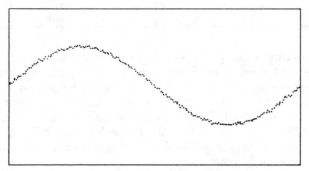

Fig. 3-8. Ensemble average of 16 noisy sine waves.

DIGITAL FILTERING

It is possible to filter noisy signals with special programs that use a single set of data, acquired from a single experiment or test. These filtering programs are useful when an experiment can be performed only once, and when the resulting information contains some noise that must be reduced. The filtering programs actually average some of the values in the data array, but instead of averaging values from multiple sets of data that were acquired at the same time, the filtering technique uses data values that were obtained both before and after the point that is to be filtered. In this way, a single array of information may be processed to reduce noise. The basic principle involved is that the points closest to the point to be filtered should also be close in value, while the points some distance away (five or six points) may have little effect upon the value of the point to be filtered. Points on each side of the point to be filtered are used in the averaging process, but as you get farther and farther away from the point of interest, the outlying points contribute less to the average. Of course, the points to be filtered in this way must have been obtained at fixed, uniform intervals from one another, and the points must be continuous.

Table 3-1. Table of Filter Coefficients for an 11-Point Filter

Data Value	Coefficient
$n-5$	0.074
$n-4$	0.111
$n-3$	0.182
$n-2$	0.333
$n-1$	0.666
n	1.00
$n+1$	0.666
$n+2$	0.333
$n+3$	0.182
$n+4$	0.111
$n+5$	0.074

The filtering technique is often called the moving average technique, since the set of coefficients "moves" along the raw array of data, performing an average of several points behind, and ahead of, the point of interest, to provide a new value for the point being averaged. In general, the coefficients that are used in the averaging process follow a continuous function themselves, generally some sort of parabolic function. A table of typical coefficients is provided in Table 3-1 for an 11-point filter.

When point $A(I)$ is being filtered, point $A(I-5)$ is multiplied by 0.074, point $A(I-4)$ is multiplied by 0.111, and so on. The sum of all the multiplications is divided by the total of the coefficients, 3.732, to generate the filtered value for point $A(I)$. The new point is stored in a separate array, since you do not want to use filtered data values in the filtering process when the next sequential point is operated upon. The main point in filtering the information is to remove noise, but you must be careful in evaluating your filtering needs, since the filtering process will alter the data, however slightly.

Example 3-4. Eleven-Point Parabolic Filter Program No. 1

```
 900 INPUT "ARRAY SIZE";W
1000 DIM C(11):C(1)=.074:C(2)=.111:C(3)=.182:C(4)=.333
1001 C(5)=.666:C(6)=1:C(7)=.666:C(8)=.333:C(9)=.182
1002 C(10)=.111:C(11)=.074
1010 DIM Q(W):X=1
1020 S=0
1030 FOR I = 1 TO 11
1050 S=S+(C(I)*A(X))
1060 X=X+1
1070 NEXT I
1090 LET Q(X-6)=S/3.732
1100 X=X-10
1110 IF X<W-9 THEN 1020
1120 PRINT "FILTER COMPLETED"
1130 N=20224
1140 FOR J=0 TO W
1150 POKE N,Q(J)
1160 N=N+1
1170 NEXT J
1180 END
```

A typical set of raw data values is shown in Fig. 3-9. These values may be filtered with the simple program shown in Example 3-4 which includes the multiplication coefficients in an 11-value array. Unfortunately, this array does not do a particularly good job of filtering the data, since it does not filter the first five, or the last five points. If the "parabola" of filtering coefficients is placed at either end of the array to be filtered, you will see that the central point, the one that will be filtered, is the sixth from the start of the array,

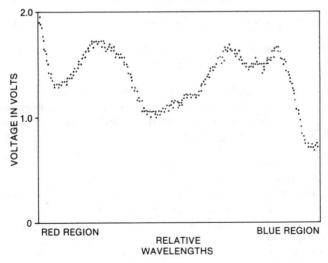

Fig. 3-9. A plot of typical, raw experimental data acquired from a spectrometer.

133

while the last point to be filtered is the sixth from the last point. This is shown in diagram form in Fig. 3-10. The first, or the last, five data points may be quite important, since the computer may have been triggered to start acquiring data at a particular time, and we wish to evaluate the data that is acquired from that point on.

The software required to filter all of the points in an array is more complex than that shown in Example 3-4, since we now require that portions of the parabolic set of coefficients be used at the start and finish of the array, so that all of the points are filtered. Thus, the first point is filtered by using its value and the values of the next five consecutive data points, the second point is filtered using the first data point, its own value, and the values of the next following five data points. Once the set of coefficients reached the sixth data value to filter it, the five points on either side will be used in the filtering process. A complete filtering program is provided in Example 3-5. You will see that special steps have been incorporated

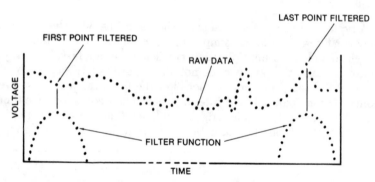

Fig. 3-10. A diagram showing the relationship between the experimental data and the parabolic filter function points.

into the program at lines 3000–3050 and at lines 2160–2210 to restructure the coefficient array so that only the points required are used at the "ends" of the array. If the information presented in Fig. 3-9 is filtered using this program, the plot shown in Fig. 3-11 represents the filtered data. Of course, you could filter this information again and again to improve its appearance, but you must remember that the filtering process also tends to broaden and flatten peaks, since it does not provide a perfect solution to the noise problem, but rather acts to average the noise to provide an average function. There are some mathematical solutions that allow the filtering to take place without serious degradation of the data, and these will be discussed in the next section. In this section, the information has been available in an array, and we have not attempted to filter the data points as they are acquired. This allowed us to use those points that occurred both before and after the data point that was averaged. If filtering is to be performed on the stream of data points as it is generated, as is the case in an R/C filter, or an active filter, then only unidirectional filtering is possible.

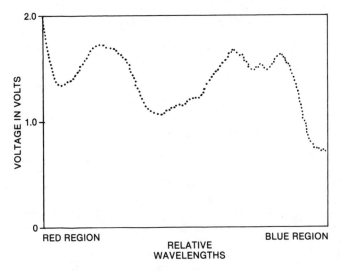

Fig. 3-11. A plot of experimental data (see Fig. 3-9) that has been filtered with a set of parabolic coefficients.

METHOD OF LEAST SQUARES

The last data processing technique that we will describe in detail is the method of least squares. This method of data analysis was developed by Carl Friederich Gauss (1777-1855) and applied to astronomical observations so that the orbits of planets and asteroids could be accurately predicted. Briefly stated, the method allows a set of data values to be used to find the best solution to an equation that fits the data.

In many experiments, the observed, or measured values do not always correspond to the theoretical values shown in textbooks and other references. This is due to noise, as we have already mentioned, and also to experimental errors. While the measured values are not all on the expected straight line (we will assume a "straight" line function here), they may be evaluated using the method of least squares, or the least squares fit, so that a *best* straight line function is obtained from the data that is available. Without going into the mathematical basis for the method of least squares in detail, the technique serves to minimize the squares of the distances

Example 3-5. Eleven-Point Parabolic Filter Program No. 2

```
2000 INPUT "ARRAY SIZE";W
2010 DIM C(10):C(0)=.074:C(1)=.111:C(2)=.182:C(3)=.333
2020 C(4)=.666:C(5)=1:C(6)=.666:C(7)=.333:C(8)=.182
2030 C(9)=.111:C(10)=.074
2040 DIM Q(W):D=6:G=0:E=10
2050 IF G<6 THEN 3000
2060 F=3.732
2070 S=0
2080 FOR I=D TO E
2090 S=S+(C(I)*A(X))
2100 X=X+1
2110 NEXT I
2120 Q(G)=S/F:X=X-10
2130 G=G+1
2140 IF G<W-4 THEN 2050
2150 IF G=W+1 THEN 5000
2160 E=E-1:F=0
2170 FOR I=D TO E
2180 F=F+C(I)
2190 NEXT I
2200 X=G-5
2210 GOTO 2070
3000 F=0:X=0
3010 D=D-1
3020 FOR I=D TO E
3030 F=F+C(I)
3040 NEXT I
3050 GOTO 2070
5000 PRINT "FILTER COMPLETE"
5010 N=20224
5020 FOR J=0 TO W
5030 POKE N, Q(J)
5040 N=N+1
5050 NEXT J
5060 END
```

between the actual data points and the best straight line function that goes through all of the points. The squares of the distances are used so that simple changes in the distances cannot be traded off against one another. For example, if two points are a distance of four units from one another, the least squares position is equally between them, since the sum of the squares of the distances between the points and the least squares position is $2^2 + 2^2 = 8$. If we choose either point as a first approximation for the least squares position, the sum of the squares of the distances would be $0^2 + 4^2 = 16$. Since this is not the *minimum* sum of the squares of the distances between the points, this is not the best position for the least squares function. Obviously, a great deal of trial and error would be required if it were necessary for us to compute the best straight line between a set of data points in this way. For straight line functions that use the simple relationship, $y = mx + b$, where m is the slope of the line, and where b is its intercept point on the y axis (y intercept), a simple equation may be used to operate upon the set of data to find the best straight line through the set of data. Actually, the least squares function provides us with the *slope* of the line, and its *y-intercept*. It is up to us to actually draw the line, or to have the computer draw it for us.

The equation below is used to evaluate the slope of the least squares fit for a set of X and Y values:

$$m = \frac{n \cdot \Sigma xy - \Sigma x \cdot \Sigma y}{n \cdot \Sigma x^2 - (\Sigma x)^2}$$

In this equation, n represents the number of data points that are being used in the calculation, and the Greek symbol sigma, Σ, means the sum of, so that Σxy means "the sum of the values obtained by multiplying the x-axis value by the y-axis value for a particular point." Likewise, the y-intercept value may be obtained for the same set of X and Y values:

$$b = \frac{\Sigma y - m \cdot \Sigma x}{n}$$

The solutions to these equations provide an exact set of slope and intercept values for the best straight line for the function. Now that two equations have been developed, it is relatively easy to write a BASIC program for the TRS-80, so that a set of data values may be processed by the least squares method. Such a program is shown in Example 3-6. When you use the method of least squares, some caution must be observed, since it is possible to find a best straight line through even random data or noise. For example, if you aimed a shotgun at a piece of graph paper, fired the gun and then plotted

Example 3-6. Least Squares Fit for a Linear Function

```
 10 DIM X(20), Y(20)
 20 INPUT "# DET'N =";N
 30 P=0:Q=0:R=0: S=0:W=0
 40 PRINT "X THEN Y"
 50 FOR I =1 TO N
 60 INPUT X(I), Y(I)
 70 P=P+X(I):Q=Q+Y(I)
 80 R=R+(X(I)↑2):W=W+(YR(I)↑2)
 90 S=S+(X(I)*Y(I))
100 NEXT I
110 NP=(N*S−P*Q):DP=(N*R−P↑2)
130 SL=NP/DP
140 IT=(Q−(SL*P))/N
150 PRINT "SLOPE =",SL:"INTERCEPT =",IT
160 END
```

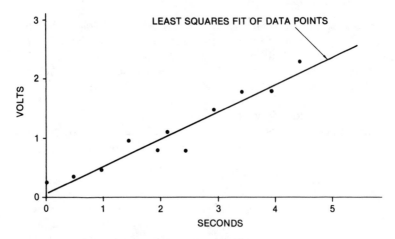

Fig. 3-12. A plot of data showing the best straight line obtained from a
least-squares calculation.

the points, the method of least squares could provide you with a
best straight line. Does it have any purpose? We doubt it. There
isn't much of a relationship between a shotgun pellet's X- and Y-
axis position. The plot shown in Fig. 3-12 shows the relationship
between a set of data points and the least squares fit straight line
that was obtained from the BASIC program shown in Example 3-6.
In this case, the data was obtained from a real experiment, but the
actual values and the coordinates are of no real importance, since
the main purpose of this plot is to show a typical relationship between real data values and the best straight line.

When applying the method of least squares, it is frequently a
good idea to go a bit further and attempt to correlate the data
values by mathematical means. The *linear correlation coefficient*, r,
provides a means of relating the X- and Y-axis information in a
linear relationship. The linear correlation coefficient is obtained
from the rather lengthy formula:

$$r = \frac{n \cdot \Sigma xy - \Sigma x \cdot \Sigma y}{\sqrt{|n \cdot \Sigma x^2 - (\Sigma x)^2| \cdot |n \cdot \Sigma y^2 - (\Sigma y)^2|}}$$

You can probably see that portions of the numerator and denomi-
nator in this equation have been calculated during the least squares
analysis of the data points, so a simple statement may be added to
the least squares analysis program in Example 3-6, so that the linear
correlation coefficient may be computed. A complete program is
shown in Example 3-7. Typical relationships are shown in Figs. 3-13
through 3-16. Another useful piece of information is the coefficient
of determination, or r^2. Thus, if the linear correlation coefficient is

Example 3-7. Least Squares Fit, with Correlation Calculation

```
20 INPUT "# DET'N =";N
30 P=0:Q=0:R=0:S=0;W=0
40 PRINT "X THEN Y"
50 FOR I =1 TO N
60 INPUT X(I), Y(I)
70 P=P+X(I):Q=Q+Y(I)
80 R=R+(X(I)↑2):W=W+(Y(I)↑2)
90 S=S+(X(I)*Y(I))
100 NEXT I
110 NP=(N*S−P*Q):DP=(N*R−P↑2)
130 SL=NP/DP
140 IT=(Q−(SL*P))/N
150 PRINT "SLOPE =", SL;"INTERCEPT =",IT
160 R=NP/(SQR(DP*(N*W−Q↑2)))
170 PRINT "CORRELATION ",R
180 END
```

0.9, the coefficient of determination is $0.9^2 = 0.81$. In other words, 81% of the variation in the Y-axis variable is due to the variation in the X-axis. The interpretation of the coefficient of determination

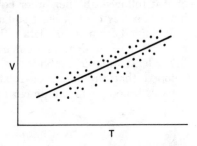

Fig. 3-13. Very low scattering of data points for a high positive correlation.

must be done with caution. For example, a store may plot the number of heads of lettuce sold *versus* the number of packages of carrots sold, obtaining a 90% variation between the two. Does this mean that if more lettuce is sold next week, that it will follow that more carrots will be sold, too? Not really, since there are probably many other variables that enter into the relationship. For ex-

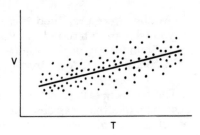

Fig. 3-14. Very low scattering of data points for a high negative correlation.

ample, carrots and lettuce are located next to each other, the store ran a special on carrots and lettuce, or there was some other relationship that didn't directly involve the actual sales of each vegetable.

In the previous discussion of the least squares method of determining the slope and Y-intercept for a best straight line through data points, we assumed that there was a *linear* relationship between

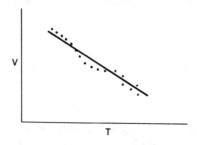

Fig. 3-15. Some scattering of points, but a relationship is established for a moderate positive correlation.

the data values. What happens if the relationship is exponential, or if it follows a higher order equation, such as $a_3x^3 + a_2x^2 + a_1x + b = y$? In this case, a least squares solution for this equation may be obtained for a set of data points, but the mathematical solution requires a great deal more manipulations than were used in the linear least squares method. In the early 1960s a technique was developed that provided for relatively easy solutions to the least squares functions for nonlinear functions. The overall mathematical

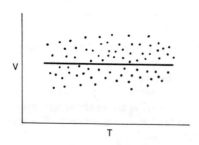

Fig. 3-16. Very high scattering of data points. Probably no correlation, or relationship between the two variables.

derivations were presented in a now classical paper, and for those of you who are interested in pursuing this further, we suggest that you obtain a copy of the original article, as it appeared in *Analytical Chemistry* (3). A complete reference is provided at the end of this chapter.

The Savitsky-Golay method uses the same type of moving average technique that was described in this chapter. However, instead of using a set of rather arbitrarily chosen parabolic coefficients for

Table 3-2. Coefficients for Least Squares Fit of a Parabolic Function (3)

Points	Coefficients				
	13-Point	11-Point	9-Point	7-Point	5-Point
−6	−11				
−5	0	−36			
−4	9	9	−21		
−3	16	44	14	−2	
−2	21	69	39	3	−3
−1	24	84	54	6	12
0	25	89	59	7	17
1	24	84	54	6	12
2	21	69	39	3	−3
3	16	44	14	−2	
4	9	9	−21		
5	0	−36			
6	−11				
NORM =	143	429	231	21	35

filtering, a set of carefully obtained coefficients is used, with the resulting data points being the least squares values for the set of data points processed. The actual coefficient values, and the "divisor," or norm, are provided for the parabolic function, $ax^2 + bx + c = y$, as shown in Table 3-2. Values for 5-, 7-, 9-, 11- and 13-point functions have been provided. These values may be substituted into the simple filtering program (Example 3-4) to provide the *exact* solution to the least squares fit of the points. Of course, the function must closely approximate the function described by the coefficients for the solution to be realistic. In most cases, the parabolic function will work quite nicely for a series of peaks and valleys.

The original Savitsky-Golay article contains many tables of coefficients for various functions. Another outgrowth of this is that there are also tables of coefficients that may be used in the "moving average" routine to provide derivatives of the data that are being processed. In this way, a simple "moving average" subroutine may be used with different arrays of coefficients to obtain various functions. Since most readers will be concerned with enhancing a simple signal, we will refer you to the original article for additional information on the other functions that this technique can provide.

There are other data processing techniques that you may find useful in your TRS-80 computer system, and rather than provide additional information about statistical analysis and Fourier transforms, we have provided some references for you. We hope that these references will furnish the information that will help you serve other data processing needs. We have not tried to make this chapter into a detailed explanation of data processing and data evaluation, but we hope that the different ideas and techniques that we have developed will help you.

REFERENCES

1. *Scientific Analysis of the Pocket Calculator*, 2nd Ed., Jon M. Smith, John Wiley and Sons, New York, NY 10016, 1977.

2. *Mathematical Methods for Social and Management Scientists*, T. Marll Mc-Donald, Houghton Mifflin Co., Boston, MA 02107, 1974.

3. "Smoothing and Differentiation of Data by Simplified Least Squares Procedures," A. Savitsky and M. J. E. Golay, *Analytical Chemistry*, July 1964, p. 1627.

4. *Fast Fourier Transforms on Your Home Computer*, W. D. Stanley and S. J. Peterson, Byte Publications, Peterborough, NH 03458, December 1978.

4

Serial Communications
and Remote Control

There are many situations in which a computer can be used to control devices that are some distance from the central processing unit. Likewise, there are situations in which it is necessary for the computer to "measure" signals that originate some distance from the CPU. In most of the interfaces that have been developed so far, many computer signals were required by the interface for proper operation. These signals, and their respective numbers, include the data bus (8 signals), the address bus (8 or 16 signals), and the control bus (up to 7 signals), for a total of up to 31 individual signals. It doesn't make much sense to try to route all of these signals to I/O devices that are more than a few feet from the computer. In this chapter, some of the alternate methods of I/O device control and data transfer will be discussed.

OBJECTIVES

At the end of this chapter, you will be able to do the following:

- Describe the bit format of an asynchronous-serial data transmission.
- Describe the sampling of an asynchronous-serial bit stream that is required to recover the information in parallel form.
- Describe the hardware and software required to use a USART chip in the TRS-80 computer system.
- Describe the use of clock signals by the USART chip.

- Develop software that can be used by USARTs in computer-to-computer communications.
- Describe the USART chip, and compare it to the UART chip.
- Design a remote control circuit that uses a UART chip, and that communicates with a computer through a USART chip.
- Design an interface that can be used with a UART to control a remote D/A or A/D converter.
- Describe the AART chip (MC14469) and how it operates.
- Design an interface circuit that will use the AART chip to control an A/D converter.
- Write software that will control the AART chip through a USART chip.
- Describe the operation of open-collector buses, when used for party-line communications.
- Use general-purpose assembly-language USART control subroutines.

Before we actually start to describe some alternate I/O techniques, though, let us examine a typical application in which a TRS-80 computer might be found. This application is the control of a solar hot-water heater. The computer would be used to measure temperatures, and to make decisions that would turn pumps on or off, and perhaps open and close valves, to route the water through portions of the heater system. In such a system, it is necessary to measure temperatures throughout the system, while also controlling I/O devices in remote locations. Even if the computer is located fairly close to the major portion of the system, probably in a basement, outdoor temperatures must be measured, along with temperatures at various places on the solar collector. Routing a 23-conductor cable from the basement to the roof can be quite a job, costing a great deal of money. If TTL-compatible signals are to be used, they must be buffered, so that the long lengths of wire can be driven without difficulty. Perhaps the temperature signal could be amplified close to the sensor, and then sent to an analog-to-digital converter that is close to the computer. While this looks like an attractive alternative, even "clean" amplified signals can pick up a great deal of noise, as well as being affected by ground loops that induce additional noise on the signal. The noise can be reduced with filters, or current level signals may be used, since they are fairly immune to induced signals, or noise. (Industrial control systems frequently use pneumatic controls in which pressures and vacuums are measured, since these "signals" are immune to electrical interference.) Obviously, there must be an alternative to both the use of multiconductor cable, or an analog signal, to acquire information from a remote device, and to control a remote I/O device.

Probably the most attractive, and interesting, alternative, is the use of *serial* digital information transfer techniques. In a serial transmission scheme, individual data bits are transmitted over a pair of wires, *one bit at a time.* The receiving device acquires the data bits, reconstructing them to form a *parallel* set of data bits. Thus, the transmitter must perform a parallel-to-serial conversion, while the receiver must perform a *serial-to-parallel* conversion. In this way, many bits of information are easily exchanged between peripheral devices, and the central processing unit of the computer. In fact, this is one of the ways in which most teletypewriters and terminals operate. Obviously, for any meaningful serial transfers to take place, there must be a well-established standard, or protocol, that dictates exactly how the individual data bits are to be transmitted, the speed of the transmission, and the format of the informational portion of the data transmission. There must also be some means of *synchronizing* the flow of serial information, so that a receiving device knows when a new transmission has started. The important points will be discussed before the actual applications of serial data transfers are explored.

ASYNCHRONOUS-SERIAL DATA TRANSFERS

The actual serial-to-parallel and parallel-to-serial data conversions are not at all difficult. Simple shift register circuits can be used to perform the conversions. However, if shift registers are used, a common clock signal must be sent to the "receivers," along with the serial stream of data bits, so that the serial bits are properly shifted into the shift register of the receiver. This seems to be defeating the purpose of using serial data transfers, since another signal must be used, and transmitted in parallel, along with the data bits. The clock signal may be affected by noise, too, so bits may be improperly shifted into the shift register of the receiver. It would be very useful to find a serial data transfer technique in which the parallel clock information is not required. Such a technique uses the *asynchronous-serial* method of transferring digital information. When asynchronous-serial transfers are used, no common clock signal is required. There must be some means of actually synchronizing an asynchronous-serial transfer, so that the bits do not become scrambled when they are received. The synchronizing information is contained within the asynchronous-serial transmission.

Each asynchronous-serial data transmission contains information about the start of the "message," and about the end of the message. When asynchronous-serial data transfers are used, the common clock signal is eliminated, but the transmitters and receivers that are to communicate with each other must be set so that their respective frequencies are very close to one another. For example, information could not be easily transmitted between a transmitter operating at 250 bits per second, and a receiver operating at 548 bits per second. The *bits-per-second* frequency notation is an industry standard that denotes the receiver/transmitter data transfer rate. Thus, for an asynchronous-serial receiver-transmitter system to operate properly, the bit rates of the receiver and the transmitter must be closely aligned. There is a small margin of error, but it is only a few percent. To reduce errors in asynchronous-serial data transfer systems, highly accurate crystal-based signal generators are used to determine the data rates.

Now, the question of how the receiver synchronizes its receipt of the transmission must be answered. A typical "stream" of data bits transmitted in an asynchronous-serial format is shown in Fig. 4-1. The important bits are the START BIT, and the two STOP BITS. The data bits represent an 8-bit data word that has been transmitted. Actually, most asynchronous-serial data systems may be used with data words that range from five to eight bits of data. This will be described later in this chapter. The START bit is used by the receiving circuitry to alert it to the start of the transmission. The logic one-to-logic zero transition signals the start of a new set of bits. Since the clock frequencies of the receiver and transmitter are fairly close, the receiver waits for one-half of a bit period, and then samples the serial input. If the logic zero is still detected, the receiver assumes that it has detected a "real" START bit, as opposed to a noise spike that might have been induced upon the signal line. When a start bit has been verified in this way, the receiver continues to sample the serial information by waiting a complete bit period from the middle of the start bit. In this way, each of the serial bits is sampled close to its midpoint. This reduces the effect of slight differences in clock frequencies between receiver and transmitter. The two STOP bits signal the receiver that it has reached the end of the data transmission. The receiver can then indicate to the receiving device that the data bits have been accepted and that they are available in a parallel format. A second series of bits

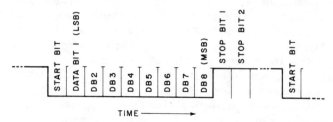

Fig. 4-1. Typical asynchronous-serial bit pattern (data bits may be logic 1 or logic 0).

may then be received, again starting with a logic zero start bit. In the asynchronous-serial data transmission format, start bits are always logic zero, and stop bits are always logic one. In the example just described, you may be wondering how the receiver distinguishes between two logic ones right next together in the data word, and the two logic ones that are used as the stop bits. This requires an explanation.

The asynchronous-serial protocol limits the number of data bits that may be transmitted to either five, six, seven, or eight. Either one or two stop bits are used in each transmission, along with a start bit. Some older serial transmission schemes specified 1½ stop bits, but we doubt that you will encounter too many of these devices. The format of the bit stream must be agreed to before the first transmission, since it would be quite difficult to transfer asynchronous-serial information between a transmitter that was sending eight bits of information and two stop bits, and a receiver that expected five bits of information and one stop bit. The data transfer rates are frequently standardized, too, although other rates can be used, if required. Transfer rates of 110, 150, 300, 600, 1200, 2400, 4800, and 9600 bits per second are quite common. Higher rates are also encountered, in a "doubling of rates," as noted in the sequence just mentioned. The rate of 110 bits per second (b/sec) is standard for most mechanical teletypewriters, and for some terminals, too. Of course, the data bits may be either logic one, or logic zero, and there are many different codes that are used to transfer the required information. Just remember that in the asynchronous-serial data protocol, the least-significant bit (LSB) of information is transmitted immediately after the start bit.

At this point, you may be wondering how much time and effort are going to have to be expended in wiring-up the transmitter and receiver circuits that follow the asynchronous-serial protocol. Very little time, indeed. There are many different types of inexpensive, commercially available asynchronous-serial integrated circuits that perform all of the necessary serial/parallel conversions, bit formatting, start bit detecting, and so on. These integrated circuits are called universal asynchronous receiver/transmitters, or UARTs, for short. The UARTs are generally found in instruments and devices that use the asynchronous-serial protocol for the transfer and exchange of information, commands, etc. The UARTs preceded the microprocessors, so the UARTs are not always compatible with microprocessor, or microcomputer, bus signals. As microcomputers evolved, serial communications chips evolved along with them, and now, most microcomputer families include some sort of serial I/O chip that supports the asynchronous-serial data format. Some of these devices also support a synchronous protocol, thus the general name, universal synchronous/asynchronous receiver/transmitter, or USART, has been applied to these types of devices. Both the UARTs and USARTs have been explained in *Interfacing and Scientific Data Communications Experiments*, Howard W. Sams & Co., Inc., Indianapolis, IN 46206, 1979. We refer you to this book for detailed descriptions of these chips, and their operation. While we will briefly describe the operation of the UART and the USART, we will not go into great detail about their operation, except as it relates to a specific application, or example.

INTERFACING AND USING THE USART

Since the USART has been designed to be compatible with the 8080-type microcomputer, we will desrcibe how it is interfaced to the TRS-80, a Z-80-based computer. Some simple BASIC-language control programs will also be discussed, so that serial transmissions may be easily controlled. The USART is a computer-programmable device, meaning that the computer will send commands, or instructions, to the USART chip, so that it can operate in any one of several possible modes. In the USART, these computer-programmed instructions take the place of jumper wires that are generally used to program the older UART devices, to configure them for various applications. We will discuss the programming of the USART functions in this section.

A block diagram of a USART, in this case, the Intel 8251A, is shown in Fig. 4-2, along with the pin designations of the 28-pin chip. Some short descriptions of the signals are also provided. The block diagram shows the USART as being divided into four main

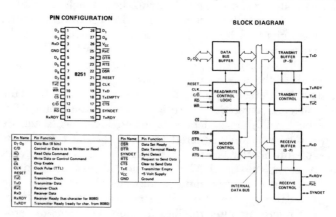

Fig. 4-2. Block diagram and pin configuration for 8251A USART chip (reprinted by permission of Intel Corp., Copyright 1978).

sections: the data bus buffer and control section, the receiver section, the transmitter section, and the modem control section. The modem control portion of the USART is not particularly important in most applications, but it will be described very briefly. The data bus buffer section provides the buffering of the input signals as well as the three-state outputs that are necessary for the proper operation of the data bus. The six control signals, RESET, CLK, C/$\overline{\text{D}}$, $\overline{\text{RD}}$, $\overline{\text{WR}}$, and $\overline{\text{CS}}$, provide the necessary signals so that the chip may be controlled by the computer. The RESET input is a logic one level, or pulse, that must be sent to the USART to reset it. This pulse may be sent to the USART at any time, causing it to be reset. The RESET signal must be activated whenever the chip is first connected to power. In many of the program examples, a simple OUT command at the start of the program is used to reset the USART. The $\overline{\text{RESET}}$ signal of the TRS-80 may be inverted and used to reset the USART.

The CLK signal is a clock input that is used to synchronize several internal functions of the USART. It is not the data rate clock, although it must be at least 30 times faster than the fastest data bit rate that will be used with the USART. The $\overline{\text{RD}}$ and $\overline{\text{WR}}$ signals control the read/write operations within the USART. These signals may be obtained from the $\overline{\text{OUT}}$ and $\overline{\text{IN}}$ signals generated by the TRS-80, if device addressing is to be used to control the USART, or from the $\overline{\text{RD}}$ and $\overline{\text{WR}}$ memory control signals of the TRS-80, if memory addressing is to be used.

The chip select signal, $\overline{\text{CS}}$, is very similar to the decoded address signals that have been used in previous examples, to enable a particular I/O device. The USART actually contains *four* I/O devices, two of which are output ports, and two of which are input ports, so two device addresses must be used to generate the chip select signal. Remember that an input port and an output port may have the same device address, since their functions are different. Two different device address signals may be gated together to provide the chip select signal, but the USART also needs some other way of determining which of the internal I/O devices the computer wishes to address, since the chip select signal simply enables the chip, it does not select individual I/O devices. A second input, C/$\overline{\text{D}}$ is used by the USART to distinguish between the two addresses. The "C" represents COMMANDs, while the "D" represents DATA. Some signal must be generated by the computer, so that it can switch the USART between the command and data addresses. This control input is generally connected to the least significant address bit, A0. In this way, two consecutive device (or memory) addresses may be used to control the USART, for example, addresses 7 and 6, or 00000111 and 00000110. Here, address line A0 would be connected to the C/$\overline{\text{D}}$ input of the USART, while address bits A7 through A1 are used to generate the chip select signal. The USART does not require that the device address be combined with the function pulses, $\overline{\text{IN}}$ and $\overline{\text{OUT}}$, since this gating takes place within the USART chip. A typical USART interface is shown in Fig. 4-3. Only the computer-USART portion of the interface has been shown.

If the TRS-80 interface breadboard is used to interface the USART, a different circuit must be used, since it is impossible to decode address bits A7 through A1, without bit A0. To overcome this problem, address bit A0 is connected to the C/$\overline{\text{D}}$ input of the USART, and decoded addresses 7 and 6 are gated together to provide a composite device select, or chip select signal. This gating will select the USART whenever device address 7 or 6 is generated by the TRS-80. Remember, when the interface breadboard is used, an $\overline{\text{INP REQ}}$ signal must be generated to properly control the bus buffering circuits. The circuit shown in Fig. 4-4 generates the proper signals for the control of a USART on the interface breadboard. In Figs. 4-3 and 4-4, the CLK signal has not been provided for the USART. This will be added later.

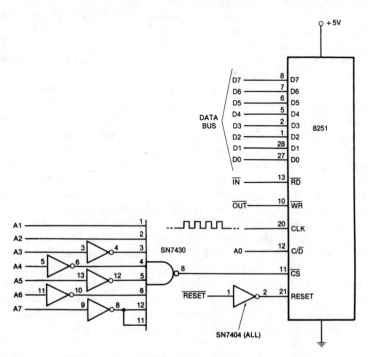

Fig. 4-3. A typical USART interface for I/O addresses 6 and 7. Communication connections not shown for clarity.

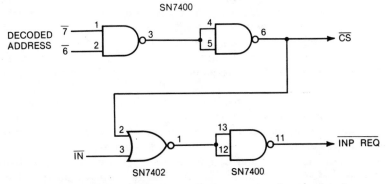

Fig. 4-4. A USART chip select circuit for the TRS-80 Interface Breadboard.

When the USART is in the data mode ($C/D = 0$), the 8-bit register of the receiver may be examined with an input command, such as PRINT INP(6), and the 8-bit register of the transmitter may be loaded with a value that is to be transmitted, OUT 6,154. Before the transmitter and receiver may be used, however, the USART must be programmed so that it knows how many bits it is to transmit and receive, how fast it is to transmit and receive information, and so on. The programming commands are sent to the USART by the computer when it is in the command mode ($C/D = 1$). Remember that there is nothing "magical" about switching between the command and data modes, since address bit A0 is used to control the mode, and it is part of the overall address used by the I/O command. Thus, I/O ports with address 7 are command ports, while I/O ports with address 6 are the data ports for the transmitter and receiver.

Programming the USART

The first thing that the computer must be programmed to do is to output a mode control instruction to the USART. The format of the mode control instruction is shown in Fig. 4-5. The eight bits in this mode control instruction allow you to set the USART so that it will transmit the data bits in the format that you desire, or the format of the receiving device—teletypewriter, terminal, line printer, etc.

Bits S2 and S1 allow you the choice of either 1, 1½, or 2 stop bits in the bit stream. The choice of bits $S2 = S1 = 0$ is invalid. The number of data bits in the bit stream may also be set, using bits L2 and L1 in the mode control instruction. If fewer than eight data bits are to be used, the least significant bits are used; for example, a 5-bit transmission would transmit bits D4 through D0, with bits D7 through D5 being ignored. The baud rate factor may also be selected, using bits B2 and B1. These bits allow you to set the frequency relationship between the bit rate, in bits per second, and the clock frequency that is used by the receiver and transmitter sections of the USART. Remember that this clock frequency is not the same as the CLK frequency that is supplied to the control section of the USART. Independent clock signals are used by the transmitter and receiver sections of the USART. Through the selection of the clock control or baud rate factor bits, the data transmission (and reception) rate may be set to be equal to 16-times *slower* than, or 64-times *slower* than the transmitter (and receiver) clock frequency. Most UART and USART systems use a clock frequency that is 16 times the data transfer rate, so we suggest that you use the B2 = 1, B1 = 0 configuration. If B2 = B1 = 0, the synchronous mode of operation is selected, a mode that we are not interested in. If the 16× baud rate factor is chosen, then for a 2400 b/sec transmission/reception rate, the clock rates of the transmitter and receiver would have to be 2400 × 16, or 38,400 Hz. In some places, you will see the notation "baud" used to represent bits per second. Actually, the meaning of the term baud is more complex than "the number of bits transmitted per second," so we will not interchange baud and bits-per-second, using the notation b/sec instead.

The mode control instruction also allows you to set the *parity* of the data, so that the number of logic ones in the data word is

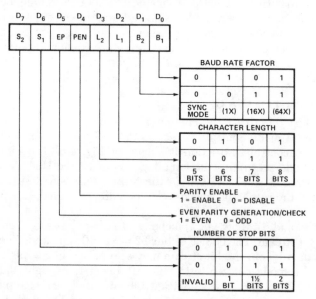

Fig. 4-5. 8251A Mode Control Instruction formats (reprinted by permission of Intel Corp., Copyright 1978).

either even, or odd, depending upon the type of parity that you choose to use. An additional *parity bit* is placed in the bit stream between the last data bit, and the stop bit, or bits. You can also choose to override the parity function by disabling it, in which case, the parity bit is not placed in the bit stream. If you choose to use the parity function, remember that it will add an additional bit to the bit stream, and that the devices that are to receive the transmission must be programmed not only to receive a parity bit, but the correct type of parity, either even, or odd. The parity function is used to help in the detection of errors in a transmission of information. It is important to remember that the mode control instruction programs both the transmitter and the receiver for exactly the same data format. It is not possible to program them separately. If different formats are required by the receiver and the transmitter, two USART chips must be used.

After the mode control instruction has been sent to the command output port of the USART, a second piece of information must be sent to this *same output port*. The USART takes care of switching the two 8-bit values to the proper places within the USART. This second set of eight bits is called the command instruction, and its bit assignments are shown in Fig. 4-6. Some of the bits will not be used at present, but the important bits are TxEN, RxE, and ER. These bits enable or disable the receiver and the transmitter, and the ER bit resets all indications of error conditions. Usually, a command instruction of 00010101, or 21, will be used in TRS-80 applications that use the USART.

After a command instruction, following a mode control instruction, has been sent to the USART, a new command instruction may be sent to it at any time, simply by sending the new command information to the command output port of the USART. In this way, it is possible to control the receiver and transmitter functions just by changing the pattern of the bits in the command instruction. In general, the mode control instruction is sent to the USART only once, just after it has been reset by the RESET signal. A logic one in the IR bit position in the command instruction will "force" the USART to be reset, allowing the computer to send the USART a new mode control instruction, so that the USART may be completely reconfigured. Of course, if the USART is reset, and a new mode control instruction is sent to it, a new command instruction must be sent to the USART, too. You cannot read the mode control, or command information back into the computer to check it, once it has been loaded into the USART.

Typical software routines that can be used to control the programming of a USART are shown in Examples 4-1 and 4-2. In Example 4-1, the program initializes the USART for one stop bit, even

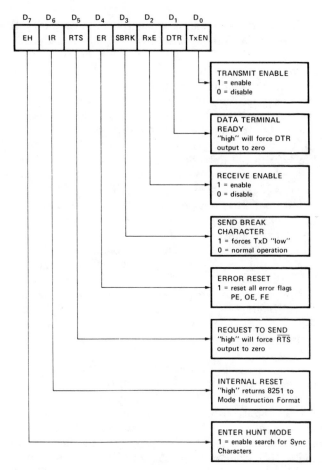

Fig. 4-6. 8251A Command Instruction format (reprinted by permission Intel Corp., Copyright 1978).

parity, seven bits of data, and a 16× baud rate factor. The receiver and transmitter are enabled, and the error conditions (if any) are reset. Later in the program, the receiver is disabled, or turned off, by a new command instruction that is sent to the USART. In Example 4-2, the USART is initialized for two stop bits, no parity, eight bits of data, and a 16× baud rate factor. Again, the receiver and transmitter of the USART are enabled, and any error conditions are cleared. Later in this program, the USART is reset, and a new mode control instruction is sent to the USART to reconfigure it for two stop bits, five data bits, and the same baud rate factor. However, the transmitter is disabled by the command instruction. You must remember to initialize the USART with a mode control instruction,

Example 4-1. USART Configuration Example No. 1

Program Steps   Comments

.
.
1050 OUT 7,122   Set Mode Control Instruction
1060 OUT 7,21   Set Command Instruction

.
.
.
2075 OUT 7,17   Change Command Instruction
.
.
.

and a command instruction, whenever it is first powered, and prior to its use for the transfer of data.

Now that the USART has been initialized, how is information actually transmitted and received, and what are the various error conditions? The USART has an input port that uses the command device address. When information is input to the computer from this input port, the status of the USART may be determined from the various bits, as shown in Fig. 4-7. The three bits of major importance are TxE, RxRDY, and TxRDY. These bits indicate the state of the receiver and transmitter. The TxRDY bit indicates that the transmitter is ready to accept a new data word from the computer, which it will then transmit. The RxRDY bit indicates that the receiver *has received* a new data word, and that it can be read by the computer. Each of these *flags* is a logic one when the condition is true. Thus, a logic one in the TxRDY position indicates that data may be loaded into the transmitter, while a logic one in the RxRDY bit position indicates the presence of a new data word. The flag bits are reset by the transmitter-loading and receiver-reading operations. Of course, the functions of the transmitter do not disturb the receiver, and *vice versa*. Simple transmitter/receiver control subroutines are

Example 4-2. USART Configuration Example No. 2

Program Steps   Comments

.
.
230 OUT 7, 206   Set Mode Control Instruction
240 OUT 7, 21   Set Command Instruction
.
.
.
510 OUT 7,64   Change Command Instruction to generate a
.   RESET
.
.
565 OUT 7,194   Set a new Mode Control Instruction
570 OUT 7, 20   Set a new Command Instruction

Example 4-3. General I/O Control Subroutines for the USART

```
1000 REM USART OUTPUT SUBROUTINE
1010 OUT 6,TX
1020 IF(INP(7) AND 1)=0 THEN 1020
1030 RETURN
1040 REM USART INPUT SUBROUTINE
1050 IF (INP(7) AND 2)=0 THEN 1050
1060 RX=INP(6)
1070 RETURN
```

provided in Example 4-3. The variable, TX, must be set to the value that is to be transmitted, and the received value is assigned the name RX. You should note the use of the flag bits of the USART in these routines.

The TxE flag indicates that the transmitter has finished its transmission, and that the transmitter has no additional information to send. Its state should not be used to indicate when the transmitter is ready to accept the next eight-bit data word for transmission. The TxE flag is often used when the USART is in the synchronous mode. The three error flags, FE, OE, and PE, are explained in Fig.

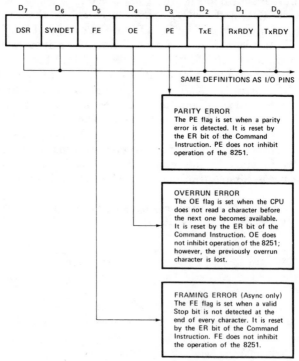

Fig. 4-7. The status bits of the USART read from the Command Input port (reprinted by permission of Intel Corp., Copyright 1978).

4-7, and in *Interfacing and Scientific Data Communications Experiments.*

Using the USART

Now that the USART can be easily interfaced to the TRS-80, and now that you understand how the USART can be configured for various data formats and for different operating modes, the USART must be connected to external devices. If you refer to Fig. 4-2, you will see that there are a number of connections to the receiver and transmitter sections of the USART. These signals provide us with the means of having the USART communicate with other asynchronous-serial devices. The TxC and RxC inputs are the clock signal connections. External clock circuits are used to supply the frequency that is used by the receiver and the transmitter. While each section has a separate clock input, and can have different data transfer rates, each clock signal will be divided by the baud rate factor that has been programmed into the USART. Thus, with a baud rate factor of 16, a transmitter section operating at 110 b/sec requires a 1760 Hz clock signal, while a receiver operating at 4800 b/sec requires a clock signal of 76,800 Hz.

The TxD output is a TTL-compatible signal that represents the serialized bit stream, including the start bit, data bits, parity bit (if any), and stop bit(s). The RxD is the TTL-compatible input of the receiver for the serial information.

Each section has some outputs that are equivalent to the flag bits in the status word. These are the TxRDY, TxE, and RxRDY signals. The receiver also has another I/O pin, SYNDET, which is used in the synchronous transfer mode. The modem control section of the USART has four signals that require some explanation. The most important of these is the $\overline{\text{CTS}}$, or clear to send, input. *This input must be a logic zero in order to enable the transmitter section.* This input simply serves as an external transmitter enable input. The $\overline{\text{DSR}}$ (data set ready), $\overline{\text{DTR}}$ (data terminal ready), and $\overline{\text{RTS}}$ (request to send), are all useful if you are going to be connecting the USART to a modem, for communications with a remote computer or terminal. In most applications, these pins will be unused, although they may be treated as general I/O pins. The $\overline{\text{DTR}}$ and $\overline{\text{RTS}}$ outputs may be controlled by bits in the command instruction. Likewise, the $\overline{\text{DSR}}$ input may be used as a 1-bit input port, the state of which may be detected in the DSR bit of the status word. Of course, the USART has no way of knowing that you are using these connections for your own purposes, so they can be used for whatever you choose, modem control, or otherwise.

A completely interfaced USART is shown in Fig. 4-8. The circuit shown is one that could be used on the TRS-80 interface bread-

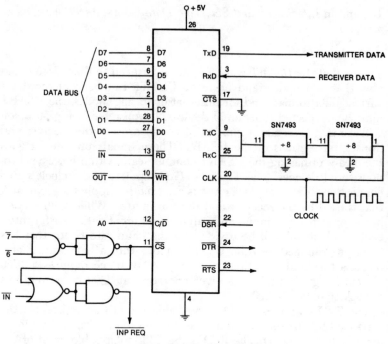

Fig. 4-8. A complete USART-to-TRS-80 interface circuit.

board. The clock signal is generated by an external circuit, such as a 555 timer chip, crystal oscillator, or equivalent. A divide-by-64 stage (two SN7493 counters) has been shown generating the lower frequency that is required by the receiver and transmitter clock inputs. The higher frequency clock signal is used for the CLK input, for internal synchronization processes. In some computers, the timing clock signal of the microprocessor is used as the CLK input of the USART, since it is a high frequency signal. Unfortunately, this signal is not readily available in the TRS-80 computer, so it must be generated externally, along with the clock signal that is used to determine the data transfer rates. Of course, the divide-by-64 stage is somewhat arbitrary, since the CLK input only has to be 30-times faster than the RxC or TxC input, whichever has the higher frequency.

The Motorola MC14411 bit rate generator chip is an easy-to-use alternative to more complex clock signal generating schemes. This 24-pin chip uses a standard 1.8432 MHz crystal to generate a basic frequency from which standard data transmission rates are derived, on the chip. Two logic inputs provide various output frequency options for the 16 different signal outputs from the MC14411. The basic crystal frequency of 1.8432 MHz, as well as a 921.6 kHz output, is always available, and may be used as the CLK input to the USART. The pin configuration and block diagram for the MC14411 are provided in Fig. 4-9, with the connections to the USART shown in Fig. 4-10. In this circuit, the 921.6 kHz signal has been used at the CLK input, while the F5 output of the MC14411 has been used to provide the 38.4 kHz frequency that is used by the USART in the 16× mode, so that data transfers can take place at 2400 b/sec. The MC14411 has been preset to the 16× rate select mode. The information in Table 4-1 shows the various relationships between the different frequency outputs and the different rate selections. The F15 and F16 output frequencies of the MC14411 are not changed by the rate selection inputs.

Once the USART has been interfaced to the TRS-80, it is a good idea to test the interface with some simple software. One of the simplest tests is to have the transmitter generate bit streams that are fed into the receiver portion of the chip. This means that TxD and RxD are jumpered together, and a simple program is developed to exercise the USART. A test program is shown in Example 4-4.

Table 4-1. Various Frequency Outputs for the MC14411 Bit Rate Generator Chip

Rate Select		Rate
B	A	
0	0	×1
0	1	×8
1	0	×16
1	1	×64

Output Number	Output Rates (Hz)			
	×64	×16	×8	×1
F1	614.4 k	153.6 k	76.8 k	9600
F2	460.8 k	115.2 k	57.6 k	7200
F3	307.2 k	76.8 k	38.4 k	4800
F4	230.4 k	57.6 k	28.8 k	3600
F5	153.6 k	38.4 k	19.2 k	2400
F6	115.2 k	28.8 k	14.4 k	1800
F7	76.8 k	19.2 k	9600	1200
F8	38.4 k	9600	4800	600
F9	19.2 k	4800	2400	300
F10	12.8 k	3200	1600	200
F11	9600	2400	1200	150
F12	8613.2	2153.3	1076.6	134.5
F13	7035.5	1758.8	879.4	109.9
F14	4800	1200	600	75
F15	921.6 k	921.6 k	921.6 k	921.6 k
F16*	1.843M	1.843M	1.843M	1.843M

*F16 is buffered oscillator output.

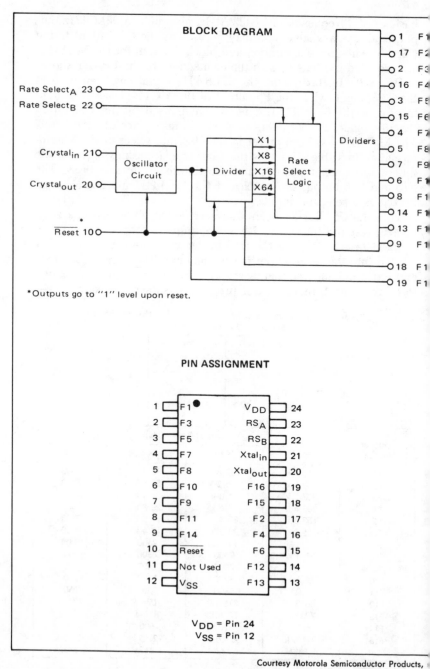

BLOCK DIAGRAM

*Outputs go to "1" level upon reset.

PIN ASSIGNMENT

V_{DD} = Pin 24
V_{SS} = Pin 12

Courtesy Motorola Semiconductor Products,

Fig. 4-9. Block diagram and pin configuration for the MC14411 bit rate generator chip.

160

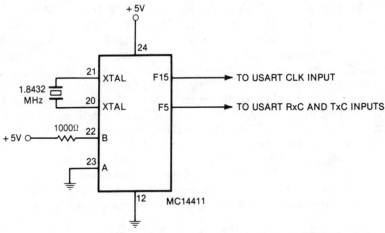

Fig. 4-10. Using the MC14411 bit rate generator chip to generate a clock signal for a 2400 b/sec USART circuit.

This program generates 256 test patterns, 0 through 255, and transmits them to the receiver. Once a pattern has been received it is compared to the pattern transmitted. Any errors are detected, and noted, stopping the test. More sophisticated test routines could be developed, but we found that the program in Example 4-4 worked quite well. Additionally, program steps could be added to this program so that the error flags in the status word could be tested as well. If an error was detected, the error flags would have to be reset with a new command instruction. Likewise, you could add program steps so that you could enter information into the computer so that in some initial "dialog'" with the computer, you would be asked questions like, "# STOP BITS?" The information gathered by the computer during this question and answer session would then be put together to "construct" a mode control instruction that would configure the USART for different modes of operation.

Example 4-4. A USART Test Program

```
  5 OUT 5,0
 10 OUT 7,206
 20 OUT 7,21
 25 FOR I =0 TO 255
 30 OUT 6,I
 35 PRINT I
 40 IF (INP(7) AND 2)=0 THEN 40
 50 IF INP(6)=I THEN 60 ELSE 100
 60 IF (INP(7) AND 1)=0 THEN 60
 70 NEXT I
 80 GOTO 25
100 PRINT "ERROR";I
```

The TxD output of the transmitter and the RxD input of the receiver are generally not connected directly to long wires for the exchange of serial information with other UART- or USART-based systems. Instead, these TTL levels are translated or converted into either current levels or voltage levels that can be transmitted for rather long distances without much interference from externally generated electrical noise. In general, either RS-232C voltage levels or 20 mA current levels are used. The RS-232C levels are standard, and they are frequently used by modems, large computers and video display terminals. The levels used range from ±6 volts to ±12 volts, depending upon the application. There are special TTL-to-RS-232C and RC-232C-to-TTL conversion chips available, and these are described more fully in the book previously mentioned, *Interfacing and Scientific Data Communications Experiments.* Current loops of

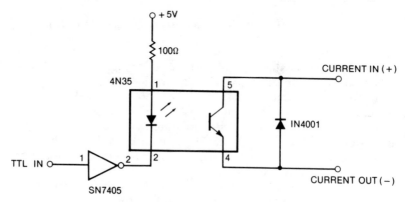

Fig. 4-11. A TTL-to-current loop transmitter circuit using an optical coupler chip.

either 20 mA flowing, or no current flowing, are frequently used with small computer systems, since these loops are immune to most electrical noise, are readily constructed, and are compatible with most teletypewriters, printers, and other serial devices. A current transmitter circuit is shown in Fig. 4-11, with a current receiver shown in Fig. 4-12. A simple resistor may be used in a transmitter/receiver circuit, along with a voltage source, to provide the 20 mA of current required, although a more elegant solution is to use a current regulator circuit, such as the one shown in Fig. 4-13.

In most modern asynchronous-serial communication systems, a separate loop is provided for the transmitter and the receiver, so that each is independent of the other. This arrangement is called a *full-duplex* circuit, and it is shown in Fig. 4-14. Note that in this example a separate voltage source and current regulator have been used for each loop. Of course, the local transmitter communicates

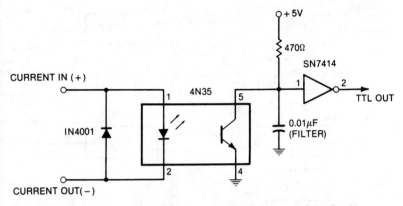

Fig. 4-12. A current loop-to-TTL receiver circuit using an optical coupler chip.

with the remote receiver, while the local receiver accepts information from the remote transmitter. If the current conversion circuits shown in Figs. 4-11 and 4-12 are used in loops such as this, the local

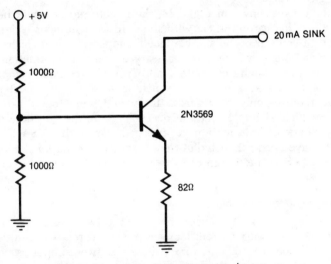

Fig. 4-13. A typical 20 mA current regulator/sink circuit.

and remote circuits are electrically isolated, since optical couplers have been used at both ends of the loop. These commonly available optical couplers, or opto-isolators, use a light-emitting diode, and a photodetector to transfer the serial information, without the need for any common electrical connections between the remote and local circuits. This removes the possibility of having *ground-loop* noise induced upon the serial information, a common problem

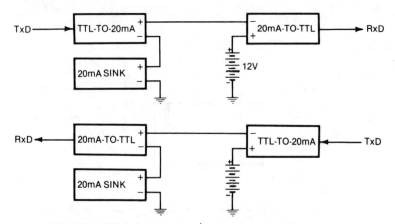

Fig. 4-14. A full-duplex transmitter/receiver circuit for 20 mA current loop communications.

in circuits that are some distance apart, but that share a common ground connection.

In the circuit shown in Fig. 4-14, the remote device could be an instrument that can interface with standard asynchronous-serial devices, or it could even be another small computer system. There are many situations in which it is necessary to transfer information between instruments and computers, and even between one computer and another. Since a full-duplex asynchronous-serial information exchange requires only four wires, this would seem to be an ideal way in which to implement the necessary interface to allow such an exchange of information to proceed. Once the USARTs or UARTs have been connected at their respective "ends" of the loops, all that is left is the design of software that can be used to control the loops.

Computer-Computer Communications

Once the USARTs have been interfaced to two separate computers, and the necessary current loops have been wired between them, it shouldn't be too difficult to see how the two computers could communicate by using the USARTs for the exchange of asynchronous-serial information. One computer would simply transmit an 8-bit data word to the other computer, using the appropriate software steps, while the USART of the receiving computer would receive the information, using its own software to control the USART. Of course, the transmitting computer would have to know when the receiving computer was ready for the next data word, so some *handshaking* might be necessary. This handshaking could be very simple, or it could be quite complex. The simplest case would be one in which the receiving computer transmitted an 8-bit data word that indicated that it was ready to accept the next transmission. More complex handshaking could involve the retransmission of the received data word to the transmitting computer so that its accuracy could be checked. Error condition flags could also be checked before the next transmission could take place. Of course, each USART must be programmed by its respective computer so that the number of data bits, parity, stop bits, and data rates are the same.

In the simplest data transfer example that we have outlined, the computers have been used to exchange 8-bit data words. Of course, 16-bit data words, or even larger data words could be exchanged, simply by breaking them down into groups of 8-bit bytes. The receiving computer would have to be properly programmed so that the series of 8-bit bytes would be reconstructed in the proper order. Decimal values are readily converted into binary numbers, so that their transmission should not present difficulty. But how would you transfer $-7.77891E-13$ to a remote computer in binary form? You could probably devise a program that would convert this into some form of binary notation, but a simpler method is available. In remote communication systems that use the asynchronous-serial transmission scheme, a standard code has been adopted to allow various instruments, computers, and terminals to communicate with one another. This code assigns 7-bit binary values to alphabetical, numerical, and symbolic characters, including the lower-case letters, and punctuation marks. When this *American Standard Code for Information Interchange* (ASCII) is used, each symbol in the message is assigned its own standard code. For example, the letter "a" is equivalent to 01100001, while "?" is equivalent to 00111111. These values are easily exchanged by computers and terminals, since their meaning has been standardized. In the examples above, eight bits have been used. In some instances, the most significant bit is preset to a logic one, or a logic zero, while in others, it is used as a parity bit.

There are other standard codes, but the ASCII arrangement is probably the one that is most widely used. A standard ASCII code chart has been provided in Appendix A, and a similar chart may be found in the Radio Shack *Level II Basic Reference Manual,* supplied with Level II TRS-80 computers.

Now, to transmit the value $-7.77891E-13$, each *character* is converted into its ASCII equivalent, and then transmitted. In this way, 12 ASCII values would be transmitted. It is important to note that the data value is being transmitted as a grouping of symbols that have nothing whatsoever to do with the actual *value* that is represented by the *group of characters*. Some software is required to perform the conversion between the numeric value and the series

Example 4-5. A Value-to-ASCII Conversion Program

```
500 INPUT "VALUE";A
520 A$=STR$(A)
530 Q=LEN(A$)
540 FOR L=1 TO Q
550 R=ASC(MID$(A$,L,1)
560 TX=R:GOSUB 1010
570 NEXT L
580 END

1010 OUT 6,TX
1020 IF (INP(7) and 1)=0 THEN 1020
1030 RETURN
```

of ASCII values that are to be transmitted. A typical "conversion" program is provided in Example 4-5. The numeric value is first converted into a string representation, and the length of the string is then determined so that the computer will know how many characters are to be transmitted. The step, R=ASC(MID$(A$,L,1)), converts the characters in the A$ string into their ASCII equivalents, one at a time, starting with the first character. Since this program step is used in a loop, each pass through the loop converts the next character into its ASCII equivalent, until all of the conversions have been performed. The standard output subroutine from Example 4-3 may be used to control the USART actual transmission of the ASCII values from one computer to another.

In Example 4-5, a value that has been entered from the keyboard is transmitted, although results of calculations could also be transmitted, by using these software steps. In fact, complete arrays of data values could be transmitted, using a somewhat longer program, such as the one in Example 4-6, in which a loop has been used to go through an array. You would have to let the computer know how long the array is, so that it would know when to stop the conversion process. In Example 4-6, a 10-element array has been used.

Example 4-6. An Array-to-ASCII Conversion Program

```
500 FOR I=1 TO 10
520 A$=STR$(A(I))
530 Q=LEN(A$)
540 FOR L=1 TO Q
550 R=ASC(MID$(A$,L,1))
560 TX=R:GOSUB 1010
570 NEXT L
580 NEXT I
590 END

1010 OUT 6,TX
1020 IF (INP(7) AND 1)=0 THEN 1020
1030 RETURN
```

The receiving terminal will print the ASCII characters, as they are received, one after the other, but there are no provisions in the program to generate a carriage return, to return the printing mechanism, or cursor, to the left-hand side of the paper or screen, and there are no steps to advance the device to the next line. These steps would have to be incorporated into your program. The ASCII code for the line-feed function is 00001010, or 10_{10}, while the code for a carriage return function is 00001101, or 13_{10}. Depending upon your application, you might want to place a carriage-return and line-feed code in the serial stream, right after each complete numeric value, or after every five or so. If another computer is used to receive this information, the carriage-return and line-feed functions can probably be left out of the program, since the computer will ignore them. However, the receiving computer must be pre-programmed to accept the ASCII values, and to re-configure them back into the proper numeric values.

Example 4-7. An ASCII-to-Value Conversion Program

```
2010 Z$=""
2020 GOSUB 1050
2030 Z$=Z$+CHR$(RX)
2040 GOSUB 1050
2050 IF RX<>32 THEN 2030
2060 A = VAL(Z$)
2070 PRINT A
2080 END

1050 IF (INP(7) AND 2)=0 THEN 1050
1060 RX=INP(6)
1070 RETURN
```

Since another TRS-80 computer might be used as the "other" computer, a program that will perform the ASCII conversion is provided in Example 4-7. In this program, the ASCII values are converted into the proper numeric values. Since the TRS-80 uses a space between characters as a *delimiter* to separate values from one another, this character's ASCII value can be detected, to indicate that a complete value has been acquired as its ASCII equivalent. A simple program that can be used to acquire 10 values from another TRS-80 computer, or from some other asynchronous-serial device, is listed in Example 4-8. In this program, the string, Z$, is used to accumulate the incoming characters, forming a longer string, as new characters are added to it. When the ASCII value for the space character is detected, the string of individual characters is converted into its actual value. Thus, the string 0.0001E4 has the actual value of 10_{10}. The standard USART receiver subroutine has been used in this example to acquire the individual characters.

Example 4-8. An ASCII-to-Array Conversion Program

```
2000 FOR I=1 TO 10
2010 Z$=""
2020 GOSUB 1050
2030 Z$=Z$+CHR$(RX)
2040 GOSUB 1050
2050 IF RX<>32 THEN 2030
2060 A(I)=VAL(Z$)
2070 PRINT A(I)
2080 NEXT I

1050 IF (INP(7) AND 2)=0 THEN 1050
1060 RX=INP(6)
1070 RETURN
```

It is important to remember that it takes the TRS-80 a significant amount of time to acquire and process this information, something that we tend to overlook. This means that while the TRS-80 may not have any difficulty in handling information that is transmitted to it from a terminal at a rate of 2400 b/sec, while you are typing 10 characters per second (at most), the TRS-80 probably couldn't acquire a steady stream of information sent to it at 2400 b/sec, one character right after the other. In cases where such high-speed data transfers are encountered, there are two choices for handling the information. You can program the TRS-80 in assembly language so that it can acquire and store the information for later processing, or you can use the handshaking technique, previously described. If handshaking is to be used, the transmitting computer must be programmed to recognize the handshaking character that the TRS-80 sends to it, indicating that the receiver is ready for another transmission.

THE UART

In those applications in which asynchronous-serial communications are to be used, as opposed to the use of multiconductor cables, there may not be another computer, or terminal-like device, at the other "end" of the communication loop. Does this mean that it is necessary to add another small computer to the system, so that a USART can be used? In some cases, this may be justified, since small computer systems can be put together with only a few chips, but in other cases, an alternative method of implementing asynchronous-serial communications is at hand. The Universal Asynchronous Receiver/Transmitter, or UART, that was mentioned previously, provides the same type of communication function as the USART, but it does not require a computer to perform the "programming" functions. You should recall that the number of data bits, parity, and number of stop bits, was programmed into the USART by the computer. In the UART, these control functions are programmed by applying various combinations of logic levels to external programming pins. Likewise, in a UART-based communication system, the flag outputs, data outputs, etc., are available as individual logic outputs. The receiver and the transmitter sections are generally separate, allowing individual access to the data outputs of the receiver, and to the data inputs of the transmitter. The functional block diagram of a UART is provided in Fig. 4-15. There are many UART chip manufacturers, but not all of them use a standard nomenclature for the I/O pins. This can lead to some confusion, unless you remember that the chips are generally pin-for-pin equivalents, and thus the pins have the same function, even if they are labeled differently. A portion of a UART data sheet is provided in Appendix B.

The UART is particularly useful in those applications in which a computer is not present, but in which asynchronous-serial communication is required. The availability of all of the control and I/O signals makes it relatively easy to design circuits that can communicate with a computer through a UART-based interface. Of course, the computer must have an asynchronous-serial I/O port.

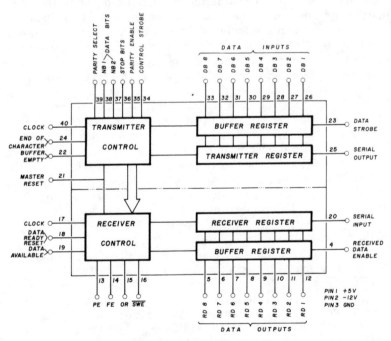

Fig. 4-15. Functional block diagram and pin configuration of the UART
(Copyright *Ham Radio Magazine*, 1976).

While UART chips can be used with computers, too, USARTs are found in most of the newer computer systems, since so many of the functions can be programmed under software control. Before the UART can be used, however, a brief explanation of its operation is necessary. In this explanation, you may find it useful to locate the various functions in Fig. 4-15, relating them to the following discussion.

The UART is particularly useful in those applications in which the number of data bits, the number of stop bits, and the parity (if any) that are used in the serial bit stream. These bits can be hardwired to either a logic one, or a logic zero, depending upon the functions required. The bits are called the control word, and their respective functions are fully described in the data sheet in Appendix B. A control strobe input is used to load these bits into the UART chip. This input is generally a logic one. Of course, these bits program the receiver and transmitter sections with the same serial format. A data word is presented to the eight transmitter input lines in parallel, and it is loaded into the transmitter by a logic zero pulse on the data strobe input. Once loaded, the transmitter starts the bit serialization process, generating the start bit, the data bits, and so on, until the transmission has been completed. The buffer-empty output of the transmitter may be used to signal an external device that the buffer register of the transmitter is empty, and that the next data word may be loaded. The receiver section of the UART accepts an asynchronous-serial stream of bits in the proper format, and provides them in parallel form. The eight parallel outputs of the buffer register of the receiver are three-state, controlled by the received data enable input, which is generally connected to a logic zero so that these outputs are always enabled. A logic one at the data available output indicates that the receiver has transferred information to the eight parallel outputs. This flag is reset by pulsing the data ready reset input with a short logic zero pulse. This does not clear the data, but only the data available flag. The three error flags of the receiver, as well as the data available flag output, are three-state, and controlled by the status word enable ($\overline{SWE}$) input. This input also controls the buffer empty output of the transmitter, which is three-state, too.

The receiver and transmitter each require a clock signal that will be used to generate the serial bit stream timing relationship. In the UART, the input clocks must be set so that their frequencies are 16-times the required data rate. This baud rate factor is not programmable, as it was for the USART. The clocks are not common, so that the receiver and the transmitter may be operated at different bit rates. A common reset signal is provided so that the internal functions may be initialized when the power is first connected to the system. Most of the first-generation UARTs used two power supplies, +5 and −12 volts. Newer devices only use the +5-volt supply, and they consume less power. For this reason, we will use them in our discussion. For a more detailed description of the UART, we refer you to Appendix B, and also to the book previously mentioned, *Interfacing and Scientific Data Communication Experiments*.

USING THE UART FOR REMOTE CONTROL

In some applications, the UART may be used to transfer information between a remote instrument and the computer, using ASCII, or some other coded format. In other applications it may be necessary to transfer information to a remote instrument that is being controlled, and to receive information from the instrument, to indicate its condition. Such an application for a UART is shown in Fig. 4-16. In this circuit, the remote UART is being used to monitor the state of the eight signals that can be either a logic one, or a logic zero. The eight outputs from the receiver are used in various ways; four of the binary outputs have been connected to a 4-to-16-line decoder, and four have been used for on/off control. One of the on/off control lines has been used to generate the data

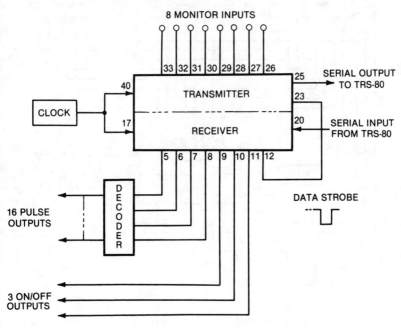

Fig. 4-16. Using a UART in a remote-control application.

strobe signal, thus controlling the transmitter section of the UART. There are many different ways in which the input and output lines of the UART can be used in remote applications.

If more than eight monitor inputs are required, the inputs may be expanded by using a multiplexing scheme such as that shown in Fig. 4-17. Three 3-state buffers control 24 monitor inputs so that any group of 8 may be selected. The selection is made by the corresponding output of the decoder that was described previously. In this circuit, additional three-state buffers could be added, so that many more monitor inputs could be checked at this remote UART. The local computer would first send a data word to the UART so that one of the sets of eight monitor inputs would be chosen. While keeping these bits constant by using logical instructions in a BASIC program, the data strobe line would be "pulsed" so that the transmitter would send the monitor input information to the computer over the serial lines that link them. More control outputs could also be added to the receiver section, by using shift registers or other latching devices. For example, the circuit shown in Fig. 4-17 could be used to control a remote 12-bit A/D converter. The 12 data bits

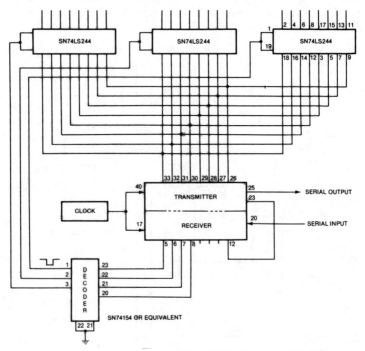

Fig. 4-17. An expanded remote-control application for the UART, in which 24 bits may be transmitted.

of the converter would be connected to two of the three-state buffers in two groups, one containing the four most-significant bits, and the other containing the eight least-significant bits. One bit could be used to monitor the BUSY/READY flag of the A/D converter, while one of the outputs of the decoder could be used to generate a start pulse that would initiate the conversion process. The software that would be used to control the remote converter would be rather simple. The program would send the proper command word to the UART so that when decoded it would start the conversion sequence of the A/D converter. The program would then send the command word that would connect the three-state buffer to the transmitter inputs of the UART so that the BUSY/READY flag could be transmitted. By pulsing the least significant bit of the receiver, the eight bits present at the transmitter would be sent to the computer so that the status flag could be checked. Once the conversion had been completed, the computer could send the UART a sequence of commands to read the two data bytes into the UART and transmit them to the computer. The additional software required here is minimal when compared to the ease of interfacing a remote A/D converter with four wires (we have assumed a full-duplex current loop).

There are other control methods that could be used in this type of a remote converter scheme. You might consider using the status flag of the converter to initiate the first transmission, with the computer controlling all of the others. Thus, once the current conversion has been completed, the A/D converter would signal this by transmitting the eight least-significant bits to the computer, through the UART. To do this, you would simply gate the status signal of the converter and the data strobe pulse provided by the receiver section of the UART. Of course, the eight outputs of the receiver would have to be present to select the eight least-significant bits, prior to the occurrence of the status flag pulse of the converter.

Another possibility involves the use of the data ready, or data received, flag signal of the receiver, which can be connected to the data strobe input of the transmitter. The receiver flag could be reset by the transmitter buffer register empty signal of the transmitter. If this type of configuration is used, the transmitter will be pulsed to transmit a data word after each new character has been received by the UART. Of course, the transmitted data can be ignored if you wish to simply change one of the outputs of the receiver. The control circuit shown in Fig. 4-18 shows how this function could be set up. The positive edge of the data ready signal triggers a monostable circuit. This provides a delay, so that the outputs of the receiver can be used by external logic prior to the transfer of any information into the buffer register of the transmitter. In the circuit shown in Fig. 4-17, the decoder and three-state circuits require some time to switch their logic states, depending upon the outputs of the receiver. The first monostable, shown in Fig. 4-18, provides this necessary delay period. The second monostable generates a pulse that loads the buffer register of the transmitter. The buffer-empty signal of the transmitter in turn clears the data ready flag of the receiver, completing the sequence. Now, whenever *any* information is received by the UART, a transmission will be initiated.

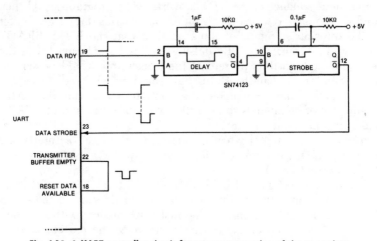

Fig. 4-18. A UART controller circuit for remote sequencing of the transmitter.

More and more circuitry can be added to the UART circuits to perform increasingly more complex functions, but there may be other ways in which these functions may be implemented, with a lot less effort. We will explore some of these alternatives.

UARTs AND ANALOG/DIGITAL CONVERTERS

An A/D converter could be connected to a UART, using a circuit that is similar to the one shown in Fig. 4-17, although this would require the use of additional chips to sequence the various data bits through the UART, and to control the A/D converter. A simpler, remote A/D converter control scheme is readily available, and it provides a great deal of measurement power in only a few chips. The Intersil ICL7109 12-bit A/D converter chip that was described in Chapter 2 may be used in a handshaking mode that is directly compatible with the control and data lines on a UART. In this mode, the ICL7109 provides the necessary sequencing signals so that once a conversion has been completed, both the low-order and high-

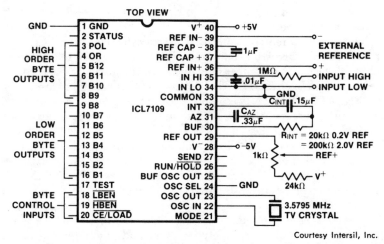

Courtesy Intersil, Inc.

Fig. 4-19. Pin configuration and test circuit for the ICL7109 A/D converter.

order bytes are transferred to the UART, and transmitted. A pin configuration diagram of the ICL7109 is provided in Fig. 4-19, for your reference.

To put the ICL7109 in the handshake mode, the mode input is connected to a logic one (+5 volts). When in this mode, the low-byte enable ($\overline{\text{LBEN}}$), high-byte enable ($\overline{\text{HBEN}}$), and chip enable/load ($\overline{\text{CE/LOAD}}$) all act as control *outputs*, rather than as control inputs. Once a conversion has been completed by the converter in the handshake mode, the high-byte three-state data outputs are enabled, and the $\overline{\text{CE/LOAD}}$ output is asserted. The $\overline{\text{HBEN}}$ output is also asserted, as a byte identification signal. The high-byte data outputs are then disabled, and the low-byte three-state data outputs are enabled, the $\overline{\text{CE/LOAD}}$, and the $\overline{\text{LBEN}}$ outputs are also asserted. Since the data outputs are three-state, corresponding bits in the high byte, and in the low byte are conveniently connected, so that a single set of eight data bits is provided for the eight inputs of the transmitter section of the UART. Since the $\overline{\text{CE/LOAD}}$ signal of the ICL7109 indicates that valid information is present on the bus, this signal is used to strobe the information of the A/D converter into the buffer register of the transmitter. Since this loading process can be rather fast, the transmitter buffer empty flag signal of the UART is connected to the SEND input of the ICL7109. This provides the handshaking, so that the converter will pause between loading the high byte and the low byte, so that the UART has a chance to transfer the high byte from the transmitter buffer register into the transmitter register itself. If the SEND input is left in the logic one state, the loading process may be so fast that the UART is not ready to accept the low byte when it is presented by the ICL7109, causing it to be "lost."

The actual circuitry involved in this UART-converter scheme is rather simple, involving only a UART, and an ICL7109 converter chip, plus the components associated with the analog signal processing of the converter. The UART/converter connections are shown in Fig. 4-20. Only 11 lines, plus a common ground, are required. The UART used in this circuit is an IM6403. This is a low-power CMOS device that has an on-chip oscillator, for use with an external crystal. An external clock signal may also be used with this chip. In the circuit shown in Fig. 4-20, the clock of the converter is used by the IM6403, as the transmitter/receiver clock. In the IM6403, the receiver and transmitter share a common clock signal, so that they will always operate at the same frequency. The basic UART/converter scheme provides a UART data rate of 110 b/sec, which is compatible with most teletypewriters and computer devices. If the UART is used to transmit to a teletypewriter, you could not expect the voltage measured by the ICL7109 to be printed as, for example, +0.97, since the information from the converter is simply a binary code, and not a series of ASCII characters.

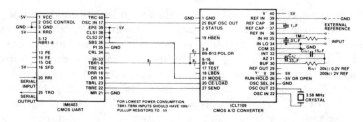

Fig. 4-20. A circuit diagram for a UART-to-ICL7109 A/D converter interface for remote measuring of voltages.

If the circuit shown in Fig. 4-20 is used for remote data acquisition, the converter will transmit information through the UART after each conversion, so it is not necessary to send a signal to the UART that will be used to start a conversion sequence. While this may appear to be an asset, it does cause some problems. For example, if you were able to look at the stream of bits, you would see two transmissions close together; a space, two transmissions close together, another space, two transmissions close together, and so on. The two close transmissions are the low-byte information, and the high-byte information, while the space is the period required for the next conversion to be completed. Unfortunately, the receiving device cannot "look" at the serial stream of bits in this way, so it has no way of telling which transmission is the high-byte, and which one is the low-byte, or of making sure that data acquired is from the same conversion. While the converter is continuously converting and transmitting information, you cannot easily interpret the information.

The continuous conversion problem can be overcome by controlling the state of the RUN/$\overline{\text{HOLD}}$ input line of the ICL7109. You may recall that this input could be used to initiate single conversions, upon the request of the computer. Even in remote data acquisition applications, the RUN/$\overline{\text{HOLD}}$ line may be controlled by the computer, simply by connecting it to one of the data outputs of the UART receiver. Now, a control word may be transmitted to the UART to control the operation of the ICL7109 A/D converter. You must remember, though, that the converter will *continue* to perform conversions for as long as the RUN/$\overline{\text{HOLD}}$ pin remains at a logic one. A control program that may be used with a computer-based USART to control a remote UART-based A/D converter is listed in Example 4-9.

There are some other important points that you should be aware of when examining the listing in Example 4-9. The USART is programmed in the first few steps. The OUT 5,0 command has been used in our system to generate a RESET pulse for the USART, and you should understand how this is done by using a device address, and the $\overline{\text{OUT}}$ function pulse. The OUT 6,0 command causes eight logic zero data bits to be transmitted to the UART, clearing the RUN/$\overline{\text{HOLD}}$ input to the ICL7109, placing the converter in the hold mode. The Q = INP(6) command reads the contents of the USART receiver, clearing the RxRDY flag, so that it is in the cleared state for the first data transmission to the USART. The OUT 6,1 command transmits a logic one to the least-significant bit in the UART receiver, with logic zeros being sent to all of the other bits.

Example 4-9. A Remote A/D Converter Control Program

```
10 OUT 5,0
20 OUT 7,206
30 OUT 7,21
40 OUT 6,0
50 REM CONTROL SEQUENCE
60 Q=INP(6)
65 OUT 6,1
70 IF (INP(7) AND 2)=0 THEN 70
80 A=INP(6)
90 IF (INP(7) AND 2)=0 THEN 90
100 B=INP(6)
120 OUT 6,0
140 PRINT (A AND 15);:PRINT B;
145 V=(((A AND 15)*256)+B)*.0006457:PRINT V
150 GOTO 60
```

This places the ICL7109 in the run mode, so that a conversion is performed. At the end of the conversion, the converter strobes the UART in the proper way, transmitting two data bytes through the UART, to the USART that is interfaced to the computer. In this program (Example 4-9) the generalized USART I/O subroutines were not used, since the additional time required to process the GOSUB and RETURN commands could cause the computer to miss the second transmission from the remote UART. Two separate sets of commands are used in the main program to receive the information from the UART.

After the two bytes of information have been received, the RUN/$\overline{\text{HOLD}}$ signal is changed to a logic zero, through a new transmission from the computer to the UART. This places the converter in the hold mode, so that no further conversions are performed. We strongly suggest that you use the 110 b/sec data transmission rate for communications under the control of BASIC-language programs, since faster data transfer rates may mean that assembly-language programming will be required so that the TRS-80 can keep up with the information that it is to receive.

In this example, the RUN/$\overline{\text{HOLD}}$ line will be asserted, or placed in the run mode state, for longer than is required for a single conversion, so additional bytes of information will be transmitted to the USART, two per conversion. The program does not use these additional bytes, but they are transmitted to the USART, which receives them. This is the reason why the RxRDY flag of the USART had to be cleared prior to the start of a conversion sequence; the flag would be *set* to indicate that these data bytes had been received by the USART. Since these bytes are not useful, the flag is cleared so that the software ignores their receipt. To prevent the multiconversion problem, additional circuitry may be added to the UART-converter circuit, so that only a single conversion is performed, generating only a single set of data byte transmissions to the USART. The required additions are diagrammed in Fig. 4-21. The positive-going edge of the least-significant data byte of the UART receiver triggers the monostable, clearing the SN7476 flip-flop. This places the RUN/$\overline{\text{HOLD}}$ input in the logic one state, starting a conversion. At the end of the conversion, the STATUS signal clocks the flip-flop, returning the RUN/$\overline{\text{HOLD}}$ input to the logic zero state, which places the converter back in the hold mode. At the end of the conversion, the information from the A/D conversion is transferred into the UART, one byte at a time, and transmitted to the USART. No other transmissions, or conversions take place. The same program listed in Example 4-9 may be used to control the modified interface, since the LSB of the UART must be returned to its logic zero state before the conversion-triggering sequence may be restarted. In this configuration, the LSB of the UART receiver has been dedicated to controlling the A/D converter, but the other seven bits may be used for any other control purposes.

There is one other way in which the ICL7109 may be controlled by the UART. This uses the data ready flag of the UART receiver to start the conversion sequence, in place of one of the output bits. The positive-going edge of the data ready flag signal is used to trigger the monostable that clears the RUN/$\overline{\text{HOLD}}$ signal to the ICL7109. This new control signal takes the place of the UART

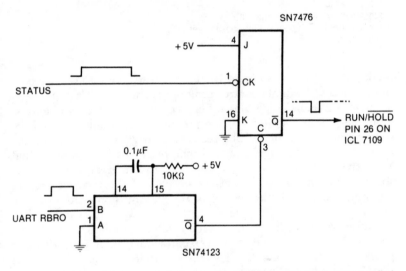

Fig. 4-21. A single conversion control circuit for the ICL7109, so that it may be controlled by the least-significant bit of the UART receiver chip.

RBR0 line that is shown in Fig. 4-21. If only the connection to the data ready flag signal is made, only one conversion will take place, since there is no provision for clearing the UART data ready flag. To clear this flag properly, the $\overline{\text{Q}}$ output from the SN74123 monostable is connected to the data ready reset input of the UART receiver, pin 18. Now, when a character is received by the UART, the positive-going edge of the data ready flag triggers the monostable so that a conversion is started. At the same time, the UART data ready flag is cleared, so that the UART is ready to signal the receipt of another character. In this example, there is *no* relationship between the value (code) of the character received, and the starting of a conversion/data transmission sequence. The receipt of *any* character, or code, by the UART receiver, will start the conversion and information transmission sequence. If this technique is

Example 4-10. A UART Control Program for the ICL7109
A/D Converter

```
10 OUT 5,0
20 OUT 7,206
30 OUT 7,21
40 OUT 6,0
50 FOR T=0 TO 300:NEXT T
60 Q=INP(6)
65 OUT 6,1
70 IF(INP(7) AND 2)=0 THEN 70
80 A=INP(6)
90 IF (INP(7) AND 2)=0 THEN 90
100 B=INP(6)
140 PRINT (A AND 15);:PRINT B;
145 V=(((A AND 15)*256)+B)*.0006457:PRINT V
150 GOTO 60
```

used, all eight outputs of the UART receiver may be used for control purposes. A simple control program is shown in Example 4-10.

There are some important differences between the programs in Examples 4-9 and 4-10. Since the program in Example 4-9 uses the state of one of the bits of the receiver to trigger a conversion, the bit must be set to a logic one, and then reset to a logic zero, so that a positive-going edge is generated properly. In Example 4-10, the states of the individual bits at the outputs of the receiver are unimportant, since it is the receipt of the transmission that triggers a new conversion. In Example 4-10, the OUT 6,0 command at line 40 causes the outputs of the UART receiver to be cleared to logic zero, but it also triggers a conversion sequence. A time delay is placed in the program to allow for the time that it will take for the ICL7109 to perform the conversion, and to transmit the information to the USART. After the time delay has elapsed, the RxRDY flag of the USART is cleared. This conversion/transmission sequence was a "dummy read," since we were only concerned with the clearing of the UART receiver outputs, and not with the result of an analog/digital conversion. The RxRDY flag in the USART is cleared, so that the computer will ignore the receipt of this "dummy" information by the USART. The main control steps in Example 4-10 contain only one output command, since the data ready flag of the UART receiver is used to control the conversion. Again, the eight data bits of the receiver are not used in any way, and they may be used to control other I/O devices. By way of an example, the program shown in Example 4-11 shows how the bits of the UART receiver may be incremented from 0 to 255, while the A/D converter is being controlled independently of the data bits.

While this method of controlling the A/D converter does make all eight data bits of the receiver available for other purposes, it

```
10 OUT 5,0
20 OUT 7,206
30 OUT 7,21
40 OUT 6,0
50 FOR T=0 TO 300:NEXT T
55 FOR M=0 TO 255
60 Q=INP(6)
65 OUT 6,M
70 IF(INP(7) AND 2)=0 THEN 70
80 A=INP(6)
90 IF (INP(7) AND 2)=0 THEN 90
100 B=INP(6)
140 PRINT (A AND 15);:PRINT B;
145 V=(((A AND 15)*256)+B)*.0006457:PRINT V
150 NEXT M
160 GOTO 55
```

does have a distinct disadvantage, since the receipt of *any* information by the receiver will trigger a conversion sequence. Even if
you simply wanted to update the information output by the receiver,
a conversion would be started by the receipt of the new information. This limitation may be overcome without much difficulty, if
you simply remember to do a "dummy" read of the USART receiver register, prior to the start of a "real" conversion sequence.
The dummy read operation will clear the RxRDY flag of the USART
so that the computer will ignore the information transmitted to the
USART when you simply wanted to update the UART receiver
outputs.

UARTs AND DIGITAL/ANALOG CONVERTERS

The receiver portion of a UART chip may be used quite effec-
tively to provide eight bits of information to the inputs of an 8-bit
D/A converter, so that an analog voltage may be generated in a
remote place, perhaps to control a servo motor, or other voltage-
dependent device. For example, an 8-bit D/A converter such as the
NE5018 can be controlled simply by connecting the eight data inputs to the eight data outputs on the receiver side of the USART,
MSB to MSB, and so on. The NE5018 has an internal latch, but it
is not necessary to use it, since the UART receiver outputs are
latched in the receiver buffer register. The NE5018 latch enable
($\overline{LE}$) input must be grounded to disable it. The information presented to the D/A converter inputs is simply changed by transmitting a new 8-bit data word to the UART receiver. The UART receiver outputs are not cleared when a new data word is received,
thus if the 8-bit data word, 10101100, is transmitted to the UART,

and then followed by another transmission of 10101100, there would be no change in the UART receiver outputs when the second 10101100 is received. This is an important point, since it means that the UART could control an 8-bit D/A converter, as well as an ICL7109 A/D converter.

To control the A/D converter, a new transmission is sent to the remote UART. The data ready flag of the UART starts the conversion/transmission sequence. To avoid disturbing the eight bits of information in the buffer register of the receiver that are being used by the D/A converter, you simply retransmit the same information to the receiver. Thus, the only effect is to pulse the UART data ready flag output, starting an A/D conversion. Likewise, when it is necessary to update the information presented to the D/A converter, information from the resulting A/D conversion is simply ignored by the computer.

The control of D/A converters with more than eight bits may present some problems, since only eight bits may be transmitted to the UART at one time, and the UART only has eight parallel data outputs, in any case. The problem of communicating between an 8-bit microcomputer and a 10-bit D/A converter was readily overcome through the use of a double-buffering circuit, shown in Chapter 2. Through the use of double buffering circuitry, the 8-bit computer was able to transfer eight bits at a time to a 10-bit (or larger) converter, finally transferring all of the bits to the converter inputs at the same time, using a second set of latch chips. The computer was able to transfer eight bits of information on the data bus, as well as generate the necessary control signals. Unfortunately, the UART only has eight outputs.

The output bits of the UART may be divided into various groups so that one group provides the information that is to be used by the converter latches, while another group provides bits that may be decoded to provide control functions. The circuit shown in Fig. 4-22 illustrates one way in which a 12-bit parallel transfer may be implemented. In this case, four bits are used to transfer information to the three latches, while the remaining four bits are decoded to provide the control signals that strobe the various latches. The double buffering is provided by the final 12-bit latch that is controlled by the "2" output of the decoder. The "6," "5" and "4" outputs of the decoder control three 4-bit latches. This circuit is controlled by the UART receiver outputs which are in turn controlled by the serial transmissions from the USART. It is your responsibility to develop the software to provide the 4-bit "nibbles" in the proper sequence, while switching the control bits in the proper sequence. The sample program in Example 4-12 provides the steps that are necessary to transfer a 12-bit data word, in parallel, to an external

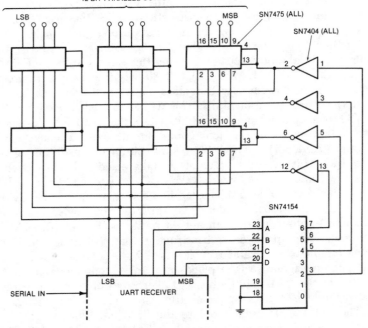

Fig. 4-22. A control circuit that allows the UART to output more than eight bits from the receiver section.

device, probably a D/A converter. The standard USART output subroutine has been used, and it is assumed that the USART has been properly initialized. The value of M is the value of the most significant four bits, divided by 256, while the value of L is the value of the eight least significant bits. You should be able to "separate" a large value into these bytes without difficulty. In this short program, the unwanted bits have been "masked" with AND instruc-

Example 4-12. A Multibyte UART Transfer Control Program

```
500 TX=0: GOSUB 1010
510 TX=((M AND 15) OR 80):GOSUB 1010
520 TX=(M AND 15):GOSUB 1010
530 TX=((L AND 15) OR 64): GOSUB 1010
540 TX=(L AND 15):GOSUB 1010
550 TX=(((L AND 240)/16) OR 96): GOSUB 1010
560 TX=((L AND 240)/16): GOSUB 1010
570 TX=32: GOSUB 1010:TX=0: GOSUB 1010
580 END

1010 OUT 6,TX
1020 IF (INP(7) AND 1)=0 THEN 1020
1030 RETURN
```

tions to set them to zero, while the individual control bits have been set to logic one by using OR instructions. Since the SN7475 latch circuits operate by latching the information present at their inputs at the negative-going edge of the clock, or latch enable, pulse, the four bits of data must be stable during this pulse transition. For example, the TX=((M AND 15) OR 80 sets the 4-bit word to be transmitted in the four least significant bits, and then sets the bit pattern 0101 in the four MSBs. This will enable latch #5, when the UART receives the composite 8-bit data word, 0101 XXXX, where the X bits represent the actual four bits of data. The next step, TX=(M AND 15) removes the control bits, while maintaining the data bits. This causes the latching to take place at latch #5, when this new composite data word, 0000 XXXX is received by the UART. The other two nibbles are handled in a similar manner. The divide-by-16 operation is used merely to shift the four most significant bits into the four least significant bit positions. Finally, the TX=32 command sets up the control instruction that will cause the 12-bit latch circuit to be enabled, while the TX=0 command will cause the latching action to take place, once these commands are transmitted to the UART, in sequence. Other types of control programs are possible, but this example clearly shows what is happening.

The nibbles are transferred to the first individual set of 4-bit latches in any sequence, as long as all of the needed information has been transmitted prior to the activation of the 12-bit latch. Some trade-offs are possible here. It would have been fairly easy to build a similar circuit that uses 6-bit latches, with two of the UART receiver bits being set aside for control purposes. Other variations are possible, but the technique is the same, using some bits for information transfer, and the remaining bits for control. The four-bit latch example shown in Fig. 4-22 contains other control outputs that may be used for other purposes, perhaps to transfer information to latches for seven-segment displays, or other uses. If this circuit and program are used with the UART that is also controlling an ICL7109 A/D converter, then each transmission to the UART will initiate a conversion/transmission sequence. Just remember to clear the computer USART RxRDY flag with a dummy read of the receiver input port, prior to any request for a "real" conversion. This allows you to ignore the conversions that take place during transfers to the latches.

MULTIPLE UART SYSTEMS

There are many cases in which a number of UARTs may be required to communicate between several remote sites, and a central computer. In general, the UARTs cannot share a "party line," in

which several UARTs have been connected to a single set of lines
for the transmitter, and a single set of lines for the receiver. If this
type of a scheme was used, there would be no way of identifying
which UART was to receive the information placed on the line by
the USART, and there would be no way in which the computer
could identify which UART was transmitting information to it.
Thus, when individual UARTs are used, a separate set of communication lines for each one is required. This does not mean that there
must be a USART, and associated circuitry, for each of the communication links, since the computer could only communicate with
one UART at a time. There are various switching methods that may
be used to multiplex a single USART among a number of communication loops. One such circuit is shown in Fig. 4-23. In this circuit,
four-pole single-throw relays are used to connect the particular
loop, A, B, or C, to the conversion circuits that are connected to
the computer USART. Each relay must be driven by a decoder/

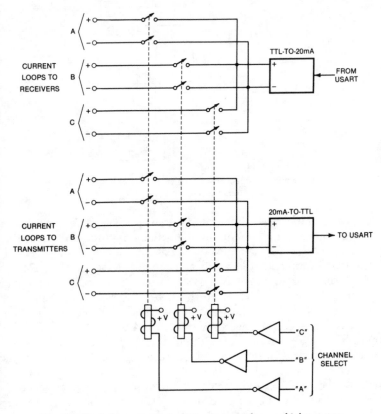

Fig. 4-23. Block diagram of typical 20 mA current loop multiplex system.

driver circuit, so that the computer can easily control the loop that it is to be communicating over. Only one 20 mA-to-TTL converter and one TTL-to-20 mA converter are used in this circuit, but one relay, plus driver circuit, is required for each loop. Of course, only one set of relay contacts may be used at one time.

An alternate multiplexing circuit is shown in Fig. 4-24. Here, each loop has been provided with a 20 mA-to-TTL or TTL-to-20 mA converter, as appropriate. The TTL signals to and from the USART are multiplexed, or switched, between the different loops using

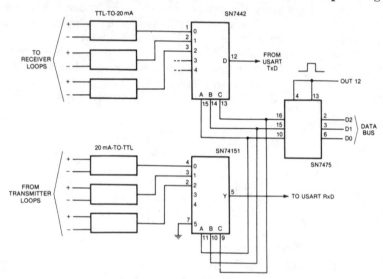

Fig. 4-24. Schematic diagram of a multiplexer circuit that multiplexes TTL communication signals.

standard SN7400-series integrated circuits. The SN7442 decoder works quite well as a one-line-to-eight-line *demultiplexer,* when the D input is wired to the transmitter data output, and the decoder outputs are routed to the various receiving devices. An SN74151 multiplexer is used to feed serial information from one of eight possible transmitting devices, to the USART serial input. Since the computer will probably be transmitting and receiving information from the same UART, the circuit in Fig. 4-24 illustrates how the multiplexer and demultiplexer circuits may be controlled by the same output port. To select a channel, the computer simply outputs the proper channel code to the output port, port 12. Up to eight individual channels may be selected in this scheme. Larger decoders and multiplexers could be used to expand the number of communication channels, almost indefinitely. In the circuits provided in Figs.

4-23 and 4-24, the current sources and current regulators have not been shown, for clarity.

AN ADDRESSABLE UART

The ideal UART-based communication system, for transmission of information between the TRS-80 computer, and remote instruments or controllers, would consist of a single set of lines (two current loops), with a number of UART-based controllers along the lines. Each UART would have a "name" that it would respond to, ignoring all other names and commands meant for other UARTs. In a system such as this, the computer could address individual, remote stations, causing specific actions to take place, without affecting other stations on the communication loops. Such systems have been developed, probably the most successful one being the SERDEX system developed by Analog Devices, Inc., in which ASCII commands are used to control remote transmitters and receivers. Unfortunately, these modules were a bit complex to use, confronting the user with literally dozens of wire-wrap pins that had to be interconnected with the instrument that was to be controlled. It would not be difficult to design an ASCII-based controller for a UART, but a simpler solution is at hand, that simplifies the communication problem, so that a number of UART-like devices may share a communication channel.

The Motorola MC14469 Addressable Asynchronous Receiver/ Transmitter, or AART, is contained in a 40-pin integrated circuit. This chip provides many UART-like functions, so that it communicates with computers in asynchronous-serial format, but it does not contain all of the buffer loading, buffer checking, and error detect-

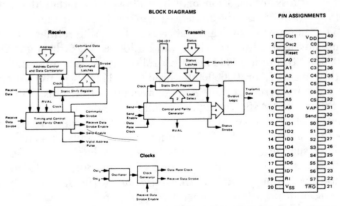

Courtesy Motorola Semiconductor Products, Inc.

Fig. 4-25. Block diagram and pin configuration of the MC14469 AART chip.

ing flag circuits that are used by a regular UART chip. This provides some additional pins that are used on the AART for various I/O and control signals. The MC14469 contains an oscillator, so that an external crystal may be used to generate the clocking needed for the timing of the bit rate. The clock frequency is *64-times* the data rate. Thus, a 307.2-kHz crystal will allow the AART to operate at 4800 b/sec transmission and reception rates. An external clock signal may be applied to the chip, in place of a crystal. The crystal connections are shown in the pin configuration given in Fig. 4-25. If an external clock is to be used, its signal is connected to pin 1, with pin 2 unconnected. A $\overline{RESET}$ signal at pin 3 is used to initially reset the chip, once power has been applied. The AART requires a +5-volt power supply, and a ground connection.

Using the Addressable UART (MC14469)

The MC14469 is truly an addressable UART, since it can be wired to recognize a 7-bit address that is sent to it by the computer. The 7-bit address is actually the seven least-significant bits of a regular 8-bit transmission, in which the most-significant bit is a logic one, indicating to the receiving AART that it is address information. The received address is compared to a 7-bit address that has been hardwired to address input pins 4 through 10 on the AART chip. If the addresses do not match, the AART remains in the standby mode. If an address match takes place, then the AART is activated, as signaled by a logic one pulse at the valid address pulse (VAP) output, pin 31. Once the chip has been activated by the proper address, several different actions are possible, but we will continue to explain the operation of the receiver section of the AART, first.

The address information may be followed by either data, or by another address. In the serial stream of bits transmitted to the AART, the most-significant bit is used to differentiate between commands and addresses. If a valid address (128 through 255, or 10000000_2 through 11111111_2) is followed by a command word (0 through 127, or 00000000_2 through 01111111_2), the command bits are transferred to the AART command output pins, 33 through 39. Since the MSB distinguishes address information from commands, only the seven LSBs are output at the command pins. As was the case for the UART outputs, these outputs are latched. To indicate that new command bits have been latched at these pins by the AART, the command strobe (CS) output, pin 32, provides a short logic one pulse. *All transmissions to the AART chip must contain eight data bits, an even parity bit, and one stop bit.*

Before an AART may be used in a communication loop with a computer-controlled USART chip, the USART must be configured for the proper data format, and the proper data transmission/ reception rate. This means that the USART must be configured with a mode control instruction of 254, and a command instruction of 21. These commands may be output to the USART chip simply by typing OUT 7,245 ENTER, and OUT 7,21 ENTER, into the TRS-80, so that they are immediately executed, to initialize the USART. These initialization steps could be contained in a program, but they have been presented in this way to show you that there are other solutions to the problem of initializing the USART, and other I/O chips. Of course, the USART must be reset, so that it can accept a new mode control instruction. Once the USART has been initialized, transmissions to the AART may be started. The first thing that must be done is to transmit the correct AART address, in this case, the address 255 has been chosen. Once the AART has received and matched the address, additional transmissions may be sent to the AART to control the command data outputs. The program listed in Example 4-13 provides an incrementing count for the seven command data outputs, once the AART has been enabled. The AART address is entered from the keyboard, starting

Example 4-13. A Simple AART Control Program

```
100 INPUT "ID CODE";C
110 TX=C: GOSUB 1010
120 FOR Y=0 TO 127
130 TX=Y: GOSUB 1010
140 NEXT Y
150 GOTO 120

1010 OUT 6, TX
1020 IF (INP(7) AND 1)=0 THEN 1020
1030 RETURN
```

the program. When the MSB in the serial transmission to the AART is a logic one, the AART treats the data bits as if they are address bits. To keep the incrementing count from setting the MSB to a logic one, the incrementing count has been limited to between 0 and 127, or 00000000 and 01111111, if all eight bits are considered.

Once an address has been received and matched by an AART chip, it will remain activated, accepting command data, as long as the MSB is a logic zero. Thus, if several command data bytes are to be transferred to an AART, it is only necessary to send out the proper address once, at the start of the transmission. *Once an AART has been activated, it is deactivated, or turned off, by the receipt of any address information, even if its own address is retransmitted to it.* Thus, to deactivate an AART, you simply transmit an address, even its own address, on the communication loop.

If the AART has been reset, and if the program in Example 4-13 is run, the seven command data outputs on the AART chip will be incremented. However, if you stop the program with the BREAK key on the TRS-80, and restart it again (RUN 100), the command data outputs will not be incremented, even when the correct address is supplied. Why is this observed? If the program is stopped when the AART is selected, and address information is transmitted to it, even if it is its own address, the AART deactivates itself. If the proper address is transmitted to it again, after it has been deactivated, the chip recognizes the address as matching its hardwired address, and it resumes incrementing the count. This is a very important point that you must keep in mind if you choose to use AART chips. Once they are activated, any address information will deactivate them.

If you are going to transfer information to the AART command data outputs, the AART will have to be activated with the proper address. Even if the computer will only be transmitting information to the AART every minute or so, it will remain activated until another address is received. In some cases, you may find that it is advantageous to deactivate the AART between data transfers, rather than keeping it active, and trying to remember which AART is activated, and which ones are not. To deactivate an AART chip, you can simply: (1) transmit an address to activate another AART, (2) transmit the AART's own address, or (3) transmit a dummy address that does not correspond to any AART in the communication loop.

Now, let us examine the AART transmitter section. This section consists of 16 data inputs, so that a 16-bit data word may be transmitted by the AART to another asynchronous-serial device, such as a USART, or UART. Of course, the USART cannot accept a 16-bit serial transmission, so the AART formats the bits into two standard 8-bit bytes, and it then transmits each byte, along with the necessary start bit, parity bit, etc. The 16 bits are divided into an input data byte, pins 11 through 18, and a status byte, pins 22 through 29. These bits may be used for any type of binary information, ASCII codes, and so on, depending upon your particular application. The bits have been labeled as input data byte and status byte just so that they can be easily referenced. A transmission sequence is started by applying a short logic one pulse applied to the AART send input, pin 30. The input data byte is transmitted first, followed by the status byte. Since some time is required for the transmission of the first byte, the status bits are latched within the AART, by the send pulse, so that there is no chance for them to change once the transmission sequence has been started. To prevent many different AARTs from transmitting at the same time, the AART must be in the active mode for the send pulse to have any effect upon the chip. This means that the proper address must be used to select an AART chip before a transmission sequence is started. This prevents those AARTs in the standby mode from transmitting information on the communication loop.

Besides starting the transmission sequence, the send pulse also has another function in an active chip; it deactivates the chip, placing it in the standby mode. This means that once an AART chip has been properly addressed, and is active, only a single transmission of the input data and status bytes may take place. Of course, the chip may be reactivated simply by retransmitting its address to it again. You may be wondering how the transmission of information from the AART to the computer is coordinated with the activation of the AART chip, itself. There are a number of simple schemes that may be used to control the transmitter section.

The simplest control scheme is to connect the valid address pulse output to the send input. Thus, whenever a valid address is received, the transmission of the input data and status bytes is started. To transmit the 16 bits of information to the computer, the computer simply *polls* the AART, by transmitting the correct address to it. Unfortunately, this mode does not allow any information to be transferred to the command data outputs, since once the address is received and matched, the transmission starts, deactivating the chip. If you wish to retain this capability, simply connect the command strobe output to the send input. Now, the transmission sequence will only be started when a valid address has been received, *and* when the command data is updated. Of course, once the transmission sequence starts, the chip is deactivated. The deactivation of the chip does not affect the transmission of the 16 bits of information. Once started, the entire transmission takes place. It would not be a good idea to connect the send input to a control signal over which you have no control. For example, the send input should not be connected to a limit switch, so that transmissions would only take place when a certain level of solvent in a vat has been reached. Since you would not have any control over this signal, transmissions might take place at some times, deactivating the chip, while no transmissions would take place at other times, possibly leaving the chip activated. If the chip was left activated when it was not supposed to be, the next transmission of its address would deactivate it, as was the case prior to our discussion of the transmitter section. If the liquid level is to be checked, a better way to test the limit switch would be to connect its output to one of the input data, or status bits. Each selection of the AART chip would transmit this status information to the computer so that it could be checked.

A short program has been provided in Example 4-14, showing how the remote AART may be controlled to initiate transmissions,

Example 4-14. An AART Transmitter Control Program

```
300 TX=200: GOSUB 1010
305 TX=0: GOSUB 1010
310 TX=255: GOSUB 1010
315 A=INP(6)
320 TX=RND(127); GOSUB 1010
330 IF (INP(7) AND 2)=0 THEN 330
340 M=INP(6)
350 IF (INP(7) AND 2)=0 THEN 350
360 L=INP(6)
370 PRINT M,:PRINT L
380 FOR T=0 TO 300: NEXT T: GOTO 310

1010 OUT 6,TX
1020 IF (INP(7) AND 1)=0 THEN 1020
1030 RETURN
```

through the use of the command strobe pulse. Recall that the command strobe pulse signals the availability of new command information. The first steps in the program send a dummy address and dummy information to the AART, to deactivate it, if it is in the activated mode. Next, the proper address is sent to the AART to activate it. An additional step has been included, to clear the USART RxRDY flag, but this is optional. A random value is computed between the limits 1 and 127, and this is sent to the AART as command information. The random value is strobed into the command data latches, generating a command strobe pulse, which starts the transmission of the input data, and status information to the computer. The standard USART transmitter subroutine has been used to control the AART, but the commands that are used to control the USART receiver are "embedded" right in the program, so that no time is lost calling and returning from a general-purpose USART receiver subroutine. At a data rate of 150 b/sec, this scheme worked quite well. A schematic diagram of the circuit that was used is provided in Fig. 4-26. Note that an external oscillator was used, and that the MC14469 transmitter output ($\overline{TRO}$) is the inverse of what has been seen for UART and USART chips. Thus, this signal is inverted.

The timing of the send input is a bit critical, so some discussion of this signal is necessary. After a valid address pulse, and after a command strobe pulse, *the send input is enabled for eight-bit times.* Thus, for a 150 b/sec transmission rate, the send input is enabled, or active, for about 53 milliseconds after the VAP, or the CS, signal has been generated. This is one reason why it is recommended that either the VAP or CS signal be used to strobe the send input. The send input senses a positive-going edge. The timing relationships between the VAP and CS signals, and the *internal* send enable sig-

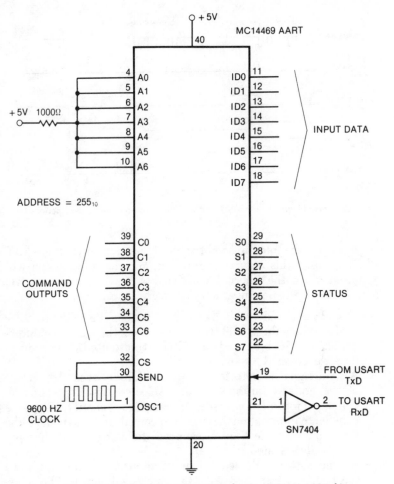

Fig. 4-26. Schematic diagram of a test circuit for the MC14469 AART chip.

nal, are shown in Fig. 4-27. Note that the VAP and CS signals are at least partially coincident with the internal send enable signal. This allows either the VAP, or the CS signal to be used to pulse the send input.

If a send signal is coincident with internal send enable signal during the 8-bit periods shown in Fig. 4-27, the transmission starts immediately. What happens if a send signal is received either when the AART is in the standby mode, or between an address for the AART, and the command word that follows it, when the internal send enable signal is not active? *The send input is always active, and sensitive to positive-going logic signals, as well as to noise.* The overall effect is this: if the positive-going edge of a send signal is

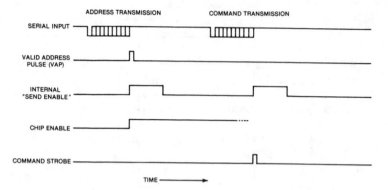

Fig. 4-27. Timing diagram for the VAP and CS pulses, showing the "active" periods for the send signal.

detected when the internal send enable signal is inactive, the AART will "remember" this request to transmit, and the transmission will be started when the internal send enable signal is again active. There are several cases in which this might take place:

1. A send signal is detected by the AART when it is in the standby mode. When the AART is next selected through an address match, the 16 bits of data will be transmitted. The chip is then deactivated (standby).

2. A send signal is detected by the AART between the receipt of the address information that selected the chip, and the command information that is to be sent to it shortly. When the command information has been received and latched at the seven outputs, the transmission will be started, and the chip will be deactivated.

3. A send signal is detected some time after a command word has been received, but while the chip is still active. The transmission will be initiated when the next command word has been received, and the bits latched. The chip will be deactivated.

4. A send signal is detected some time after a command word, or after an activating address has been received, but the chip is deactivated by the receipt of a nonmatching address before a transmission is initiated. The "send request" is saved, and the next activation of the chip will start the transmission, and chip will be deactivated.

We hope that you will see that when the send input is used with control signals other than VAP and CS, its control can be complex, and it is not always possible to tell when the send signal was detected by the AART. We strongly suggest that the simple control scheme, in which the VAP or CS signal is used, be used for all except the most specialized applications. For example, we don't think that you would want to use an end-of-conversion flag in an A/D converter to pulse the send input. If the conversion took a few hundred milliseconds, it would not be easy to determine what action would have to be initiated at the AART to read the data. In fact, it may have already been sent to the computer, if the end-of-conversion flag happened to coincide with the VAP or CS signal! Rather, we would recommend monitoring the flag, and then acquiring the information from the converter when the conversion process has been completed.

The use of an A/D converter with the AART is illustrated in Fig. 4-28. The ICL7109 A/D converter has been chosen again because of its simplicity and flexibility. In this circuit, the converter is operated in the free-running mode, with the outputs constantly enabled. The polarity, overrange, and status flags are also connected to the AART, so that they may be monitored. The status flag may be monitored in many ways to indicate that a conversion has been completed, but since these methods have been described in Chapter 2, we will not review them here. In the present example, the CS output has been used to trigger the transmission, since there may

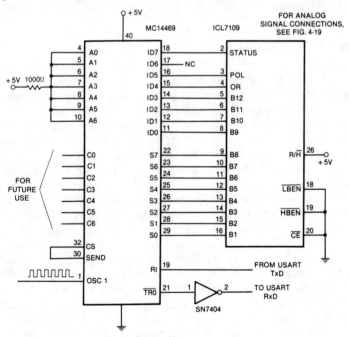

Fig. 4-28. Using the AART with a 12-bit A/D converter for remote measurements.

Example 4-15. An AART/Analog-to-Digital Converter Control Program

```
300 TX=200: GOSUB 1010
305 TX=0: GOSUB 1010
310 TX=255: GOSUB 1010
310 A=INP(6)
320 TX=RND(127): GOSUB 1010
330 IF (INP(7) AND 2)=0 THEN 330
340 M=INP(6)
350 IF (INP(7) AND 2)=0 THEN 350
360 L=INP(6)
370 PRINT ((M AND 128)/128);:PRINT (M AND 15);:PRINT L
380 FOR T=0 TO 300: NEXT T: GOTO 310

1010 OUT 6,TX
1020 IF (INP(7) AND 1)=0 THEN 1020
1030 RETURN
```

be additional uses for the seven outputs in the future. A control program is listed in Example 4-15. This program is very similar to the one provided in Example 4-14, except that a step has been added so that the status flag may be displayed, along with the high byte, and the low byte. If you are interested in the use of the status signal, we refer you to Example 2-25. The necessary conversion equation that will display the actual voltage is listed in Example 4-11.

Party-Line Control Systems

One of the reasons why the MC14469 AART device has been chosen for use in remote interfacing is that a number of these chips may be connected to the same pairs of transmitter and receiver communication lines. Each AART may be assigned a different address, so that up to 128 different instruments or controllers could be serviced on a single transmitter/receiver loop. Just as one gate's output may be connected to several inputs on other chips, the computer can transmit information to a number of AART chips without great difficulty. If you choose to use a 20-mA current loop for the transmission, each optocoupler in the loop will require a minimum amount of current and voltage. Each of the LEDs will require 20 mA, and each will have a forward (conducting) voltage drop of about 1.6 to 0.7 volts. Thus, you must be sure that the loop can handle any additional voltage or current, depending upon whether you have connected the LEDs to the communication line in parallel, or in series. The series configuration is probably the worst, since it is like the old Christmas tree lights that were connected in series. When one bulb burned out, all of the bulbs had to be tested, until the burned out bulb was found and replaced. Two burned out bulbs were almost impossible to find. In a parallel scheme, additional current-handling capability may be required at the transmitter. Of course, we don't expect that you will be connecting several dozens of optical coupler LEDs to the transmitter loop. Other transmission schemes may also be used, but most of them require a common ground signal connection which may induce ground-loop noise into the communication system.

The loop that allows each AART chip transmitter to communicate with a single receiver presents some problems. For example, how can all of these outputs be connected to the same line, without causing some of them to be burned out? If the 20-mA current loop scheme is used, there are few major difficulties, but not too many phototransistors can be connected to the same loop. Since current is flowing in the loop (20 mA) to indicate a logic one, any station could interrupt the flow to indicate a logic zero. This means that the photodetectors would have to be connected in series. For three or four stations, or "drops," in the line, this shouldn't present too many difficulties, and a typical loop system is shown in Fig. 4-29. Of course, the current loop configuration does not require a common ground, and it isolates the stations, and the computer, from one another.

Another approach to communicating with a number of stations involves the use of open-collector drivers. These were discussed briefly in Chapter 1. The open-collector devices allow the signal line to "float" at a logic one level, as supplied by a pull-up resistor at the receiving device. This means that the "normal" condition for the bus is logic one. To communicate information, the transmitting device pulls the bus down to a logic zero by turning on its open-collector transistor. The collector is connected to the bus, and it is pulled down to ground by having current flow through the transistor. In this way, the transistor appears to be off, or disconnected from the line, or it appears to be on, providing a logic zero signal for the line. Many open-collector devices may be connected to the line, but only one may be conducting at any time. This system also requires a common ground signal. A typical open-collector system is shown in Fig. 4-30. Note that coaxial cable has been used, along with a common ground. For short distances of 10 feet, or so, single wires may be used, without the need for terminating resistors, although a pull-up resistor is still needed (Fig. 4-31).

When *open-collector inverters* are used on a bus to transmit the serial data of the AART, no enabling of the open-collector devices is required. Since the transmitted serial output ($\overline{TCO}$) signal is a logic zero in its quiescent state, the open-collector output of the inverter is "off," or disconnected from the bus.

An alternate approach is to use a balanced line, consisting of a twisted pair of wires. When such a line is used, standard *line-driver,*

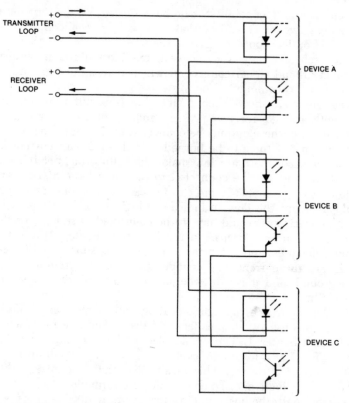

Fig. 4-29. Using a 20 mA current loop transmitter/receiver scheme with three stations.

and *line-receiver* circuits may be used. A typical transmitter/receiver system is shown in Fig. 4-32. In some applications, shielded, twisted-pair wires may be useful, to reduce the noise on the lines. Texas Instruments recommends the use of Belden No. 8227 (shielded), or Belden No. 8795 (unshielded) wire in these types of applications. These cables have an impedance of about 100 ohms, so the termination resistors at each end of the line would be 50 ohms each. These

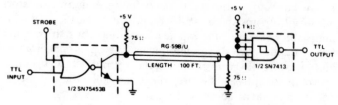

Courtesy Texas Instruments, Inc.

Fig. 4-30. A simple open-collector line-driver circuit.

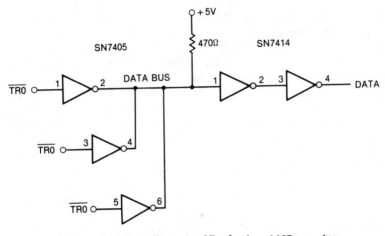

Fig. 4-31. A short open-collector signal line for three AART transmitters.

resistors are used only at the ends of the transmission line. Several other receivers and transmitters could be connected to this balanced line for a party-line network. In the USART/AART system, however, one transmitter feeds many receivers, and many transmitters feed one receiver, using separate loops. Using the scheme shown in Fig. 4-32, lines over 1000 feet long are possible. In the transmitter loop of the USART, the INHIBIT and STROBE inputs to the line-driver and line-receiver circuit may be hard-wired to logic one, so that they are always enabled.

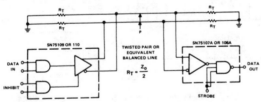

Courtesy Texas Instruments, Inc.

Fig. 4-32. A simple balanced line transmission system.

The USART receiver loop presents one difficulty. How are the individual AART transmitter line-driver chips to be enabled in remote locations? Each line driver may be enabled upon command from the remote computer, simply by using one of the command outputs as an enable signal for the line-driver chip. In this way, the command word that is used to initiate the transmission (CS is connected to send) also supplies the enable signal for the line-driver. Of course, this bit would have to be reset after the transmission was completed, to disable the line driver, so that it would not interfere, or conflict with, other transmissions on the loop. If additional transmissions are required from the same AART, the line-driver chip may be left enabled until all of the transmissions have been completed, or it may be re-enabled, as required. Of course, only one transmitter may be enabled at any time.

If the command strobe pulse is used to start a transmission, how can a transmission be blocked when you simply wish to send a new command data word to the AART to disable the line-driver chip? Actually, the transmission is started, but the line-driver is disabled so quickly by the new command data word, that it will not get through to the transmission line. Thus, the transmission takes place, but it is not gated through the line-driver circuit. We used this scheme quite easily with two AART chips, and an open-collector bus, as shown in Fig. 4-33. The circuit shown in Fig. 4-32 may be used in the AART-to-USART transmission loop simply by connecting one INHIBIT input to one of the command data outputs. The other INHIBIT input, and one of the DATA inputs may be hardwired to logic one, as may the STROBE input on the line receiver that is connected to the USART receiver input pin.

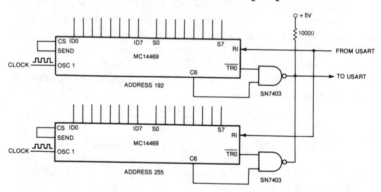

Fig. 4-33. Controlling an open-collector serial bus for multiple MC14469 AART chips.

A multiline control program is listed in Example 4-16. While random information is again generated to provide a visual check for the operation of the command data outputs, output C6 has been "dedicated" to control the open-collector bus driving chip. To control the state of the C6 bit, a logical OR operation is used to set the bit, while a logical AND operation is used to clear the bit. The random information is temporarily stored and then used in the various logical operations so that bit C6 may be cleared and set, as needed. Note, though, that when the control bit is cleared, the AART address must also be output first, to reactivate the chip so that it can receive the new command information.

```
300 TX=200: GOSUB 1010
305 TX=0: GOSUB 1010
307 INPUT "ID #";N:IF N<128 THEN 307
310 TX=N: GOSUB 1010
315 A=INP(6)
320 R=RND(63):TX=(R OR 64): GOSUB 1010
330 IF (INP(7) AND 2)=0 THEN 330
340 M=INP(6)
350 IF (INP(7) AND 2)=0 THEN 350
360 L=INP(6)
370 PRINT ((M AND 128);:PRINT (M AND 15);:PRINT L
380 TX=N: GOSUB 1010: TX=(R AND 63): GOSUB 1010
390 GOTO 310

1010 OUT 6,TX
1020 IF (INP(7) AND 1)=0 THEN 1020
1030 RETURN
```

Assembly Language and the USART

There may be times when an assembly-language program to control the USART is the only answer to communicating with serial devices at high data rates. Perhaps an ICL7109 converter is set up to transmit its information through a UART at 4800 b/sec. At this rate, it is doubtful if the BASIC USART control program would be able to acquire the two bytes of converter information fast enough to keep up with the high data rate. To aid you in applications where this may be the case, we have provided a number of useful assembly-language subroutines in this section. The program listed in completely assembled hexadecimal form in Example 4-17 is a two-byte USART receiver subroutine that may be called by a BASIC program. The assembly-language program has been written to accept two bytes of information from the USART, and then store them for later use, perhaps by some BASIC program. The program uses a general purpose USART input subroutine, called USART. The TWOBYT subroutine calls the USART subroutine to obtain a data byte. When the byte has been received, it is transferred from the A register of the Z80 to a R/W memory location that we have labeled, LOC1. In a similar manner, the next byte received from the USART is transferred to LOC2. These two memory locations may be accessed through the use of PEEK commands.

Before this assembly-language program may be used, some portion of the R/W memory of the TRS-80 must be set aside for our use. Thus, when the computer asks, "MEMORY SIZE?" at the start of operation, you should respond with, "32000." You may use other addresses if you have more or less memory, but the addresses in

Example 4-17. Assembly-Language Program for Two-Byte USART Inputs

```
                     *7DH 00H
7D   00   CD   TWOBYT,  CALL      /CALL THE USART SUBROUTINE
7D   01   32            USART
7D   02   7D            0
7D   03   32            STA       /STORE THE RECEIVED VALUE FROM THE
7D   04   64            LOC1      /USART IN A LOCATION FOR LATER USE
7D   05   7D            0
7D   06   CD            CALL      /CALL THE USART SUBROUTINE AGAIN FOR
7D   07   32            USART     /THE SECOND BYTE
7D   08   7D            0
7D   09   32            STA       /STORE IT, TOO
7D   0A   65            LOC2
7D   0B   7D            0
7D   0C   C9            RET       /RETURN TO "BASIC"

                     *7DH 32H
              /THIS IS A GENERAL PURPOSE USART INPUT ROUTINE
7D   32   DB   USART,   IN        /TEST THE RECEIVER FLAG
7D   33   07            007
7D   34   E6            ANI       /MASK IT
7D   35   02            002
7D   36   CA            JZ        /IF IT IS ZERO, TEST IT AGAIN
7D   37   32            USART
7D   38   7D            0
7D   39   DB            IN        /FLAG IS DETECTED, SO INPUT DATA
7D   3A   06            006
7D   3B   C9            RET       /RETURN WITH DATA IN THE A REGISTER

                     *7DH 64H
              /THESE ARE THE STORAGE LOCATIONS FOR THE TWO BYTES
7D   64   00   LOC1,    0
7D   65   00   LOC2,    0
```

the assembly-language program must be changed, too. Before an assembly-language program can be called, the low and high address bytes of the start of the subroutine must be stored in locations 16526 and 16527, respectively.

The BASIC program in Example 4-18 shows how the assembly-language program may be used. The BASIC program also contains the necessary steps to transfer the decimal equivalents of the hexadecimal instruction codes into their proper locations in memory. These steps take lines 10 through 120. Except for the commands at line No. 150 that load the user's subroutine address into the two memory locations, and the actual user subroutine call at line No. 180, the program is very similar to other AART control programs discussed previously. The data bytes are retrieved from R/W memory by PEEK instructions.

While the USART subroutine in the assembly-language program is a general-purpose USART input subroutine, this subroutine cannot be used by itself, being called from a BASIC program to input a single character from the USART. There are no commands in this subroutine that allow the data byte, or argument, to be passed back to the BASIC program, so that it may be used. Instead, the information is stored in a read/write memory location, where it can be accessed with a PEEK command. Two general-purpose assembly-language USART control programs are provided in Example 4-19.

Example 4-18. Main Control Program. Uses the Assembly-Language Programs in Example 4-17

```
 10 DATA 205,50,125,50,100,125,205,50,125,50,101,125,201
 20 DATA 219,7,230,2,202,50,125,219,6,201
 30 N=32000
 40 FOR I=0 TO 12
 50 READ D
 60 POKE N+I,D
 70 NEXT I
 80 N=32050
 90 FOR I=0 TO 9
100 READ D
110 POKE N+I,D
120 NEXT I
130 TX=200: GOSUB 1010
140 TX=0: GOSUB 1010
150 POKE 16526,0:POKE 16527,125
155 R=INP(6)
160 TX=255: GOSUB 1010
170 TX=0:GOSUB 1010
180 Z=USR(0)
190 PRINT (PEEK(32100) AND 15);:PRINT PEEK(32101)
200 GOTO 160
1010 OUT 6,TX
1020 IF (INP(7) AND 1)=0 THEN 1020
1030 RETURN
```

These programs may be used at any time for the control of a USART receiver or transmitter. This doesn't mean that BASIC can't be used to control the USART, too. The USART input subroutine, USIN, performs the same input function as the USART subroutine in Example 4-17, except that the resulting value is placed in the "L" register of the Z-80, and the "H" register is cleared. The final JMP command transfers control of the program to a portion of the BASIC interpreter so that the value that was input from the USART is assigned the "name" used in the subroutine call, for example, Z, in the user subroutine call operation, Z =USR(0), assuming this called the USIN subroutine. The USOUT subroutine operates much like the BASIC subroutine that performed the same operation. The only difference is that the value that is to be transmitted may be incorporated into the user's subroutine call operation, for example, W = USR(20). Here, the binary equivalent of decimal twenty would be

Example 4-19. General-Purpose Assembly-Language USART Control Programs

```
                    /GENERAL PURPOSE USART INPUT SUBROUTINE
                       *7DH 32H
7D    32   DB   USIN,   IN        /TEST THE FLAG
7D    33   07           007
7D    34   E6           ANI       /MASK OUT OTHER BITS
7D    35   02           002
7D    36   CA           JZ        /IF NO FLAG, TEST AGAIN
7D    37   32           USIN
7D    38   7D           0
7D    39   DB           IN        /INPUT DATA BYTE
7D    3A   06           006
7D    3B   6F           MOVLA     /STORE IT IN REG L
7D    3C   26           MVIH      /CLEAR REG H
7D    3D   00           000
7D    3E   C3           JMP       /TO RETURN THE ARGUMENT, JUMP TO
7D    3F   9A           9AH       /THIS ADDRESS, INSTEAD OF A RETURN
7D    40   0A           0AH


                    /GENERAL PURPOSE USART OUTLINE SUBROUTINE
7D    41   CD   USOUT,  CALL      /THIS CALL GETS THE ARGUMENT INTO
7D    42   7F           7FH       /THE H & L REGISTERS FROM "BASIC"
7D    43   0A           0AH
7D    44   7D           MOVAL     /GET THE DATA BYTE
7D    45   D3           OUT       /OUTPUT IT
7D    46   06           006
7D    47   DB   TEST,   IN        /CHECK THE FLAG
7D    48   07           007
7D    49   E6           ANI       /MASK OUT THE OTHER BITS
7D    4A   01           001
7D    4B   CA           JZ        /STILL XMTING?, CHECK AGAIN
7D    4C   47           TEST
7D    4D   7D           0
7D    4E   C9           RET       /DONE, SO RETURN
```

transmitted by the USART. The assembly-language subroutine that is used to control the USART transmitter must first call a subroutine that is located within the BASIC interpreter, so that the argument that is to be transmitted is transfered to the Z-80 H and L registers. In both cases, when transferring a value to, or from, a subroutine, the Z-80 H and L registers are used to contain a 16-bit signed number. Since the USART is an I/O device, and thus limited to values between 0 and 255, only the 8-bit L register is considered. The H register may be ignored.

In the transmitter subroutine, once the value in the L register is copied into the A register, and then into the USART, the subroutine is simply ended with a return (RET) instruction. These subroutines are quite useful, and an example of their use is provided in Example 4-20. In this program, these subroutines are loaded into R/W memory and executed in a BASIC program that transmits random

Example 4-20. A BASIC Program that Uses the Assembly-Language USART Subroutines

```
 10 DATA 219,7,230,2,202,50,125,219,6,111,38,0,195,154,10
 15 DATA 205,127,10,125,211,6,219,7,230,1,202,71,125,201
 20 FOR I=0 TO 28
 30 READ D
 40 POKE 32050+I,D
 50 NEXT I
 60 A=INP(6)
 70 A=RND(255)
 80 POKE 16526,65:POKE 16527,125
 90 W=USR(A)
100 POKE 16526,50
110 Z=USR(0)
120 IF Z=A THEN 70 ELSE 200
200 PRINT "ERROR":END
```

data, and then checks it against what is received by the receiving side of the USART. If the output of the transmitter and the input of the receiver are connected, this provides an easy means of testing the USART. Error is detected when the received value and the transmitted value are unequal.

If you are concerned about the use of a jump or a call to the BASIC interpreter in these subroutines, these instructions may be replaced with equivalent assembly language instructions that will store a received value in a R/W memory location, or retrieve one from a R/W memory location. We suggest that you might want to review your 8080 or Z-80 assembly-language programming before you get much more involved in assembly-language subroutine calls.

In this chapter, you have been introduced to the use of asynchronous-serial data communications, and the devices that are used to implement various interfaces and controllers that are compatible with this mode of communication. Our basic purpose was to show you how easy it is to use this type of interfacing to link remote devices and small computers. In fact, many, many devices are readily interfaced to computers in this way, since the only requirement is an asynchronous-serial I/O port at both ends of two pairs of wires. We have also provided some typical examples of what you can do with a serial transmitter/receiver loop once it has been constructed.

5

TRS-80 Interrupts

Most modern computers have some form of interrupt input, so that an external signal may be used to force the computer to jump, or branch, to some other portion of a program. Unlike the use of input ports and sensing software steps that are used to determine the state of external devices and signals, the interrupts are independent of the operation of the computer program. In general, there are no specific steps in a program that are used to sense when an interrupt has taken place. Hardware associated with the microprocessor chip, or central processing unit (CPU), forces a specific sequence of actions to take place, independent of the byte of instruction that the computer may be operating upon. Interrupts can be particularly useful in situations in which it is necessary to immediately alert the computer to some specific condition. Examples of signals that might be used to generate an interrupt signal are an A/D converter end-of-conversion flag, a floppy disk data-ready flag, or perhaps even a heat sensor signal. Each of these signals could be used by the microcomputer interrupt input to force the computer to stop what it is doing, and to point it to a new set of software steps that are related to the device or signal that has generated the interrupt signal. The A/D converter end-of-conversion signal might be used to interrupt the computer so that it would acquire the data that is ready, and then start a new conversion. Our purpose in this chapter is to introduce you to some of the various ways in which the TRS-80 interrupts may be used. The Z-80 central processor has a number of different interrupt modes, and these will be discussed in some detail. Before you go any further, though, you should realize that the use of the TRS-80 interrupts involves assembly-language programming. Our program examples will not be very complex, so a detailed understanding of the Z-80 instruction set will not be required.

The use of interrupts is a complex subject, and we have covered many of the software and timing considerations elsewhere, in *The 8080 Bugbook*: Microcomputer Interfacing and Programming*, and in *8080/8085 Software Design, Book 2*, Howard W. Sams & Co., Inc., Indianapolis, IN 46206, so there is little reason to cover them here in the same detail. Interrupts must be used with a great deal of care, since they can be used to take control away from the BASIC interpreter, so that assembly-language programs may be executed to accomplish a specific task. Since assembly-language programming is involved, you may find that your BASIC programs are destroyed through the careless use of interrupts and interrupt subroutines. It is our philosophy that only one or two interrupts should be used with small computers, since similar functions may be implemented in other ways, through sense inputs, flags, and the like.

OBJECTIVES

At the end of this chapter, you will be able to do the following:

- Describe, in general terms, the operation of a simple interrupt.
- Describe the operation of the three interrupt modes of the Z-80.
- Design an interrupt instruction port circuit, and flip-flop controller.
- Write a simple interrupt control program.
- Show how BASIC programs may be used to preset various read/write memory locations for use by interrupt service subroutines.
- Describe the Z-80 interrupt control instructions.
- Tell why the TRS-80 cannot be used for interrupts, except for simple Mode 1 interrupts.
- Describe a simple modification that can be made to the TRS-80, so that all types of interrupts can be used.
- Describe the use of a priority encoder chip in a priority interrupt system.

ELEMENTARY INTERRUPTS

Before we start a discussion of the various types of interrupts of the TRS-80, we must be sure that the concept of interrupting a program is fairly well understood. Let us suppose that you have the

---

* Bugbook is a registered trademark of E&L Instruments, Inc., Derby, CT 06418.

lawn to mow, and that you are well underway when the telephone rings, and you have to leave the mower to answer it. This is an interrupt of your main task, which is mowing the lawn. The phone call interrupted your job, but you were able to answer the call, and then return to the lawn mower with little difficulty, picking up where you were originally interrupted by the ringing phone. Computer interrupts operate in a similar way; a main program is being executed, when an interrupt occurs. This interrupt signals the computer to stop its current operation, and to transfer its attention to a new program, subprogram, or subroutine, as indicated by the interrupting device. After this *interrupt service program* has been completed, the computer transfers control back to the main program that was being executed when the interrupt was sensed. There were no signs posted on the lawn that said, "Stop and listen for phone,'" and there are no interrupt "sensing" steps in the main task program of the computer. The detection of an interrupt signal is taken care of with hardware, and this is independent of the program steps that are being executed.

There are some complex problems associated with interrupts, and it is important that these be understood prior to the use of interrupts in complex control schemes. Using the lawn-mowing example, it is fairly easy to describe some of these problems and limitations.

1. When you leave the lawnmower to answer the phone, the mower must be shut down in an orderly fashion, so that it won't "burn" the lawn, waste gas, and interfere with your conversation. This is also the case with programs. They must be shut down in an orderly fashion, so that they may be restarted once the interrupt servicing sequence has been completed.

2. If you have a number of phone calls to answer during the time that you have set aside to mow the lawn, you may spend more time answering the phone, than in mowing the lawn. Your main task of cutting the grass has been extended by the time to answer all of the calls, plus the time to mow the grass. You also have to add in the time that has been used to shut off the mower and to restart it. The original task has been considerably lengthened by the interrupting phone calls, so that it has taken much longer to mow the lawn than it should have. One solution is to "disable" the interrupting device, perhaps by ignoring the phone ringing, or by taking the phone off the hook. The analogy with computer programs should be quickly apparent. Interrupted software tasks take longer than uninterrupted ones. There are ways in which the computer interrupt hardware can be disabled, so that it will ignore any external interrupt signals. Programs can also become *interrupt bound,*

spending so much time servicing the interrupts, that the computer never gets back to the main task that it originally started.

3. While you are answering the phone, one of your children may come into the house, crying, interrupting your phone conversation. This means that a new interrupt has taken place, so that after soothing the child, you go back to the phone, and then back to the lawn mower. Interrupts can be interrupted by other interrupts, and so on, *ad nauseam*. In fact, there can be cases in which one device can interrupt the computer while it is half-way through servicing the first interrupt of that same device, much like the child who asks for a glass of water, and when you have started to fill the glass, asks for a sandwich. This can cause you to become interrupt bound quickly, and it is quite possible to lose track of exactly what it is that you are doing. Likewise, computers can become disoriented quickly, too, when handling too many interrupts.

4. It is necessary in some cases to assign a priority to interrupts, since there is always the possibility of having two different interrupts occurring at the same time. For example, while you are mowing the lawn, a friend may drop over to borrow a rake at the same time that the phone rings. Which of the interrupts is serviced first?

These are some of the things that we have discussed in detail, in the two books cited previously in this chapter. Since assembly-language programming is used extensively in these examples, we will not discuss it beyond our simple examples. Interrupts are difficult to debug, since they can occur at almost any time, and they generally request interrupt service when you (and the program) least expect it. We hope that you will treat interrupts with a great deal of respect, and that you will be careful in your use of them.

Z-80 INTERRUPTS AND TRS-80 INTERRUPTS

The Z-80 microprocessor chip has two interrupt inputs, called nonmaskable interrupt ($\overline{\text{NMI}}$) and interrupt ($\overline{\text{INT}}$). In the TRS-80 computer, the reset push button, located inside the interface hatch cover, is connected to the $\overline{\text{NMI}}$ input. The BASIC interpreter program has been programmed to recognize this input as a reset function. If you actuate this push button, the computer will respond with "READY." This input is not available to the TRS-80 user. The other interrupt, $\overline{\text{INT}}$, has not been used in the basic TRS-80 computer, so it is available for experimental use, and it is available at the interface edge connector. A logic zero pulse on this input indicates an interrupt request to the Z-80 chip. Unlike the nonmaskable interrupt, which is always active, the interrupt input may be turned on or off, so that the computer may be set to accept interrupts, or to ignore them. The $\overline{\text{INT}}$ input may be used in one of three possible ways, all of which may be programmed through the use of the appropriate assembly-language steps. These different types of interrupts are called Mode 0, Mode 1, and Mode 2. Each operates in a specific way, as described in the sections that follow.

Mode 0 Interrupts

This mode is identical to the 8080A and 8085A interrupt response, so that when the Z-80 is in this mode, any single-byte instruction may be forced into the computer for execution. Thus, the interrupting device provides the next instruction for execution by the computer. Of course, this must be an assembly-language instruction. In general, the single-byte restart instructions will be used with the Z-80 when it is in this mode, since these instructions are 1-byte

Table 5-1. Restart Instruction and Address Vectors for the BASIC Interpreter

Instruction	Hex Op-code	Decimal Op-code	Points to Address		Contents		Comments
RST0	C7	199	0H	0	Start of		BASIC ROM
			1H	1			
			2H	2			
RST1	CF	207	8H	8	C3H	195	Jump to 16384_{10}
			9H	9	00H	0	
			AH	10	40H	64	
RST2	D7	215	10H	16	C3H	195	Jump to 16387
			11H	17	03H	3	
			12H	18	40H	64	
RST3	DF	223	18H	24	C3H	195	Jump to 16390
			19H	25	06H	6	
			1AH	26	40H	64	
RST4	E7	231	20H	32	C3H	195	Jump to 16393
			21H	33	09H	9	
			22H	34	40H	64	
RST5	EF	239	28H	40	C3H	195	Jump to 16396
			29H	41	0CH	12	
			2AH	42	40H	64	
RST6	F7	247	30H	48	C3H	195	Jump to 16399
			31H	49	0FH	15	
			32H	50	40H	64	
RST7	FF	255	38H	56	C3H	195	Jump to 16402
			39H	57	12H	18	
			3AH	58	40H	64	

Table 5-2. Vector Addresses and Their Contents in R/W Memory

Pointer	Address	Contents		Comments
4000H	16384	C3H	195	Jump instruction—Used by BASIC
		96H	150	
		1CH	28	
4003H	16387	C3H	195	Jump instruction—Used by BASIC
		78H	120	
		1DH	29	
4006H	16390	C3H	195	Jump instruction—Used by BASIC
		90H	144	
		1CH	28	
4009H	16393	C3H	195	Jump instruction—Used by BASIC
		D9H	217	
		25H	37	
400CH	16396	C9H	201	Return instruction—Available for user's
		—	—	jump command
		—	—	
400FH	16399	C9H	201	Return instruction—Available for user's
		—	—	jump command
		—	—	
4012H	16402	FBH	251	Enable interrupt instruction
		C9H	201	Return instruction
				Available for user's jump command

subroutine call instructions that point to subroutines at specific points within the Z-80 memory. The locations that may be used in this mode are already preset with instructions in the TRS-80 BASIC interpreter read-only memories (ROMs), as shown in Tables 5-1 and 5-2. These addresses are inaccessible to you, since they are located within a ROM chip. However, there are jump instructions at each of the *vector points*, 0, 8, 10, etc., pointing the computer to a section of read/write memory that may be used to store either a short interrupt service subroutine, or *another jump instruction* that will be used to point to the main interrupt service subroutine. The use of a restart instruction is detailed in Fig. 5-1. When the Z-80 is turned on, it is set to the Mode 0 interrupt mode. We will show you how the restart instructions are "jammed" into the computer, shortly.

Mode 1 Interrupts

When this mode has been selected, no external instructions can be jammed into the Z-80 when it is interrupted. Instead, the computer is immediately pointed to address 0038H, or 56_{10}. An interrupt service subroutine may be located here. In the TRS-80, this

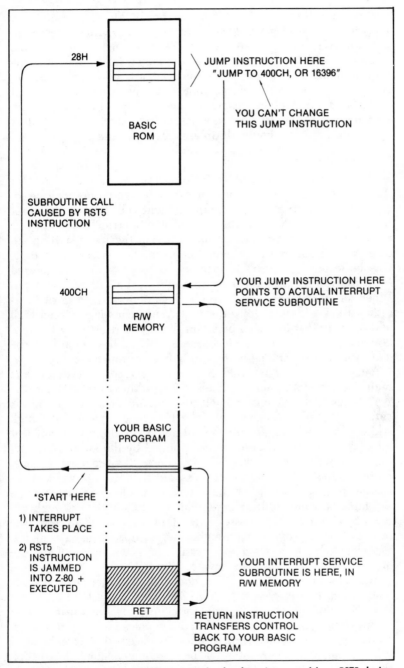

Fig. 5-1. Flow diagram for a BASIC program that has been interrupted by a RST5 device.

location is within the BASIC interpreter ROM, so it contains a jump instruction to get the computer into read/write memory. In fact, the computer goes to the same address that is used by the Restart 7, or RST7, command, when the Z-80 is in Mode 0. In Mode 1, even though only a single interrupt vector is provided, many devices can be used with the interrupt, since the individual interrupt could be ORed together, generating an interrupt to the Z-80 whenever any one of the devices requests interrupt service. The Mode 1 operations are very simple, flexible, and easy to use.

Mode 2 Interrupts

This mode is the most powerful interrupt response available for the Z-80. In this mode, an interrupt service subroutine may be located at any address in the computer, and called by an interrupt request signal to the Z-80 chip. When this interrupt mode is to be used, the programmer must set up a table of the 16-bit starting addresses for each of the different interrupting devices. This table may be located anywhere in memory, although it must be located in read/write memory for it to be useful in the TRS-80 computer. When an interrupt request is received, the interrupting device furnishes a low address byte to the Z-80. When combined with a high address byte that has been preset in the Z-80 I register by the programmer, a 16-bit address is formed. This address points to the *address of the subroutine* in the subroutine address table. Assembly-language steps must be used to preset the Z-80 I register to the high address of the interrupt subroutine address table. When the Z-80 is reset, the I register is cleared to zero. Since each address entry in the address table will take two bytes, one for the high address byte, and one for the low address byte, the least significant bit of the low address information supplied by the interrupting device is preset to zero by the Z-80. Of course, the programmer must fill the address table with the addresses of the interrupt service subroutine prior to the use of this interrupt mode. The first byte in the table is a low address byte, which is followed by a high address byte. Since the addresses in the table may be changed by the program, as it progresses through a set of operations, a complex, sophisticated control scheme is possible. An illustration of the use of the Mode 2 interrupt is shown in Fig. 5-2.

You may be wondering, "How does the computer remember its place when it is interrupted?" The Z-80 chip has a built-in circuit that will *push*, or save, the program counter contents in a section of read/write memory that is called the *stack*. It does this automatically, when an interrupt request is received, but only after it has completed the execution of the assembly-language instruction that it is operating on. The execution of a *return instruction*, RET,

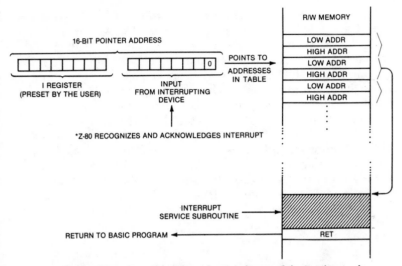

Fig. 5-2. Mode 2 interrupt program flow, showing the use of the I register and an externally supplied low address to point to the address table.

at the end of an interrupt service subroutine causes the computer to go back to the stack to retrieve the 16-bit value of the program counter, so that it can execute the next instruction that would have been executed in the main task program, if no interrupt had taken place. In this way, the computer keeps track of where it is in a program, so that it can return. In the same way, the GOSUB command in BASIC forces the computer to perform a subroutine, and the RETURN command forces the computer to go back to the "calling point" in the BASIC program. The stack area that is set aside by the BASIC interpreter program may be used to store return addresses for interrupt service subroutines, without difficulty, so you don't have to be concerned with exactly where the stack is located at this point.

INTERRUPT CONTROL HARDWARE

The hardware that is used to control interrupts is fairly easy to construct. A simple input port is used to provide an *8-bit instruction*, or an *8-bit address*, to the Z-80, depending upon the interrupt mode that is to be used. A three-state input port is used, but instead of being controlled by a device select pulse, such as $\overline{\text{IN 78}}$, the *interrupt instruction port* is controlled by the computer interrupt acknowledge signal, $\overline{\text{INTAK}}$, which is a short logic zero pulse. Once an interrupt has been recognized by the TRS-80, it generates the $\overline{\text{INTAK}}$ signal to indicate to the interrupting device that it has been recognized, and that it is to place its address or instruction byte on the data bus. This logic zero pulse on the $\overline{\text{INTAK}}$ line is used to enable the three-state interrupt instruction port, so that the information flows onto the data bus, and to the Z-80 chip in an orderly fashion. In most interfaces, the interrupt requesting device does not assert the interrupt request signal ($\overline{\text{INT}}$) directly, using an interrupt flip-flop instead. The $\overline{\text{Q}}$ output of the flip-flop is used to indicate that the device is requesting an interrupt. The $\overline{\text{INTAK}}$ signal is used to clear the flip-flop, so that multiple interrupts do not occur for the same interrupt request signal. A typical interrupt instruction port, and interrupt flip-flop, are shown in Fig. 5-3. This interrupt instruction port may be used when the Z-80 is in either the "0" or "2" interrupt mode. The port should be disabled when Mode 1 operations are to be used, although the flip-flop may still be used to generate the interrupt request signal.

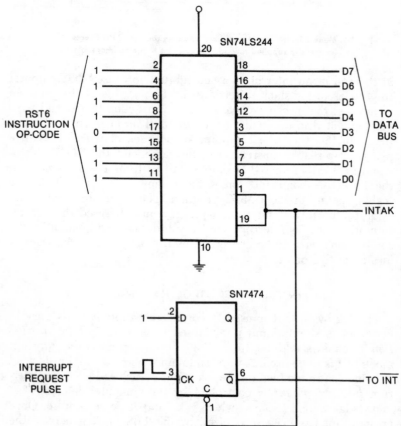

Fig. 5-3. Schematic diagram for an interrupt instruction port and control flip-flop.

While the Z-80 microprocessor may be used in any of the three interrupt modes, the TRS-80 cannot. Apparently, the TRS-80 has been set up so that all interrupting devices will operate with it in the Mode 1 configuration. This arises from the way in which the TRS-80 data bus is controlled. The internal operations of the TRS-80 control the data bus so that it is normally in the output state. The bus is only turned around for the input state, when a read (memory or I/O) takes place. *Unfortunately, the TRS-80 data bus is not turned around when the interrupt acknowledge signal is generated.* The TRS-80 can be modified to allow all of the different interrupt modes to be used with it, simply by using the $\overline{\text{INTAK}}$ signal to "turn the bus around," placing it in the input mode so that interrupt instructions and addresses may be accepted by the computer. Two possible modifications, both of which are simple, may be made to the TRS-80. The schematic diagrams for both of these changes are provided in Figs. 5-4 and 5-5. The simplest modification gates the $\overline{\text{INTAK}}$ and $\overline{\text{RD}}$ signals together, while removing the TEST signal. The second modification requires the addition of an AND gate so that the function of the TEST input may be retained. The TEST signal is used by direct memory access (DMA) devices, so that they can "disconnect" the Z-80 microprocessor chip from the various buses, so that they may be controlled externally. If such DMA de-

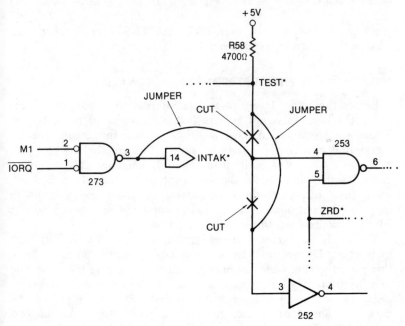

Fig. 5-4. Simple interrupt modification for the TRS-80. (No DMA operations are possible.)

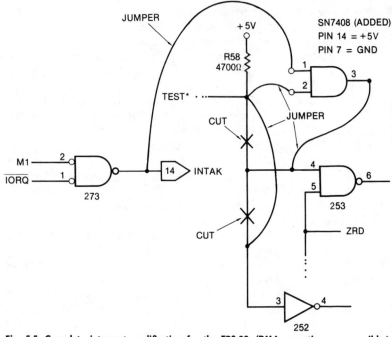

Fig. 5-5. Complete interrupt modification for the TRS-80. (DMA operations are possible.)

vices are not going to be used with your TRS-80 system, the simplest modification is recommended.

INTERRUPT CONTROL SOFTWARE

Before the actual interrupt service subroutine steps can be outlined, the basic interrupt control instructions should be reviewed. These are assembly-language instructions, and they cannot be incorporated in a BASIC program, except through the use of a call to a user's subroutine, written in assembly language. The interrupt control instructions allow the interrupt to be turned on and off, allow the interrupt mode to be preset, and allow the program to be properly controlled at the end of an interrupt service subroutine. The instructions are summarized in Table 5-3.

The enable interrupt instruction, EI, and the disable interrupt instruction, DI, are used to turn the Z-80 interrupt on and off. In this way, the computer response to interrupts during the execution of a program may be carefully controlled. For example, if the computer system involves interrupting devices, the interrupt will be turned on almost as soon as the program is started, so that any external interrupts may be serviced. However, if a time-sensitive por-

Table 5-3. Assembly-Language Interrupt Control Instructions

Mnemonic	Op-Code Hex	Op-Code Decimal	Operation
EI	FB	251	Enables the Z-80 interrupt so that external interrupts may be sensed.
DI	F3	243	Disables the interrupt, so that future interrupts will be ignored.
IM0	ED 46	237 70	Sets Mode 0 interrupts, so that restart instructions can be jammed into the Z-80.
IM1	ED 56	237 86	Sets Mode 1 interrupts. Any maskable interrupt will cause a subroutine call at address 38H, or 56.
IM2	ED 5E	237 94	Sets the Z-80 for Mode 2 interrupts. The I register contains the high address for an address entry in a table that specifies the starting address of the interrupt service subroutine. The interrupting device supplies the low address, with bit DO = 0.
RET	C9	201	A normal return instruction, for use with subroutines of all types.
RETI	ED 4D	237 77	Return instruction for use in maskable interrupt subroutines. Used with Z-80 family chips.
RETN	ED 45	237 69	Return from nonmaskable interrupt subroutine. Not used in TRS-80 systems.

tion of the program is to be executed, the interrupt may be disabled at the start of this program segment, and then turned on at the end of it. This protects portions of programs from the effects of interrupts. Whenever an interrupt is serviced, the interrupt is disabled by the Z-80, so that further interrupts cannot be serviced. If you wish to have the Z-80 recognize subsequent interrupts, then the interrupt must be re-enabled, by using another enable interrupt instruction. This feature allows you to "protect" interrupt service subroutines, so that they will not be interrupted by other devices.

Before any interrupts can be serviced, the interrupt mode must be set. The Z-80 uses three instructions to preset the interrupt mode. These instructions are set interrupt Mode 0, IM0; set interrupt Mode 1, IM1; and set interrupt Mode 2, IM2. The interrupt mode may be changed at any time, simply by executing one of these two-byte instructions. Even though the Z-80 is placed in the "0" mode when the chip is reset, we recommend using the IM0 instruction, since it is impossible to tell what interrupt mode the TRS-80 has preset in the Z-80, although we suspect that it is Mode 1.

Once the interrupt mode has been set, and the interrupt enabled, the TRS-80 can accept and process interrupt request signals, calling interrupt service subroutines that are located in an area that you have "protected" in read/write memory. Once the interrupt service subroutine has been completed, an assembly-language return, RET, instruction is used to cause the Z-80 to retrieve the return address from the stack area. Prior to the return instruction, you will probably want to place an enable interrupt instruction in the subroutine, so that the Z-80 interrupt input is re-enabled. The EI instruction does not take effect until *after* the execution of the *next* instruction. This means that if an EI instruction is executed just before a RET instruction, the computer will return to the main program before another waiting interrupt will be processed.

The Z-80 instruction set contains two special return instructions that are available for use at the end of interrupt subroutines. These two instructions, RETN, and RETI, are used at the end of non-maskable, and regular interrupt service subroutines, respectively. Since the nonmaskable interrupt is not available for interfacing use in the TRS-80, the RETN instruction is of no use to us. The RETI instruction is generally used only when Z-80 family devices are to be used with the Z-80 chip. The instruction is used to "inform" these family chips that the end of an interrupt service subroutine has been reached. Since we will not be discussing any of the special Z-80 family chips, this instruction will not be used, either. These instructions are important if you have any plans to apply the Z-80 chip, itself, to any interfacing tasks, and you should be aware that they are available, and that they have special functions.

Now that the Z-80 interrupt control instructions have been described, it is a fairly simple matter to apply them to a situation in which an interrupt is to be used with the TRS-80. We will assume that an interrupt instruction port has been interfaced to the TRS-80, and that the TRS-80 has been appropriately modified (Figs. 5-4 or 5-5). (If you are using the TRS-80 interface breadboard, remember to connect the $\overline{\text{INTAK}}$ signal to one of the $\overline{\text{INP}}$ $\overline{\text{REQ}}$ inputs, too.) The first thing that the program must do is to set up the particular interrupt mode that is to be used, and then enable the interrupt. This can be done by using DATA statements, and POKE-ing the decimal equivalents of the op-codes into memory, so that they may be executed by a call to a user's subroutine. This is shown in Example 5-1. Once the interrupt mode has been set, and the interrupt enabled, the interrupt may be used. In this case, we have assumed that Mode 0 interrupts will be used, so two

Example 5-1. A Sample Program To Load the Interrupt Set-Up Information Into a Protected Section of the TRS-80 Memory

```
200 POKE 32100,237:POKE 32101,70:POKE 32102,251:POKE 32103,201
220 POKE 16526,100:POKE 16527,125
240 POKE 16399,195:POKE 16400,0:POKE 16401,125
250 Z = USR(0)
```

other tasks must be performed prior to the actual use of the interrupt. First, the interrupt service subroutine must be loaded into memory, and second, a jump instruction (three 8-bit bytes) must be stored in memory, starting at address 400CH, 400FH, or 4012H, depending upon which restart instruction is used at the interrupt instruction port, RST5, RST6, or RST7. Once one of the restart instructions has been chosen, it is a simple matter to find the corresponding vector addresses in Tables 5-1 and 5-2. In the schematic diagram shown in Fig. 5-3, the RST6 instruction has been preset, so the proper jump-to-interrupt service subroutine instruction must be placed in the three consecutive memory addresses, starting at address 400FH, or 16399_{10}. Of course, when you started the TR-80, you had to set aside a portion of the read/write memory for your assembly-language programs.

Before we go any further, let's review the steps in using the interrupt. First, an interrupt instruction port had to be constructed, along with a flag flip-flop circuit. Second, the interrupt mode had to be preset, and the interrupt enabled. Third, the interrupt service subroutine had to be stored in read/write memory, in an area that had been protected. Fourth, the proper restart instruction, assuming Mode 0, had to be chosen, and the required jump instruction placed in the vector points in read/write memory, to link the pointer in the BASIC interpreter ROM with the actual location for the start of the interrupt service subroutine.

A simple interrupt-based program has been illustrated in Example 5-2. While the program has been written in BASIC, there are

Example 5-2. A Simple Interrupt-Based Program

```
10 DATA 229,33,50,125,52,225,251,201
20 DATA 237,70,251,201
30 FOR I=0 TO 7
40 READ D:POKE 32000+I,D
50 NEXT I
60 FOR I=0 TO 3
70 READ D:POKE 32100+I,D
80 NEXT I
90 POKE 16526,100:POKE 16527,125
100 POKE 16399,195:POKE 16400,0:POKE 16401,125
110 Z = USR(0)
120 PRINT@ 832,PEEK(32050)
130 GOTO 120
```

two assembly-language sections that are loaded into protected read/write memory at the start of the BASIC program. The interrupt service subroutine is loaded starting at address 32000 (7D00H), while the interrupt initialization steps are loaded starting at address 32100 (7D64H). At line No. 90, the address of the initialization subroutine is loaded into two special read/write memory locations, so that this may be called with the user call instruction. At line No. 100, the jump instruction and the low and high address bytes are loaded into the locations that start at address 16399 (400FH), to link the interrupt with the proper interrupt service subroutine. The last steps in the BASIC program call the subroutine that sets up the interrupt for Mode 0, and enables the interrupt. Then, the computer simply remains in an endless loop, printing the value that is contained in a memory location, at address 32050 (7D32H).

Now, let's examine exactly what the two assembly-language subroutines do. The initialization subroutine, and the interrupt service subroutines are listed in Example 5-3. The initialization subroutine sets the interrupt for Mode 0 operation, enables the interrupt, and then returns to the BASIC program. The interrupt service subroutine may be required at any time, whenever an interrupt is requested, and an RST6 instruction is jammed into the Z-80. The simple interrupt service subroutine that we have illustrated has only one purpose; it will increment the contents of a memory location by one, each time an interrupt is detected. The memory location that the interrupt service subroutine uses is the same one that is PEEKed at in the BASIC program, so that the effects of any interrupts may be observed. The interrupt service subroutine uses the Z-80 internal H and L registers to temporarily point to the memory location that is to be incremented. Since the values that are present in the H and L registers may be important to the BASIC program, they

Example 5-3. Assembly-Language Programs for an RST6 Interrupt Device, and for Interrupt Initialization

7D	00	E5	INTSUB,	PUSHH	/SAVE REG H & L ON THE STACK
7D	01	21		LXIH	/LOAD THE ADDRESS OF THE LOCN
7D	02	32		32	/TO BE INCREMENTED
7D	03	7D		7D	/DECIMAL 32050
7D	04	34		INRM	/INCREMENT IT
7D	05	E1		POPH	/RESTORE REG H & L FROM STACK
7D	06	FB		EI	/RE-ENABLE INTERRUPT
7D	07	C9		RET	/RETURN TO BASIC PROGRAM
7D	64	ED		IMO	/SET INTERRUPT MODE 0
7D	65	46		46	
7D	66	FB		EI	/ENABLE INTERRUPT
7D	67	C9		RET	/RETURN FROM BASIC SUBROUTINE CALL

are stored on the stack with a PUSHH instruction. The H and L registers are then loaded with the address of the location that is to have its contents incremented, and the increment operation is performed. The POPH instruction retrieves the previous values for the H and L registers, so that as far as the BASIC program is concerned, they were not used, or disturbed in any way. The subroutine then enables the interrupt, and returns to the BASIC interpreter. The interrupt enabling action does not actually take place until the computer has returned control back to the program that was interrupted. Let us make it clear that the interrupt may take place during one of the many hundreds, or thousands of assembly-language steps that make up the endless loop of printing and jumping in the BASIC program. When this program is interrupted by the device shown in Fig. 5-3, you will observe an increasing count displayed at one point on the video display screen. One count is added to the number displayed, after each interrupt, up to a maximum of 255 counts, the maximum for eight binary bits.

The simple BASIC program will be able to print the increasing value, without any difficulty. A PRINT statement could be used, although the printed values would be rapidly changing, and "flowing" up the video screen. Just to prove that the interrupts will be serviced during the execution of the BASIC program, a time delay routine may be added to the program to slow down the display rate:

```
125 FOR T=0 TO 1000: NEXT T
```

Now, when multiple interrupts are serviced, the *total* accumulated count will be displayed by the PRINT command. The interrupts that have caused the count to be incremented have occurred during the time delay, GOTO and PRINT commands. If the interrupts were to be generated at a fast enough rate, you would be able to observe a significant slowing down of the time between the "printing" of the different values, due to the time that the computer would use to service the many interrupts.

Multiple Mode 0 Interrupts

Now that a simple interrupting device has been interfaced to the TRS-80, we will examine the use of two interrupting devices, operating in Mode 0. To handle a second interrupting device, it is necessary to decide which one of the remaining vector addresses will be used to point to the interrupt service subroutine for the new interrupt device. In this case, the RST7 vector has been chosen, since it is very easy to switch back and forth between the binary values for an RST6 (11110111) and an RST7 (11111111) instruction at the interrupt instruction port. To use the new interrupt, the interrupt service subroutine must be given some task, say, decrementing the number that is incremented by the other interrupt service subroutine. In order to decrement the contents of memory location 32050, the same type of interrupt service subroutine is used, except that (1) the increment instruction must be changed to a decrement instruction, and (2) the new subroutine must be located in an unused section of read/write memory. In this example, the two subroutines will be located close together. The new address information and the jump instruction must be placed in the proper memory locations so that the computer is pointed to the decrementing subroutine whenever an RST7 interrupt occurs.

A schematic diagram for a simple interrupt controller is shown in Fig. 5-6. In this control circuit, two separate flip-flops are used to generate individual interrupt signals, one for the RST6 interrupt device, and one for the RST7 interrupt device. The individual interrupt request signals are gated together to provide a single interrupt request line to the Z-80 microprocessor chip $\overline{\text{INT}}$ input. Once an interrupt has been acknowledged, the three-state interrupt instruction port transmits its information to the CPU over the data bus lines. In this case, the RST7 flip-flop determines the state of the D3 data bit, to generate an RST6, or an RST7 instruction. This circuit has been kept quite simple by ignoring the possibility that the

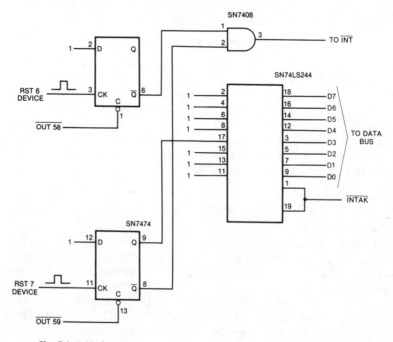

Fig. 5-6. A Mode 0 interrupt control circuit for two devices, RST6 and RST7.

two flip-flops might be clocked simultaneously. While this can occur in real interrupt systems, we will not consider it in this example.

A BASIC program is listed in Example 5-4 which incorporates steps that load various assembly-language program steps into read/write memory. This is a new version of the program listed in Example 5-2. The main differences are that an additional line of assembly-language op-codes has been added to this program to provide the necessary program steps to decrement the count for

Example 5-4. A BASIC Program To Load Interrupt Control Programs for Two Devices

```
 10 DATA 229,33,50,125,52,225,251,201
 15 DATA 229,33,50,125,53,225,251,201
 20 DATA 237,70,251,201
 30 FOR I=0 TO 15
 40 READ D:POKE 32000+I,D
 50 NEXT I
 60 FOR I=0 TO 3
 70 READ D:POKE 32100+I,D
 80 NEXT I
 90 POKE 16526,100:POKE 16527,125
100 POKE 16399,195:POKE 16400,0:POKE 16401,125
105 POKE 16402,195:POKE 16403,8:POKE 16404,125
110 Z=USR(0)
120 PRINT@ 832,PEEK(32050)
130 GOTO 120
```

RST7 interrupts. There are also steps that load the proper three-byte jump instruction into the vector address table, starting at address 16402_{10} (see Table 5-2). There are no changes in the steps that are used to initialize the Z-80 interrupt mode. When this program is running, an interrupt from the RST6 device will cause the displayed count to be incremented, while an interrupt from the RST7 device will cause the count to be decremented. This example is rather simple, but it illustrates a number of important things: how assembly-language program steps may be loaded into the TRS-80 read/write memory, how two interrupting devices may be handled, and how a short user subroutine may be called to initialize the Z-80 interrupt mode.

Mode 1 Interrupts

The Z-80 may be configured so that when it responds to an interrupt signal at its $\overline{INT}$ input, it will always call an interrupt service subroutine at a fixed address. This interrupt mode is particularly useful when only a single interrupting device will be used with the Z-80, since the starting address of the subroutine is already defined in the Z-80 memory address "space," starting at address 38H, or 56_{10}.

Only an interrupt request flip-flop is required. In the TRS-80, the BASIC interpreter ROM contains a jump instruction at address 38H that points the computer to address 4012H, or 16402_{10}. Another jump instruction may be placed at that address, to point the computer to the start of the actual interrupt service subroutine.

If multiple interrupts are required, the Mode 1 interrupt may still be used. All of the interrupt request flip-flop outputs would be gated together, to generate a composite interrupt request, as was the case in the Mode 0 interrupt example (see Fig. 5-6). In this way, any of the flip-flops can generate an interrupt request signal. Once the interrupt service subroutine is started, the Z-80 starts to execute user-provided assembly-language program steps that test various bits at an input port, so that it can determine which flip-flop is requesting interrupt service. If a bit is detected as being a logic one, this indicates that the corresponding flip-flop is requesting service, and this can cause the computer to branch to a portion of the interrupt service subroutine that is set up to service the corresponding device. This type of polled interrupt action was used extensively by many early minicomputers, such as Digital Equipment Corporation's PDP-8 family.

Even though the program shown in Example 5-4 has been written so that two interrupting devices can be controlled, it can be easily modified so that it can control the RST7 interrupt device in Mode 1 operation. Actually, the only change that is necessary is one that involves the second byte in the interrupt mode control instruction. This is changed in the DATA statement at line No. 20 from a 70 to an 86 (see Table 5-3). Once this change has been made, the program may be run as it is. It will only respond to the interrupt that starts its service subroutine at address 38H, or 56. In this program, that is the same as the RST7 interrupt. Thus, whenever the TRS-80 is interrupted, the value displayed by the BASIC program will be decremented. Changing the binary bit pattern at the interrupt instruction port has no effect on the Z-80, since in the "1" mode, only the single interrupt service subroutine is implemented.

It would be quite nice if BASIC instructions could be used to poll the input port, checking for the interrupting device, and taking the appropriate actions to service it. The INP, AND, IF, and THEN commands would be particularly useful. However, once interrupted, the TRS-80 starts to execute user-supplied assembly-language program steps, and it does not get back to the BASIC interpreter until after the interrupt task has been completed. In any case, the assembly-language program steps are going to be able to detect the interrupting device much more quickly than could equivalent BASIC-language steps. Since speed of response is probably the reason that leads to the use of interrupts and assembly-language programs, the use of BASIC-language steps to process interrupts is self-defeating.

Looking at the information in Table 5-2, it appears that only three of the vector locations are available in the TRS-80 for Mode 0 interrupt vectors. However, if the Mode 1 operation is selected, many additional interrupts may be added to the TRS-80, as shown in Fig. 5-7. The interrupt request signals from all of the flip-flops are gated together, as mentioned previously, and a second signal is routed to an input port, so that it may be sensed by software commands. There are some important points that should be noted here. The flip-flops are cleared with individual output commands, as was the case for Mode 0 interrupts, and assembly-language steps, rather than BASIC-language steps, would be used to generate these control pulses that clear the interrupt flip-flops. Each flip-flop would be cleared, either after it was detected, or after its corresponding interrupt service subroutine was completed.

There is a definite *priority* assigned to the interrupting devices, since there is a definite order in which the individual flag bits will be detected. Suppose that two interrupts occur at the same time. As the computer sequences through the individual flag bits, testing

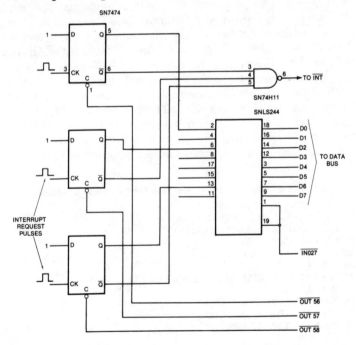

Fig. 5-7. Schematic diagram of an interrupt control circuit for three Mode 1 polled interrupt devices.

227

each, say from bit D7 to bit D0, bit D5 will be tested before bits D4, D3, D2, D1, and D0, and so on. This establishes the priority, so that if bits D5 and D3 are the two simultaneous interrupt flag bits, the device that corresponds to flag bit D5 will be serviced before the device that corresponds to bit D3. If you are using only a few simple interrupts, and if the interrupting devices can "wait" while others are serviced, then the Z-80 Mode 1 type of interrupt is quite useful, and easy to implement.

Mode 2 Interrupts

The Mode 2 interrupt is very similar to the Mode 0 interrupt, except that the Mode 0 interrupt is limited to the use of eight restart instructions that call interrupt service subroutines at specific locations within the computer memory. In the TRS-80, only three of these locations are "free" for the user's own interrupt schemes. When the Z-80 is used in Mode 2, an almost unlimited number of interrupting devices may be accommodated, and their service subroutines may be located almost anywhere in memory. To illustrate the use of this type of interrupt, the basic interrupt programs that have been used previously are used again as interrupt service subroutines that will be controlled by Mode 2 interrupts. The BASIC control program is illustrated in Example 5-5. Some simple changes have been made so that the display will not display the incremented or decremented value, but rather the ASCII character which corresponds to the 8-bit value. The four assembly-language steps that were loaded in previous examples to initialize the Z-80 interrupt mode and then enable the interrupt, have been expanded so that the Z-80 I register may be loaded. This requires an additional four bytes to load the I register with the value 7DH, or 125. This is the high address byte of the address that will be used to locate the starting address of the interrupt service subroutine in a table of

Example 5-5. A BASIC Control Program for Two Mode 2 Interrupts

```
10 DATA 229,33,0,62,52,225,251,201
20 DATA 229,33,0,62,53,225,251,201
30 DATA 62,125,237,71,237,94,251,201
40 FOR I=0 TO 15
50 READ D:POKE 32000+I,D
60 NEXT I
70 FOR I=0 TO 7: READ D:POKE 32100+I,D
90 NEXT I
100 POKE 16526,100:POKE 16527,125
110 POKE 32050,0:POKE 35051,125
120 POKR 32052,8:POKE 32053,125
130 Z=USR(0)
140 CLS
150 GOTO 150
```

such addresses (see Fig. 5-2). The low address is supplied by the interrupting device, with bit D0 being preset to a logic zero. In this example, the starting addresses of the two interrupt service subroutines are placed in the address table, which starts at address 32050_{10}. The low address byte is located at this specific address, with the high address byte located at address 32051_{10}, and so on for any other addresses stored in the table.

Now, let us see what happens when the Z-80 is interrupted by an external device, when the Z-80 is ready for Mode 2 interrupts. When the interrupt is sensed, the Z-80 completes the execution of the present assembly-language operation, and pushes a return address onto the stack. It then acknowledges the interrupt, and accepts eight bits of information from the interrupt instruction port. When Mode 2 interrupts are used, however, this byte that is transferred to the Z-80 is actually a *low address byte, and not an actual instruction.* The Z-80 "combines" the low address that has been provided by the interrupting device, with the high address stored in the internal I register, to generate a 16-bit address pointer. This address points to entries in the address table, and the addresses in the table are the ones that actually define the start of the individual interrupt service subroutines. In Example 5-5, there are only two address entries in the table, one for the subroutine at address 7D00H, or 32000_{10}, and one for the subroutine at address 7D08H, or 32008_{10}. These are the starting addresses of the "incrementing" and "decrementing" subroutines used in previous examples. Since the *address* for the start of the incrementing subroutine is located in the table, starting at address 7D32H, the I register must be pre-programmed with the value 7DH, or 125_{10}. The initialization steps in the BASIC program provide for this initialization. The interrupting device provides the low address byte, 32H, or 00110010_2. To access the decrementing subroutine, the interrupting device supplies a low address byte of 34H, or 00110100_2. We refer you to Fig. 5-2, for a schematic diagram of the operation of a Mode 2 interrupt. While this mode is quite powerful, and easy to use, it does require the use of the Z-80 I register, and also the use of an address table, for the starting addresses of the interrupt service subroutines. Our initial experiments suggest that the Radio-Shack BASIC interpreter program for the TRS-80 does not use the I register, but there is no way to be sure that it will not be modified by some portion of the interpreter that we have not used, or by other available programs.

PRIORITY INTERRUPTS

The use of multiple interrupts for Mode 1 interrupt operation has already been discussed. This type of multiple interrupt scheme is fairly simple, since each of the possible interrupting devices is checked by the same interrupt service subroutine, to determine which devices require servicing. Simultaneous interrupts may occur, but each device must wait its turn, to be checked, and serviced, if necessary. When the Z-80 is used with either Mode 0 or Mode 2 interrupts, multiple interrupt systems are more complex, since each interrupting device must supply either an op-code for an instruction, or the low address btye for an address table entry. The external interrupt-controlling circuits must have some way in which to arbitrate between interrupting devices, so that only one device at a time is serviced by an interrupt service subroutine. It is fortunate that a *priority encoder* chip is available to perform most of these arbitrating functions. The SN74148 chip is illustrated in a pin configuration diagram, Fig. 5-8. A truth table for this chip is also provided in Fig. 5-8. This chip can be thought of as working in a manner that is the reverse of a decoder chip such as the SN7442. Whenever one of the eight inputs to the SN74148 chip is grounded, the corresponding binary code is provided at the three outputs. *The codes are inverted,* so that if the "7" input is grounded, the 3-

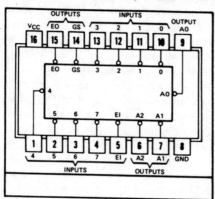

(A) Pin configuration.

INPUTS									OUTPUTS				
EI	0	1	2	3	4	5	6	7	A2	A1	A0	GS	EO
H	X	X	X	X	X	X	X	X	H	H	H	H	H
L	H	H	H	H	H	H	H	H	H	H	H	H	L
L	X	X	X	X	X	X	X	L	L	L	L	L	H
L	X	X	X	X	X	X	L	H	L	L	H	L	H
L	X	X	X	X	X	L	H	H	L	H	L	L	H
L	X	X	X	X	L	H	H	H	L	H	H	L	H
L	X	X	X	L	H	H	H	H	H	L	L	L	H
L	X	X	L	H	H	H	H	H	H	L	H	L	H
L	X	L	H	H	H	H	H	H	H	H	L	L	H
L	L	H	H	H	H	H	H	H	H	H	H	L	H

(B) Truth table.

Courtesy Texas Instruments, Inc.

Fig. 5-8. Pin configuration and truth table for SN74148 priority encoder chip.

bit binary output is 000. In this circuit, it is possible to have a number of inputs grounded at the same time, so the chip must decide which binary code it is to output at pins A0, A1, and A2. Thus, the chip decides upon the *priority*, so that when more than one of the eight inputs are grounded, only one specific code is output by the chip. Thus, if the "7" and "3" inputs are both grounded, only the code that corresponds to the "7" will be output. The exact behavior of the SN74148 is described by the information in the truth table. The $\overline{GS}$ output is a logic zero whenever any of the inputs is grounded.

The SN74148 priority encoder chip may be used in a multiple interrupt system to provide the necessary encoding of the address or op-code information that is required by the Z-80 for Mode 0 and Mode 2 interrupts. A simple interrupt circuit is shown in Fig. 5-9. In this example, the Z-80 is used for Mode 0 interrupts, so that the interrupt instruction port will furnish the Z-80 with the various op-codes for the restart instructions. Some of the bits at the interrupt instruction port have been hard-wired to logic one, since these bits remain constant in the op-codes for restart instructions. The SN-74148 priority encoder chip has been used to furnish the "changing" bits in the instruction, so that the op-codes for RST0 (11000111) through RST7 (11111111) may be easily generated, one at a time. Since the TRS-80 uses all of the vector addresses, except for those that correspond to restart instructions, RST5, RST6, and RST7, only those three op-codes should be generated. Thus, the nonallowed inputs to the SN74148 chip have been permanently hard-wired to

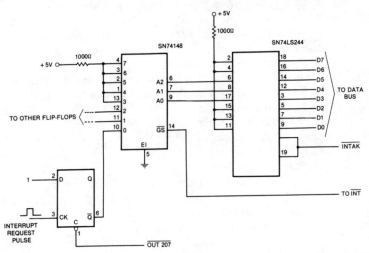

Fig. 5-9. A three-input priority interrupt controller circuit, for devices RST7 (shown), RST6, and RST5.

logic one. The three remaining inputs, "2," "1," and "0," may be used. Remember, that since the SN74148 generates inverter binary outputs, the respective outputs for these three inputs are 101, 110, and 111. This means that if the "0" input is grounded, the op-code for the RST7 instruction (11111111) will be present at the inputs to the interrupt instruction port. In this circuit, the "2" input has the highest priority, causing a vector to address 28H, or 40_{10}. The vector addresses, and their respective priorities are listed in Table 5-4.

Table 5-4. Priority Interrupt Vector Addresses (Fig. 5-9)

Active Input	Code Generated	Restart Instruction	Address	
			Hex	Decimal
0	111	RST7	0	0
1	110	RST6	8	8
2	101	RST5	10	16
3	100	RST4*	18	24
4	011	RST3*	20	32
5	010	RST2*	28	40
6	001	RST1*	30	48
7	000	RST0*	38	56

*Not available for use with the TRS-80.

When this circuit is used, the priority encoder $\overline{GS}$ output is used as the interrupt signal that is sent to the Z-80. It will be a logic zero, as long as there is an interrupting device that is waiting to be serviced. In Fig. 5-8, an interrupt flip-flop has been shown. When this flip-flop receives an interrupt request from its corresponding device, its $\overline{Q}$ output becomes a logic zero, causing the SN74148 to assert the $\overline{GS}$ output, and also causing it to output 111 to the interrupt instruction port. Once the interrupt service subroutine has serviced this device, several assembly-language program steps are used to generate an $\overline{OUT\ 207}$ pulse that clears the interrupt flip-flop. Each of the other interrupt inputs to the SN74148 chip would also use flip-flops in a similar configuration, except that different output control signals would be used to clear them.

Let us suppose that two interrupting devices request an interrupt at the same time, using the circuit shown in Fig. 5-8. One is the "0" interrupting device, and the other is the "2" interrupting device. Since the "2" input of the SN74148 chip has a higher priority than the "1" or "0" input, the encoder outputs the binary code 101 (remember that this is the inverse of the value for the input, which would be 010). This output is combined with the logic one bits at the interrupt instruction port to generate an RST5 instruction, which is read into the computer by the $\overline{INTAK}$ signal. To service this interrupt, the computer vectors to the proper interrupt service sub-routine and completes its tasks. One of the first things that the interrupt service subroutine does is to clear the interrupt flip-flop associated with this interrupt. At the end of the subroutine, the interrupt is re-enabled with an EI instruction, and the computer returns to the main BASIC interpreter program. Since another interrupt is waiting, the computer immediately recognizes the "0" interrupt, vectoring to the proper address for the RST7 instruction. Again, one of the first tasks in this interrupt service subroutine is to clear the interrupt flip-flop, in this case, with an $\overline{\text{OUT 207}}$ pulse. At the end of this interrupt service subroutine, the interrupt is re-enabled, but no other interrupts are awaiting service, so the BASIC interpreter again takes control of the computer.

This same type of a priority encoder scheme may be used in the Z-80 Mode 2 interrupt operations. The SN74148 priority encoder simply furnishes bits D1, D2, and D3 to the interrupt instruction port, while the other bits are wired to represent the low address of the interrupt address table, located in the computer read/write memory. Bit D0 is not used, being preset to a logic zero, by the Z-80 during the Mode 2 interrupts.

There are other multiple interrupt schemes that may be used with the Z-80, in either Mode 0, or Mode 2 operation. Some of these schemes are more complex than the example that we have provided, while others are less complex. Our main purpose here has been to introduce you to the idea of using a number of interrupts at the same time. As we noted at the start of this chapter, there are good reasons for avoiding multiple interrupts, if that is at all possible.

INTERRUPT APPLICATIONS

It is difficult to discuss specific interrupt applications, without going into a great deal of assembly-language programming, so examples will be described in general terms so that you will better understand the possible uses of interrupts in a TRS-80 computer system. A high-speed printer application, and a USART application will be described.

In the first interrupt application, a small high-speed electrostatic printer is interfaced to the computer. The printer can print three 21-character lines in about 1 second, including time for the carriage returns and line feeds. Once the printer has been started, the print-head moves across the entire width of the paper, regardless of whether new characters have been provided to the interface. The printer interface circuit provides a flag signal to the computer to indicate that the printer is ready for the next character. This signal allows the computer to provide each new character as the printer is ready for it. If a new character is not provided to the printer when it is ready, it will continue to print the previous character, until the new character has been supplied. Thus, the computer must act quickly to service the printer requests for new characters. It is impossible to control this printer by using a Level II BASIC program. The BASIC program just can't keep up with the high-speed data requirements of the printer. A printed line that should be printed as ABCDEFGHIJKLMNOPQ, turns out as AAAAAAABBB-BBBBCCCCCCC, instead. The solution to the problem is to use the printer "ready" flag as an interrupt to the TRS-80. The simplest interface/software scheme would use a single Mode 1 interrupt, and a single interrupt service subroutine.

The interrupt service subroutine would obtain the next ASCII character from a "protected" area of read/write memory, and output it to the printer. The system would also clear the interrupt flag, re-enable the Z-80 interrupt, and return to the BASIC program. Another solution might involve an assembly-language subroutine that would control *all* of the printer functions. Of course, the ASCII values would have to be set up in a short file, or array, in read/write memory, so that they would be available to both the interrupt service subroutine, and to the BASIC program that would actually generate the information that must be printed. In this example, the printer operated at a rate that was faster than that which could be managed by a BASIC program. Thus, the interrupt provided an alternate method of controlling the printer.

In the previous chapter, a great deal of time was spent discussing the USART chip, and how it is interfaced to, and used with, the TRS-80 computer. There may be times when the USART receiver is operated at such a high data rate that it will receive characters faster than they can be input and processed by a BASIC-language program. This means that a BASIC-language control program would lose a number of characters. Luckily, the USART receiver ready (RxRDY) flag is provided as an output pin, as well as a bit that can be checked with software. The RxRDY signal may be used to interrupt the TRS-80, indicating that a new piece of information has been received. An assembly-language input routine could be used to service the USART interrupt, storing the information, clearing the flag, re-enabling the interrupt, and so on. At fairly high data transfer rates it is doubtful whether the TRS-80 BASIC interpreter could keep up with a steady stream of information transmitted to the USART chip.

It is only fair to say that there are other solutions to these two interfacing problems, as presented by the printer and USART. While software solutions have been described here, hardware solutions are also possible. In fact, the TRS-80 could be interfaced to the printer through a small buffer memory that would be used to contain a complete line of ASCII characters. The memory could then "dump" them to the printer as they were required, completely independent of the computer. Likewise, a small buffer memory could be used between the USART and the TRS-80, but this would be more complex, since the USART must be controlled by a computer (unless you want to add *a lot* of additional hardware). In this case, a *slave* processor might be considered, simply to control the USART. (See *8085A Cookbook*, Howard W. Sams & Co., Inc., Indianapolis, IN 46206.) The main point is that there are frequently a number of possible solutions to hardware and software problems. By having a good understanding of each area, you increase your skills at solving computer interfacing problems.

American Standard Code
for Information Interchange
(ASCII) Code Chart

		LEAST SIGNIFICANT BITS								
		000	001	010	011	100	101	110	111	
	00000	NUL	SOH	STX	ETX	EOT	ENQ	ACK	BEL	CONTROL
	00001	BS	HT	LF	VT	FF	CR	SO	SI	FUNC-
	00010	DLE	DC1	DC2	DC3	DC4	NAK	SO	ETB	TIONS
	00011	CAN	EM	SUB	ESC	FS	GS	RS	US	
	00100	SP	/	"	#	$	%	&	"	
	00101	(	)	*	s	'	'	.	/	
MOST	00110	0	1	2	3	4	5	6	7	
SIGNIF-	00111	8	9	:	;	<	=	>	?	
ICANT	01000	@	A	B	C	D	E	F	G	
BITS	01001	H	I	J	K	L	M	N	O	
	01010	P	Q	R	S	T	U	V	W	
	01011	X	Y	Z	[	\	]	↑	—	
	01100	'	a	b	c	d	e	f	g	
	01101	h	i	j	k	l	m	n	o	
	01110	p	q	r	s	t	u	v	w	
	01111	x	y	z	{	:	}	∼	DEL	

Control Character Functions

NUL = Null
SOH = Start of Heading
STX = Start of Text
ETX = End of Text
EOT = End of Transmission
ENQ = Enquiry
ACK = Acknowledge
BEL = Bell (ring)
BS = Backspace
HT = Horizontal Tabulation
LF = Line Feed
VT = Vertical Tabulation
FF = Form Feed
CR = Carriage Return
SO = Shift Out
SI = Shift In

DLE = Data Link Escape
DC1 = Device Control 1
DC2 = Device Control 2
DC3 = Device Control 3
DC4 = Device Control 4 (Stop)
NAK = Negative Acknowledge
SYN = Synchronous Idle
ETB = End of Transmission Block
CAN = Cancel
EM = End of Medium
SUB = Substitute
ESC = Escape
FS = File Separator
GS = Group Separator
RS = Record Separator
US = Unit Separator
DEL = Delete

IM6402/IM6403 Universal Asynchronous Receiver Transmitter (UART) Data Sheet*

---

* Reprinted by permission of Intersil, Inc.

INTERSIL

FEATURES

- Low Power — Less Than 10mW Typ. at 2MHz
- Operation Up to 4MHz Clock — IM6402A
- Programmable Word Length, Stop Bits and Parity
- Automatic Data Formatting and Status Generation
- Compatible with Industry Standard UART's — IM6402
- On-Chip Oscillator with External Crystal — IM6403
- Operating Voltage —
  - IM6402-1/03-1: 4-7V
  - IM6402A/03A: 4-11V
  - IM6402/03: 4-7V

GENERAL DESCRIPTION

The IM6402 and IM6403 are CMOS/LSI UART's for interfacing computers or microprocessors to asynchronous serial data channels. The receiver converts serial start, data, parity and stop bits to parallel data verifying proper code transmission, parity, and stop bits. The transmitter converts parallel data into serial form and automatically adds start, parity, and stop bits.

The data word length can be 5, 6, 7 or 8 bits. Parity may be odd or even. Parity checking and generation can be inhibited. The stop bits may be one or two (or one and one-half when transmitting 5 bit code). Serial data format is shown in Figure 7.

The IM6402 and IM6403 can be used in a wide range of applications including modems, printers, peripherals and remote data acquisition systems. CMOS/LSI technology permits operating clock frequencies up to 4.0MHz (250K Baud) an improvement of 10 to 1 over previous PMOS UART designs. Power requirements, by comparison, are reduced from 670mW to 10mW. Status logic increases flexibility and simplifies the user interface.

The IM6402 differs from the IM6403 on pins 2, 17, 19, 22, and 40 as shown in Figure 5. The IM6403 utilizes pin 2 as a crystal divide control and pins 17 and 40 for an inexpensive crystal oscillator. TBREmpty and DReady are always active. All other input and output functions of the IM6402 and IM6403 are identical.

PIN CONFIGURATION

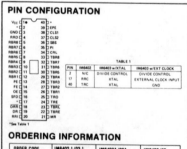

PIN	IM6402	IM6403 w/XTAL	IM6403 w/EXT CLOCK
2	N/C	DIVIDE CONTROL	DIVIDE CONTROL
17	RRC	XTAL	EXTERNAL CLOCK INPUT
40	TRC	XTAL	GND

TABLE 1

*See Table 1

PACKAGE DIMENSIONS

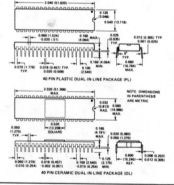

40 PIN PLASTIC DUAL-IN-LINE PACKAGE (PL)

NOTE: DIMENSIONS IN PARENTHESIS ARE METRIC

40 PIN CERAMIC DUAL-IN-LINE PACKAGE (DL)

ORDERING INFORMATION

ORDER CODE	IM6402-1/03-1	IM6402A/03A	IM6402/03
PLASTIC PKG	IM6402-1/03-1IPL	IM6402/03-AIPL	IM6402/03-IPL
CERAMIC PKG	IM6402-1/03-1IDL	IM6402/03-AIDL	—
MILITARY TEMP	IM6402-1/03-1MDL	IM6402/03-AMDL	—
MILITARY TEMP. WITH 883B	IM6402-1/03-1 MDL/883B	IM6402/03-AMDL/ 883B	—

INTERSIL, INC., 10710 N. TANTAU AVE., CUPERTINO, CA 95014

Printed in U.S.A.

(408) 996-5000 TWX: 910-338-0171

IM6402/IM6403

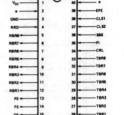

*DIFFERS BETWEEN IM6402 AND IM6403.

FIGURE 1. Pin Configuration

IM6403 FUNCTIONAL PIN DEFINITION

PIN	SYMBOL	DESCRIPTION
1	V_{CC}	Positive Power Supply
2	IM6402-N/C IM6403-Control	No Connection Divide Control High: 2^4 (16) Divider Low: 2^{11} (2048) Divider
3	GND	Ground
4	RRD	A high level on RECEIVER REGISTER DISABLE forces the receiver holding register outputs RBR1-RBR8 to a high impedance state.
5	RBR8	The contents of the RECEIVER REGISTER appear on these three-state outputs. Word formats less than 8 characters are right justified to RBR1.
6	RBR7	See Pin 5 — RBR8
7	RBR6	See Pin 5 — RBR8
8	RBR5	See Pin 5 — RBR8
9	RBR4	See Pin 5 — RBR8
10	RBR3	See Pin 5 — RBR8
11	RBR2	See Pin 5 — RBR8
12	RBR1	See Pin 5 — RBR8
13	PE	A high level on PARITY ERROR indicates that the received parity does not match parity programmed by control bits. The output is active until parity matches on a succeeding character. When parity is inhibited, this output is low.

IM6403 FUNCTIONAL PIN DEFINITION
(Continued)

PIN	SYMBOL	DESCRIPTION
14	FE	A high level on FRAMING ERROR indicates the first stop bit was invalid. FE will stay active until the next valid character's stop bit is received.
15	OE	A high level on OVERRUN ERROR indicates the data received flag was not cleared before the last character was transferred to the receiver buffer register. The Error is reset at the next character's stop bit if DRR has been performed (i.e., DRR: active low).
16	SFD	A high level on STATUS FLAGS DISABLE forces the outputs PE, FE, OE, DR, TBRE to a high impedance state. See Figure 4 and Figure 5.
17	IM6402-RRC IM6403-XTAL or EXT CLK IN	The RECEIVER REGISTER CLOCK is 16X the receiver data rate.
18	DRR	A low level on DATA RECEIVED RESET clears the data received output (DR), to a low level.
19	DR	A high level on DATA RECEIVED indicates a character has been received and transferred to the receiver buffer register.
20	RRI	Serial data on RECEIVER REGISTER INPUT is clocked into the receiver register.
21	MR	A high level on MASTER RESET (MR) clears PE, FE, OE, DR, TRE and sets TBRE, TRO high. Less than 18 clocks after MR goes low, TRE returns high. MR does not clear the receiver buffer register, and is required after power-up.
22	TBRE	A high level on TRANSMITTER BUFFER REGISTER EMPTY indicates the transmitter buffer register has transferred its data to the transmitter register and is ready for new data.
23	TBRL	A low level on TRANSMITTER BUFFER REGISTER LOAD transfers data from inputs TBR1-TBR8 into the transmitter buffer register. A low to high transition on TBRL requests data transfer to the transmitter register. If the transmitter register is busy, transfer is automatically delayed so that the two characters are transmitted end to end. See Figure 2.
24	TRE	A high level on TRANSMITTER REGISTER EMPTY indicates completed transmission of a character including stop bits.
25	TRO	Character data, start data and stop bits appear serially at the TRANSMITTER REGISTER OUTPUT.

241

IM6403 FUNCTIONAL PIN DEFINITION
(Continued)

PIN	SYMBOL	DESCRIPTION
26	TBR1	Character data is loaded into the TRANS-MITTER BUFFER REGISTER via inputs TBR1-TBR8. For character formats less than 8-bits, the TBR8, 7, and 6 Inputs are ignored corresponding to the program-med word length.
27	TBR2	See Pin 26 — TBR1
28	TBR3	See Pin 26 — TBR1
29	TBR4	See Pin 26 — TBR1
30	TBR5	See Pin 26 — TBR1
31	TBR6	See Pin 26 — TBR1
32	TBR7	See Pin 26 — TBR1
33	TBR8	See Pin 26 — TBR1
34	CRL	A high level on CONTROL REGISTER LOAD loads the control register. See Figure 3.

IM6403 FUNCTIONAL PIN DEFINITION
(Continued)

PIN	SYMBOL	DESCRIPTION
35	PI*	A high level on PARITY INHIBIT inhibits parity generation, parity checking and forces PE output low.
36	SBS*	A high level on STOP BIT SELECT selects 1.5 stop bits for a 5 character format and 2 stop bits for other lengths.
37	CLS2*	These inputs program the CHARACTER LENGTH SELECTED. (CLS1 low CLS2 low 5-bits)(CLS1 high CLS2 low 6-bits)(CLS1 low CLS2 high 7-bits)(CLS1 high CLS2 high 8-bits)
38	CLS1*	See Pin 37 — CLS2
39	EPE*	When PI is low, a high level on EVEN PARITY ENABLE generates and checks even parity. A low level selects odd parity.
40	IM6402-TRC IM6403-XTAL or GND	The TRANSMITTER REGISTER CLOCK is 16X the transmit data rate.

*See Table 2 (Control Word Function)

TABLE 2. Control Word Function

CONTROL WORD					DATA BITS	PARITY BIT	STOP BIT(S)
CLS2	CLS1	PI	EPE	SBS			
L	L	L	L	L	5	ODD	1
L	L	L	L	H	5	ODD	1.5
L	L	L	H	L	5	EVEN	1
L	L	L	H	H	5	EVEN	1.5
L	L	H	X	L	5	DISABLED	1
L	L	H	X	H	5	DISABLED	1.5
L	H	L	L	L	6	ODD	1
L	H	L	L	H	6	ODD	2
L	H	L	H	L	6	EVEN	1
L	H	L	H	H	6	EVEN	2
L	H	H	X	L	6	DISABLED	1
L	H	H	X	H	6	DISABLED	2
H	L	L	L	L	7	ODD	1
H	L	L	L	H	7	ODD	2
H	L	L	H	L	7	EVEN	1
H	L	L	H	H	7	EVEN	2
H	L	H	X	L	7	DISABLED	1
H	L	H	X	H	7	DISABLED	2
H	H	L	L	L	8	ODD	1
H	H	L	L	H	8	ODD	2
H	H	L	H	L	8	EVEN	1
H	H	L	H	H	8	EVEN	2
H	H	H	X	L	8	DISABLED	1
H	H	H	X	H	8	DISABLED	2

X = Don't Care

ABSOLUTE MAXIMUM RATINGS

Operating Temperature
Industrial IM6402AI/03AI .... -40°C to +85°C
Military IM6402AM/03AM .... -55°C to +125°C
Storage Temperature .... -65°C to 150°C
Operating Voltage .... 4.0V to 11.0V
Supply Voltage .... +12.0V
Voltage On Any Input or Output Pin .. -0.3V to V$_{CC}$ +0.3V

NOTE: Stresses above those listed under "Absolute Maximum Ratings" may cause permanent device failure. These are stress ratings only and functional operation of the devices at these or any other conditions above those indicated in the operation sections of this specification is not implied. Exposure to absolute maximum rating conditions for extended periods may cause device failures.

D.C. CHARACTERISTICS

TEST CONDITIONS: V$_{CC}$ = 4V to 11V, T$_A$ = Industrial or Military

	SYMBOL	PARAMETER	CONDITIONS	MIN	TYP	MAX	UNITS
1	V$_{IH}$	Input Voltage High		70% V$_{CC}$			V
2	V$_{IL}$	Input Voltage Low				20% V$_{CC}$	V
3	I$_{IL}$	Input Leakage[1]	GND≤V$_{IN}$≤V$_{CC}$	-1.0		1.0	μA
4	V$_{OH}$	Output Voltage High	I$_{OH}$ = 0mA	V$_{CC}$-0.01			V
5	V$_{OL}$	Output Voltage Low	I$_{OL}$ = 0mA			GND+0.01	V
6	I$_{OL}$	Output Leakage	GND≤V$_{OUT}$≤V$_{CC}$	-1.0		1.0	μA
7	I$_{CC}$	Power Supply Current Standby	V$_{IN}$=GND or V$_{CC}$		5.0	500	μA
8	I$_{CC}$	Power Supply Current IM6402A Dynamic	f$_C$ = 4MHz			9.0	mA
9	I$_{CC}$	Power Supply Current IM6403A Dynamic	f$_{CRYSTAL}$=3.58MHz			13.0	mA
10	C$_{IN}$	Input Capacitance[1]			7.0	8.0	pF
11	C$_O$	Output Capacitance[1]			8.0	10.0	pF

NOTE: 1. Except IM6403 XTAL input pins (i.e. pins 17 and 40).

A.C. CHARACTERISTICS

TEST CONDITIONS: V$_{CC}$ = 10V ± 5%, C$_L$ = 50pF, T$_A$ = Industrial or Military

	SYMBOL	PARAMETER	CONDITIONS	MIN	TYP	MAX	UNITS
1	f$_C$	Clock Frequency IM6402A		D.C.	6.0	4.0	MHz
2	f$_{CRYSTAL}$	Crystal Frequency IM6403A			8.0	6.0	MHz
3	t$_{PW}$	Pulse Widths CRL, DRR, TBRL		100	40		ns
4	t$_{MR}$	Pulse Width MR	See Timing Diagrams	400	200		ns
5	t$_{DS}$	Input Data Setup Time	(Figures 2,3,4)	40	0		ns
6	t$_{DH}$	Input Data Hold Time		30	30		ns
7	t$_{EN}$	Output Enable Time			40	70	ns

TIMING DIAGRAMS

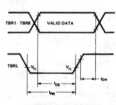

FIGURE 2. Data Input Cycle

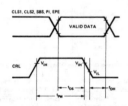

FIGURE 3. Control Register Load Cycle

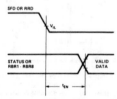

FIGURE 4. Status Flag Enable Time
or Data Output Enable Time

ABSOLUTE MAXIMUM RATINGS

Operating Temperature
Industrial IM6402-1I/03-1I .... -40°C to +85°C
Military IM6402-1M/03-1M .... -55°C to +125°C
Storage Temperature .... -65°C to +150°C
Operating Voltage .... 4.0V to 7.0V
Supply Voltage .... +8.0V
Voltage On Any Input or Output Pin .. -0.3V to V_CC +0.3V

NOTE: Stresses above those listed under "Absolute Maximum Ratings" may cause permanent device failure. These are stress ratings only and functional operation of the devices at these or any other conditions above those indicated in the operation sections of this specification is not implied. Exposure to absolute maximum rating conditions for extended periods may cause device failures.

D.C. CHARACTERISTICS

TEST CONDITIONS: $V_{CC} = 5.0 \pm 10\%$, T_A = Industrial or Military

	SYMBOL	PARAMETER	CONDITIONS	MIN	TYP	MAX	UNITS
1	V_{IH}	Input Voltage High		$V_{CC}-2.0$			V
2	V_{IL}	Input Voltage Low				0.8	V
3	I_{IL}	Input Leakage[1]	GND<V_{IN}<V_{CC}	-1.0		1.0	μA
4	V_{OH}	Output Voltage High	I_{OH}=-0.2mA	2.4			V
5	V_{OL}	Output Voltage Low	I_{OL} = 2.0mA			0.45	V.
6	I_{OL}	Output Leakage	GND<V_{OUT}<V_{CC}	-1.0		1.0	μA
7	I_{CC}	Power Supply Current Standby	V_{IN}=GND or V_{CC}		1.0	100	μA
8	I_{CC}	Power Supply Current IM6402 Dynamic	f_C = 2MHz			1.9	mA
9	I_{CC}	Power Supply Current IM6403 Dynamic	$f_{CRYSTAL}$=3.58MHz			5.5	mA
10	C_{IN}	Input Capacitance[1]			7.0	8.0	pF
11	C_O	Output Capacitance[1]			8.0	10.0	pF ·

NOTE: 1. Except IM6403 XTAL input pins (i.e. pins 17 and 40).

A.C. CHARACTERISTICS

TEST CONDITIONS: $V_{CC} = 5.0V \pm 10\%$, $C_L = 50pF$, T_A = Industrial or Military

	SYMBOL	PARAMETER	CONDITIONS	MIN	TYP	MAX	UNITS
1	f_C	Clock Frequency IM6402		D.C.	3.0	2.0	MHz
2	$f_{CRYSTAL}$	Crystal Frequency IM6403			4.0	3.58	MHz
3	t_{PW}	Pulse Widths CRL, $\overline{DRR}$, $\overline{TBRL}$		150	50		ns
4	t_{MR}	Pulse Width MR	See Timing Diagrams	400	200		ns
5	t_{DS}	Input Data Setup Time	(Figures 2,3,4)	50	20		ns
6	t_{DH}	Input Data Hold Time		60	40		ns
7	t_{EN}	Output Enable Time			80	160	ns

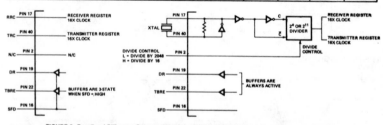

FIGURE 5. Functional Difference Between IM6402 and IM6403 UART (6403 has On-Chip 4/11 Stage Divider)

The IM6403 differs from the IM6402 on three inputs (RRC, TRC, pin 2) as shown in Figure 5. Two outputs (TBRE, DR) are not three-state as on the IM6402, but are always active. The on-chip divider and oscillator allow an inexpensive crystal to be used as a timing source rather than additional circuitry such as baud rate generators. For example, a color TV crystal at 3.579545MHz results in a baud rate of 109.2Hz for an easy teletype interface (Figure 11). A 9600 baud interface may be implemented using a 2.4576MHz crystal with the divider set to divide by 16.

ABSOLUTE MAXIMUM RATINGS

Operating Temperature
IM6402/03 .... -40°C to +85°C
Storage Temperature .... -65°C to 150°C
Operating Voltage .... 4.0V to 7.0V
Supply Voltage .... +8.0V
Voltage On Any Input or Output Pin .. -0.3V to V_{CC} +0.3V

NOTE: Stresses above those listed under "Absolute Maximum Ratings" may cause permanent device failure. These are stress ratings only and functional operation of the devices at these or any other conditions above those indicated in the operation sections of this specification is not implied. Exposure to absolute maximum rating conditions for extended periods may cause device failures.

D.C. CHARACTERISTICS

TEST CONDITIONS: $V_{CC} = 5.0 \pm 10\%$, $T_A = -40°C$ to $+85°C$

	SYMBOL	PARAMETER	CONDITIONS	MIN	TYP	MAX	UNITS
1	V_{IH}	Input Voltage High		V_{CC}-2.0			V
2	V_{IL}	Input Voltage Low				0.8	V
3	I_{IL}	Input Leakage[1]	GND<V_{IN}<V_{CC}	-5.0		5.0	μA
4	V_{OH}	Output Voltage High	I_{OH} = -0.2mA	2.4			V
5	V_{OL}	Output Voltage Low	I_{OL}=1.6mA			0.45	V
6	I_{OL}	Output Leakage	GND<V_{OUT}<V_{CC}	-5.0		5.0	μA
7	I_{CC}	Power Supply Current Standby	V_{IN}=GND or V_{CC}		1.0	800	μA
8	I_{CC}	Power Supply Current IM6402 Dynamic	f_C = 500 KHz			1.2	mA
9	I_{CC}	Power Supply Current IM6403 Dynamic	$f_{CRYSTAL}$=2.46MHz			3.7	mA
10	C_{IN}	Input Capacitance[1]			7.0	8.0	pF
11	C_O	Output Capacitance[1]			8.0	10.0	pF

NOTE: 1. Except IM6403 XTAL input pins (i.e. pins 17 and 40).

A.C. CHARACTERISTICS

TEST CONDITIONS: $V_{CC} = 5.0V \pm 10\%$, $C_L = 50pF$, $T_A = -40°C$ to $+85°C$

	SYMBOL	PARAMETER	CONDITIONS	MIN	TYP	MAX	UNITS
1	f_C	Clock Frequency IM6402		D.C.	3.0	1.0	MHz
2	$f_{CRYSTAL}$	Crystal Frequency IM6403			4.0	2.46	MHz
3	t_{PW}	Pulse Widths CRL, DRR, TBRL		225	50		ns
4	t_{MR}	Pulse Width MR	See Timing Diagrams	600	200		ns
5	t_{DS}	Input Data Setup Time	(Figures 2,3,4)	75	20		ns
6	t_{DH}	Input Data Hold Time		90	40		ns
7	t_{EN}	Output Enable Time			80	190	ns

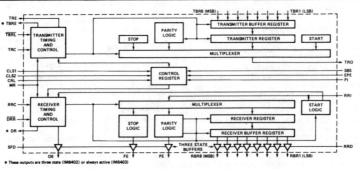

● These outputs are three state (IM6402) or always active (IM6403)

FIGURE 6. IM6402/03 Functional Block Diagram

IM6402/IM6403

TRANSMITTER OPERATION

The transmitter section accepts parallel data, formats it and transmits it in serial form (Figure 7) on the TROutput terminal.

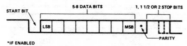

FIGURE 7. Serial Data Format

Transmitter timing is shown in Figure 8. Ⓐ Data is loaded into the transmitter buffer register from the inputs TBR1 through TBR8 by a logic low on the $\overline{TBR}$Load input. Valid data must be present at least t_{DS} prior to and t_{DH} following the rising edge of $\overline{TBR}$L. If words less than 8 bits are used, only the least significant bits are used. The character is right justified into the least significant bit, TBR1. Ⓑ The rising edge of $\overline{TBR}$L clears TBREmpty. 0 to 1 clock cycles later data is transferred to the transmitter register and TREmpty is cleared and transmission starts. TBREmpty is reset to a logic high. Output data is clocked by TRClock. The clock rate is 16 times the data rate. Ⓒ A second pulse on TBRLoad loads data into the transmitter buffer register. Data transfer to the transmitter register is delayed until transmission of the current character is complete. Ⓓ Data is automatically transferred to the transmitter register and transmission of that character begins.

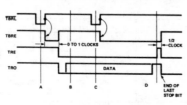

FIGURE 8. Transmitter Timing (Not to Scale)

RECEIVER OPERATION

Data is received in serial form at the RI input. When no data is being received, RI input must remain high. The data is clocked through the RRClock. The clock rate is 16 times the data rate. Receiver timing is shown in Figure 9.

Ⓐ A low level on $\overline{DRR}$eset clears the DReady line. Ⓑ During the first stop bit data is transferred from the receiver register to the RBRegister. If the word is less than 8 bits, the unused most significant bits will be a logic low. The output character is right justified to the least significant bit RBR1. A logic high on OError indicates overruns. An overrun occurs when DReady has not been cleared before the present character was transfered to the RBRegister. A logic high on PError indicates a parity error. Ⓒ 1/2 clock cycle later DReady is set to a logic high and FError is evaluated. A logic high on FError indicates an invalid stop bit was received. The receiver will not begin searching for the next start bit until a stop bit is received.

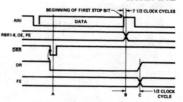

FIGURE 9. Receiver Timing (Not to Scale)

START BIT DETECTION

The receiver uses a 16X clock for timing (see Figure 10.) The start bit Ⓐ could have occurred as much as one clock cycle before it was detected, as indicated by the shaded portion. The center of the start bit is defined as clock count 7½. If the receiver clock is a symmetrical square wave, the center of the start bit will be located within $\pm 1/2$ clock cycle, $\pm 1/32$ bit or $\pm 3.125\%$. The receiver begins searching for the next start bit at the center of the first stop bit.

FIGURE 10. Start Bit Timing

TYPICAL APPLICATION

Microprocessor systems, which are inherently parallel in nature, often require an asynchronous serial interface. This function can be performed easily with the IM6402/03 UART. Figure 11 shows how the IM6403 can be interfaced to an IM6100 microcomputer system with the aid of an IM6101 Programmable Interface Element (PIE). The PIE interprets Input/Output transfer (IOT) instructions from the processor and generates read and write pulses to the UART. The SENSE lines on the PIE are also employed to allow the processor to detect UART status. In particular, the processor must know when the Receive Buffer Register has accumulated a character (DR active), and when the Transmit Buffer Register can accept another character to be transmitted.

In this example the characters to be received or transmitted will be eight bits long (CLS 1 and 2: both HIGH) and transmitted with no parity (PI:HIGH) and two stop bits (SBS:HIGH). Since these control bits will not be changed during operation, Control Register Load (CRL) can be tied high. Remember, since the IM6402/03 is a CMOS device, all unused inputs should be committed.

The baud rate at which the transmitter and receiver will operate is determined by the external crystal and DIVIDE CONTROL pin on the IM6403. The internal divider can be set to reduce the crystal frequency by either 16 (PIN 2:HIGH) or 2048 (PIN 2:LOW) times. The frequency out of the internal divider should be 16 times the desired baud rate. To generate 110 baud, this example will use a 3.579545MHz color TV crystal and DIVIDE CONTROL set low. The IM6402 may use different receive (RRC) and transmit (TRC) clock rates, but requires an external clock generator.

To assure consistent and correct operation, the IM6402/03 must be reset after power-up. The Master Reset (MR) pin is active high, and could be driven reliably from a Schmitt trigger inverter and R-C delay. In this example, the IM6100 is reset through still another inverter. The Schmitt trigger between the processor and R-C network is needed to assure that a slow rising capacitor voltage does not re-trigger RESET. A long reset pulse after power-up (~100ms) is required by the processor to assure that the on-board crystal oscillator has sufficient time to start.

The IM6402 supports the processor's bi-directional data bus quite easily by tying the TBR and RBR buses together. A read command from the processor will enable the RECEIVER BUFFER REGISTER onto the bus by using the RECEIVER REGISTER DISABLE (RRD) pin. A write command from the processor clocks data from the bus into the TRANSMITTER BUFFER REGISTER using $\overline{\text{TBRL}}$. Figure 11 shows a NAND gate

driving $\overline{\text{TBRL}}$ from the $\overline{\text{WRITE}}_2$ pin on the PIE. This gate is used to generate a rising edge to $\overline{\text{TBRL}}$ at the point where data is stable on the bus, and to hold $\overline{\text{TBRL}}$ high until the UART actually transfers the data to it's internal buffer. If $\overline{\text{TBRL}}$ were allowed to return low before TBRE went high, the intended output data would be overwritten, since the TBR is a transparent latch.

Although not shown in this example, the error flags (PE, FE, OE) could be read by the processor using the other READ line from the PIE. Since an IM6403 is used, TBRE and DR are not affected by the STATUS FLAGS DISABLE pin. Thus, the three error flags can be tied to the data bus and gated by connecting SFD to $\overline{\text{READ}}_2$.

If parity is not inhibited, a parity error will cause the PE pin to go high until the next valid character is received.

A framing error is generated when an expected stop bit is not received. FE will stay high after the error until the next complete character's stop bit is received.

The overrun error flag is set if a received character is transferred to the RECEIVER BUFFER REGISTER when the previous character has not been read. The OE pin will stay high until the next received stop bit after a $\overline{\text{DRR}}$ is performed.

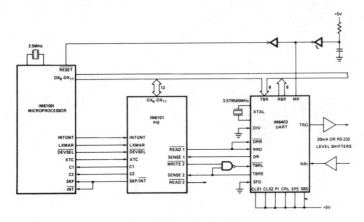

FIGURE 11. 110 Baud Serial Interface for IM6100 System

INTERSIL

10710 N. Tantau Ave., Cupertino, CA 95014 (408) 996-5000 TWX 910-338-0171

Intersil cannot assume responsibility for use of any circuitry described other than circuitry entirely embodied in an Intersil product. No other circuit patent licenses are implied. Intersil reserves the right to change the circuitry and specifications without notice at any time.

11-78/00C

Index

TO THE READER

This book is one of an expanding series of books that will cover the field of basic electronics and digital electronics from basic gates and flip-flops through microcomputers and digital telecommunications. We are attempting to develop a mailing list of individuals who would like to receive information on the series. We would be delighted to add your name to it if you would fill in the information below and mail this sheet to us. Thanks.

1. I have the following books:

_____

_____

_____

_____

_____

_____

_____

_____

_____

_____

_____

_____

2. My occupation is: ☐ student ☐ teacher, instructor ☐ hobbyist

☐ housewife ☐ scientist, engineer, doctor, etc. ☐ businessman

☐ Other: _____

Name (print): _____

Address _____

City _____ State _____

Zip Code _____

Mail to:

Books
P.O. Box 715
Blacksburg, Virginia 24060